C0-GBU-814
10/09

Hybrid Nations

Hybrid Nations

Gender Troping
and the Emergence of Bigendered Subjects
in Latin American Narrative

Patricia Lapolla Swier

Madison • Teaneck
Fairleigh Dickinson University Press

PQ
7082
.N7
S98
2009

Fairleigh Dickinson
University Library

Teaneck, New Jersey

© 2009 by Rosemont Publishing & Printing Corp.

All rights reserved. Authorization to photocopy items for internal or personal use, or the internal or personal use of specific clients, is granted by the copyright owner, provided that a base fee of $10.00, plus eight cents per page, per copy is paid directly to the Copyright Clearance Center, 222 Rosewood Drive, Danvers, Massachusetts 01923. [978-0-8386-4209-2/09 $10.00 + 8¢ pp, pc.]

Associated University Presses
2010 Eastpark Boulevard
Cranbury, NJ 08512

The paper used in this publication meets the requirements of the American National Standard for Permanence of Paper for Printed Library Materials Z39.48-1984.

Library of Congress Cataloging-in-Publication Data

Swier, Patricia Lapolla.
Hybrid nations : gender troping and the emergence of bigendered subjects in Latin American narrative / Patricia Lapolla Swier.
p. cm.
Includes bibliographical references and index.
ISBN 978-0-8386-4209-2 (alk. paper)
1. Spanish American fiction—20th century—History and criticism. 2. Spanish American fiction—19th century—History and criticism. 3. Gender identity in literature. 4. Sex role in literature. 5. National characteristics, Latin American, in literature. 6. Martí, José, 1853–1895. Amistad funesta. 7. Gallegos Rómulo, 1884–1969. Doña Bárbara. 8. Asturias, Miguel Angel. Señor presidente. I. Title.
PQ7082.N7S98 2009
863′.009353—dc22

2009007100

PRINTED IN THE UNITED STATES OF AMERICA

Contents

Preface

DURING THE NINETEENTH CENTURY AND THROUGHOUT THE nation-building era in Latin America, many nationalist writers utilized "gender troping," or opposing conceptualizations of gender, in the creation or exclusion of national subjects. Gender troping, which can be defined as the implementation of gender codes used in order to persuade the reader of the political objectives of the author, relies heavily on the binary status of gender as perceived by Western patriarchal culture of the late nineteenth and early twentieth centuries. This technique becomes particularly problematic during these years because while conceptualizations of gender were in a constant state of transition, concepts of nationhood were also being challenged. During the nineteenth century, these perceptions fluctuated in Latin America due to the tumultuous nature of the post-independence era, the epistemological discourse of science that emerged in the age of positivism, as well as the philosophical perceptions of gender offered by many popular nineteenth-century philosophers including Immanuel Kant, Georg Wilhelm Friedrich Hegel, Arthur Schopenhauer, and Friedrich Wilhelm Nietzsche.[1]

Following independence, the shift from religious power to the new hegemonic discourse of nationalism led by a secularized intelligentsia problematized traditional concepts of authority, race, and class, and it is not surprising that perceptions about gender many times became contradictory depending on the philosophical ideals and political perspectives of the writer. According to Michael Aronna, gender played a pivotal role in defining Spain and Latin America within the scientific and philosophical theories about gender and race that culminated in the ideas of Kant and Hegel in the nineteenth century. Kant argued that only a select minority of elite Caucasian men was capable of the civilizing qualities of reason, whereas women and all nonwhite peoples shared a propensity for immorality. Similarly, Hegel expounded on the "immature" status of Latin American countries for their perceived relationship to nature. In addition, Schopenhauer and Nietzsche advocated the idea of chastity, or denying the will, as a means of strengthening the intellect, thus promoting self-healing and self-knowledge.

It is not surprising that the masculine subject in many Latin American texts was often depicted as the man of reason, who exercised control of his will by repressing his sexual libido. Conversely, the uncontrollable desires and sexuality of women existed in opposition, and many times were assigned to the weakened, degenerative, feminine status of the nation. In addition, the epistemological discourse of science and medicine that emerged in the nineteenth century reinforced negative perceptions of the feminine with its portrayal of the pathological woman as the undesirable Other. Throughout the century, many writers utilized these conceptualizations of gender in order to promote their ideas and philosophies about the nation, oftentimes introducing in their writings a new national subject that would replace what they perceived as the current unacceptable political order. Consequently, perceptions of masculinity and femininity held by intellectuals often differed from traditional conceptions of gender inherited from Catholicism and Spanish culture, and these contradictions surfaced in apparently homogeneous texts based on the paradigmatic construction of binary oppositions.

This work uses feminist, queer, masculinist, and psychoanalytic theories of gender in an attempt to examine the contradictions and fluctuations of interpretations of gender in José Martí's *Amistad funesta* (1885), Rómulo Gallegos's *Doña Bárbara* (1929), and Miguel Ángel Asturias's *El Señor Presidente* (1946). I have chosen these particular texts because they represent the political strife of their respective nations, and they show how conceptualizations of gender evolve and transform according to the sociopolitical and historical context. Although it may be problematic for some critics to consider these modern European and Anglo approaches in the analysis of early Latin American texts, I feel that they are helpful in understanding the gendered relationship of power that arose in the postindependence era. The authors of these texts employed gender troping in order to contest a hegemonic power that threatened their very subjectivity, and in my opinion each author responded to these powers in ways that disturb traditional concepts of gender based on binary oppositions.[2] Thus, through an examination of the constant shifting of gender codes, due in part to the diverse shifting of institutions of power during the late nineteenth and early twentieth centuries, I provide new, open-ended readings of these texts.

This study foregrounds the study of the novels by embarking upon an analysis of the use of gender troping in Esteban Echevería's *El matadero* and Domingo Faustino Sarmiento's *Facundo,* two mid-nineteenth-century texts, which have become representative of the abuse and violence that reigned during the dictatorship of Juan Manuel de Rosas in Argentina. Sarmiento's paradigmatic struggle between civilization and barbarism has been widely accepted and appropriated by many Latin American writers in the formation of nations and has been reinscribed in such novels as *Amalia* (1851) and *Doña Bárbara* (1929). These texts offer clear examples of how the employment of binary oppositions with regard to gender disrupts common perceptions of the relationship between gender and power. Both Sarmiento and Echeverría set out to portray Rosas and his followers (Federalists) as the irrational Other, thus casting them in the realm of the feminine, for their use of force and violence. These writers exploit the metaphorical image of gendered bodies in order to contest (virile) hegemonic institutions of power. Surprisingly, the gendered bodies of the hypo-virile protagonists Facundo Quiroga and Matasiete are constructed in order to reflect the irrational feminine characteristics of the exaggerated status of power held by Rosas. In this way the texts allude to the feminine aspects of barbarism that exist in opposition to the masculine conceptions of reason held by those select few.

During the end of the nineteenth century one can see a shift in conceptualizations of gender that becomes evident in the essays of José Martí, as well as in his only novel, *Amistad funesta.* In the narrative of Martí the use of gender troping becomes even more apparent as he celebrates the virile qualities of the new man, while simultaneously denigrating the feminine nature of those men who depend entirely on reason and progress. The use of gender oppositions in Martí's narrative is indicative of a deeper and more important polarity of materialism and spirit, or capitalism and the soul, a theme that is later employed by José Enrique Rodó in his prominent essay *Ariel* (1900). I believe that Martí's only novel, *Amistad funesta* (1885), is an early example of these opposing ideas of gender and nation that will later surface in his famous essay "Nuestra América" (1891). By creating the female irrational protagonist of Lucía Jérez in the novel, Martí unwittingly introduces a new type of woman into modern literary narrative, one endowed with masculine characteristics and a sense of agency.

Most studies about *Amistad funesta* ignore the relationship between the novel and the political posture of José Martí.[3] Martí, a revolutionary who dedicated his adult life to the independence and stability of Cuba, had written prolifically about the image of Latin America and the concept of man in the modern age. I argue that Martí utilizes gendered bodies in this novel in order to denounce the (feminine) materialist characteristics of the United States. The pathological tendencies of Lucía Jerez in the novel reflect the materialistic essence and irrational posture of US foreign policy between 1881 and 1885. Thus, by adopting this symbolic friendship, Cuba (and by extension Latin America) would be harmed by the unilateral aspirations of their northern neighbor, a nation perceived by most to be the land of promise and progress. However, in order to construct a pathological image of this imposing power, Martí assigns Lucía masculine characteristics not typical of her gender. Lucía's strength and agency in the novel contrast with Juan's more gentle qualities, thus disturbing traditional concepts of gender in fin-de-siècle Latin America.

A gendered analysis of Rómulo Gallegos's *Doña Bárbara* also reveals the inculcation of a bigendered national subject at the national level, who carefully straddles both sides of the gendered scale. Critics of Gallegos's novel have focused primarily on the metaphorical use of gender in the depiction of civilization and barbarism, which is a reinscription of the basic tenets of Sarmiento's text. Most studies have overlooked the disruption of perceptions of gendered bodies in the novel as well as the exchange of traditional gendered characteristics of the two main protagonists, Santos Luzardo and Doña Bárbara. My study examines the ways in which gender is simultaneously shed and appropriated in order to construct the new man of Venezuela, one who encompasses the civilizing masculine qualities of reason and education, as well as the feminine, barbaric qualities of the virile man of the *llanos* [plains]. In this novel, we see the fusion of those traditional perceptions of virility, such as physical strength, power, and the ability to strive in the *llanos,* with philosophical conceptualizations of masculinity formulated in accordance with Darwinism and positivism. However, in the process of emasculating the hypo-virile female protagonist Doña Bárbara, the text subverts traditional conceptualizations of gender based on binary oppositions. A reexamination of this novel according to gender provides possibilities of a new reading of this text, which has traditionally been perceived as homogeneous.[4]

El Señor Presidente has been analyzed with regard to power, politics and as a dictator novel and within the aesthetics of surrealism or vanguardism, but few have commented on the role that gender plays in this mid-twentieth-century novel. My work studies Asturias's novel as an example of Hélène Cixous' theory of feminine writing, or *écriture féminine.* The novel marks a rupture from the objective eye of realism by its innovative play with language and its echoes of pre-Columbian civilizations, which, in turn, function to displace the patriarchal authority, characterized in this text by the corruption of a dictatorship. Thus, the subjective world associated with the feminine challenges a traditional authoritative order, which is represented in this novel as oppressive. In my work I explore the ways in which narrative attributed to the feminine sphere (*écriture féminine*) is utilized in *El Señor Presidente* in order to reveal the fallacies of an exaggerated patriarchal authority and to displace traditional paradigms of conceptualization.

The purpose of my study then is to present gender as a complex dialectic construction that frequently shifts according to the social and political landscapes of the historical period. Gender is not always seen within the concepts of binary oppositions, but as a frequently evolving positioning that very often contests what R. W. Connell refers to as hegemonic masculinity. Throughout history, many intellectuals have utilized oppositional gender codes in order to appropriate, reappropriate, or maintain the status of power in the political arena, and in doing so they have consciously or unconsciously broken away from these codes, thus opening up new spaces for interpretation. Consequently, many writers have produced ambiguously constructed subjects that defy traditional conceptualizations of gender and therefore should be noted for their innovative role in modern literary narrative. This study examines the slippery consistency of gender codes in late nineteenth- and early twentieth-century texts in Latin America, where the postindependent climate, the profusion of scientific studies and the nature of philosophical postulations invoked competing interpretations of masculinity and femininity.

In this work, I examine the fissures or conflicts that arise due to the use of gender troping, thereby revealing the inherent contradictions of dichotomous perceptions of gender characteristic of Western thought. Gender is the main focus of this study. I do not pretend to present or to read these works within a vacuum; therefore, in an attempt to narrow my study I have chosen some of the most representative works that reveal the manipulation of gender as a means of supporting the political objectives of the authors.

Acknowledgments

WITHOUT THE CONTINUAL SUPPORT AND ENCOURAGEMENT OF MY colleagues, friends, and family, I could not have completed this project. I am especially grateful to Jorge Marbán, Gloria Pastorino and Juan Carlos González Espitia for their time and expertise with the Spanish translations. I am unduly grateful to the guidance of Maria A. Salgado who provided valuable suggestions and support throughout the writing process. As well I would like to thank Harry Keyishian, Julien Yoseloff, Christine Retz, and the editorial staff of Fairleigh Dickenson Press and Associated University Presses, whose patience and interest made this experience possible. Finally, I would like to give special thanks to my parents, Joan and Joe Lapolla, who continue to be a source of encouragement and inspiration; and to my husband Tom, and my children Rachel, Nick and Joey, who always believed in me.

* * *

I also want to thank the Wellcome Institute Library of London for permission to use the image "Charcot lecturing on hysteria at the Salpêtrière" and The New York Academy of Medicine for permission to use the photograph by P. Regnard, entitled "Extase," Augustine. Grateful acknowledgment is made to Herederos de Miguel Ángel Asturias and the Orion Publishing Group for permission to use quoted material and to the following publishers for permission to use reprinted material:

Hispanic Journal: "Transgendering and the Emergence of Ambiguous National Subjects in Rómulo Gallegos' *Doña Bárbara." Hispanic Journal* v. 29, issue 1, Spring 2008, 91–105.

Vanderbilt Press: "Unveiling the Mask of Modernity: A Critical Gendered Perspective of José Martí's *Amistad funesta*" in *Building Nineteenth-Century Latin America: Re-rooted Cultures, Identities, and Nations,* Eds. William Acree and Juan Carlos Gonzáles Espitia, Vanderbilt Press, 2009.

Hybrid Nations

Introduction: Who's on Top? Nation Building and the Gendered Struggle for Power

DIANA TAYLOR BEGINS HER BOOK *DISAPPEARING ACTS* (1997) BY stating that she had stumbled into the wrong play, *Paso de dos.*[1] In this hit production of the 1990s, Argentine playwright Eduardo Pavlovsky recalls the atrocities committed during the military occupation in Argentina in his portrayal of a masochist erotic relationship between an aggressive male torturer and a passive female victim. Taylor suggests that "the performance reproduced rather than dismantled the military's authoritarian discourse" and "the visual frenzy provoked by her [the female protagonist] abuse seemed closer to pornography" than a contestation of the military junta (4). According to Taylor, the oppressor needs the female body in order to define his own sexual identity; She, silent and passive, is "the inert mute mass in which he inflicts his sexual pleasure" (5). Throughout the play, He, the maniacal military man, beats, strips, rapes, and finally kills She; and She, oddly enough, likes it. Taylor takes issue with this play for merely reenacting the gendered difference of power and infliction of violence that took place during the military dictatorship in Argentina between 1976 and 1983. She states: "In the national struggle for identity, both groups [the military junta and the opposition] of males were fighting to define and occupy the 'masculine' position while emasculating, feminizing and marginalizing the 'Other'" (9). The presence of the female body, argues Taylor, is necessary in this struggle for power in order to complete the transaction. While Argentine psychotherapist, actor, and playwright Eduardo Pavlovsky uses this play as a platform to deal with the nation's issues of memory regarding the atrocities committed during the dictatorship, a disappointed Taylor compares it to a "theatrical disappearing act," which "all too clearly illustrated the mechanics of nation-building" she previously associated with the "Dirty War" (2).

Flashback approximately 150 years ago to 1837 to Esteban Echeverría's *Slaughterhouse* (*El matadero*) in Buenos Aires, where the setting depicts an aura of confusion and chaos created by the slaughter of fifty young calves.[2] The floods and the violence of the *chusma* [mob] add to the grotesque aspects of Romanticism, reflecting the literary aesthetics of the day. In the midst of the confusion, a civilized member of the Unitarian party enters riding his horse European style. This young Unitarian "como de 25 años de gallarda y bien apuesta persona" [about twenty-five years old, elegant, debonair of carriage] depicts the epitome of civilization and seems somewhat feminine compared to the barbaric nature of the Federalists (19).[3] His refined appearance and his initial calm manner differ drastically with that of Matasiete, the head butcher, whose brutal image can be described within traditional perceptions of hypermasculinity, or *machismo:* "el carnicero con el cuchillo en mano, brazo y pecho desnudos, cabello largo y revuelto, camisa y chiripá y rostro embadurnado de sangre" (12) [the butcher with the knife in his hand, his chest and arms bare, his hair long and wild, his shirt, chiripá[4] and face smeared with blood] (9).

In the climax of the story, the young man is dragged off to the slaughterhouse [arrastraron al infeliz joven al banco del tormento como los sayones de Cristo] (13) and ultimately dies in a manner similar to that in which Christ is sacrificed on the cross. Beforehand, Matasiete and the crowd attempt to transform the weakened androgynous figure of the Unitarian into the brutal image of the Federalists. First they shave his European-style beard, and then they warn him not to forget to grow a mustache, which was the sign of masculinity prescribed by the regime: "Ya estás afeitado a la federala, sólo te falta el bigote. Cuidado con olvidarlo" [He's already been shaved Federalist-style—all that you need is the mustache. See that you don't forget it] (15). When asked why he does not wear the *divisa,* the insignia of the Rosas regime, he responds: "La librea es para vosotros, esclavos, no para los hombres libres" [Livery is for slaves like you, not for free men] (15). Matasiete and his followers then try to strip the Unitarian and beat him. In order to constrain him, they put him "boca abajo" [face down] on the table, depicting the homoerotic nature of this scene. The Unitarian prefers death rather than adopt the barbaric codes of the opposition, and in a flustered, frenzied struggle to free himself, he tragically dies.

In their works, Eduardo Pavlovsky and Esteban Echeverría provide highly visible gendered reenactments of the violence and barbarity of the abusive dictatorial governments that oppressed them. It is somewhat ironic that the gendered performativity of Pavlovsky's late twentieth-century play can be traced back to the early nineteenth-century short story and that both works reveal similar struggles for power represented in gendered terms. Pavlovsky, a member of the opposition, had spent nearly twelve years in exile after barely escaping abduction by the military junta in 1978. Very much aware of the humiliation and emasculation felt by the nation during this period, he utilized his plays as a means of confronting repressed feelings of denial, shame, and complicity. Similarly, Echeverría was one of the leaders of the *Asociación de Mayo,* a secret society founded to combat the dictator Juan Manuel de Rosas. He spent the last years of his life in exile in Montevideo, where he wrote *El matadero* (1837), a short story fervently attacking the Rosas regime. In both works the writers portray the powerless, inactive image of the feminine in order to contest a hegemonic masculinized institution. Both works utilize what I call gender troping in their depiction of the severe inequity of power distribution within their respective political regimes, which is used, as Taylor so aptly put it, in their struggle for the masculine position for power (9). But what happens to the feminine in this quest of the masculine search for the masculine position? Is she/he always inert, passive, and powerless and synonymous with the Other? And even more intriguing, what happens to the masculine figure? Is he/she always positioned on top of this metaphorical struggle for power?

In this study I address the critical role that gender plays in the formation of national identities in Latin America that are negotiated and challenged within extreme gendered struggles for power as presently discussed. In the subsequent chapters, I will explore the writers' use of dichotomous conceptualizations of gender in José Martí's *Amistad funesta* (1885), Rómulo Gallegos's *Doña Bárbara* (1929), and Miguel Ángel Asturias's *El Señor Presidente* (1946), focusing on the fissures that emerge as a result of their use of oppositional gender codes. Like Echeverría and

Pavlovsky, the authors of these texts utilized gender troping in order to contest a masculine hegemonic power that threatened their very subjectivity, and each author responded to these powers in ways that disturb traditional concepts of gender based on binary oppositions. During the nineteenth century and throughout the nation-building era in Latin America, conceptualizations of gender fluctuated in large part due to the scientific and philosophical trends that circulated in Europe as well as the tumultuous atmosphere provoked by independence.

While scientific and philosophical theorizations of gender posited the intellectual man of reason over the more rugged men of the land, the need for strong charismatic leaders during the independence years placed the latter in strategic positions of power that they may not have held otherwise. In the years following independence, many budding nations were faced with *caudillista* rulers and, as a result, the metaphorical, gendered struggle for power often surfaced in many well-known political treatises during this period as a means of contesting these hypomasculine governmental orders. Interestingly enough, the opposition adopted similar methods for effacing their rivals, depending in large part on their current perceptions of gender and power in a changing and evolving world. The introduction of this work is therefore dedicated to providing some groundwork for the frequently transforming and often intersecting conceptualizations of gender that were instrumental in the formation of nations in Latin America and incorporated in such paradigmatic works as Esteban Echeverría's *El matadero* and Domingo Faustino Sarmiento's *Facundo: Civilización y barbarie.*

Gender Troping

Gender troping, which I define as the utilization of gender codes in order to persuade the reader of the (political) objectives of the author, is a manipulative strategy utilized by many writers in the formation or exclusion of a desired subject. The basic premise of gender troping relies heavily on the accepted binary status of gender as perceived by Western patriarchal culture, which is believed to be inherent in language, a phenomenon that has been theorized extensively by psychoanalysts and feminists alike. According to Elaine Showalter, "the term 'sexual difference' comes out of the discourses of poststructuralism and psychoanalysis, and originates with the question of difference in language, subjectivity and identity."[5] Following the theories of Jacques Lacan, she posits that gender is primarily constructed through the acquisition of language or when the speaking subject enters the symbolic system ruled by the law of the father, marked by the signifier of the phallus and the castration complex. In taking up a linguistic position as "he" or "she" in relation to the symbolic, the subject learns to be gendered (3).

Anne Cranny-Francis asserts that traditional perceptions of gender that are both constructed and perpetuated in patriarchal society portray women as passive, helpless, emotional, and nurturing, whereas men are constructed as active, competitive, rational, and heroic.[6] These gendered dichotomies are reinforced by what Hélène Cixous refers to as patriarchal binary thought that has its roots firmly grounded in language. According to Cixous' theory of the hierarchal nature of patriarchal binary thought, oppositions such as passive/active and masculine/feminine reach their significance only in opposition to each other.[7] Cixous argues that each opposition can be analyzed as a hierarchy where the feminine side is always seen as the negative powerless instance (104).

Thus, one could deduce that the persistent conceptualizations of gender in terms of binary oppositions work to reinforce the gendered relationship of power as male/active and female/passive and continue to position the feminine subject on the passive side of the power scale. This theory certainly could be used in *Paso de dos* and *El matadero* because in both works the feminized powerless body of the Other is offered up as a symbolic representation of the oppressed subjects in Argentina; and in both cases, the highly charged erotic relationship between the masculine and the feminine leads to the death of, or the exclusion of, the feminine subject. Both writers, no doubt, utilized this gendered reenactment to portray the function of domination and coercion in these hegemonic political institutions, as well as revealing the helplessness that the feminine subject felt within this struggle.

For centuries women in Latin America have pointed out the dichotomous nature of gender and the consequential inequity of power distribution. As early as the seventeenth century, Sor Juana Inés de la Cruz's "Respuesta a Sor Filotea de la Cruz," as well as her famous poem "Hombres necios," addresses the injustice of the double standard resulting in the inability of women to advance in colonial Mexico. Similarly in her much-cited contemporary essay "La crítica literaria feminista y la escritora en América Latina" (1985), Sara Castro-Klarén refers to the opposition between male and female seen by certain French feminists as the foundation of Western ideology. In this essay, she claims that a polarity of opposites based on sexual analogy organizes our language and, through it, directs our ways of perceiving the world.[8] More importantly, Francine Masiello recognizes that the binary logic that separates man from woman is also established within the discourse of power.[9] However, is it possible to find fissures or contradictions within this discourse of power that may have depicted the feminine subject as the positive active agent (using the terminology of Cixous)? Or are we so intricately a part of this discourse of power that we cannot appreciate that some very influential theorists and male writers in Latin America have either advocated for a recovery of the feminine in their texts or have inadvertently disturbed traditional conceptualizations of gender based on binary oppositions?

Sara Castro-Klarén asserts that the male/female opposition would always be present, but terms and meanings would vary as multiplicity increased. She and other Latin American female critics, including Josefina Ludmer and María Lugones, search for the creation of new gendered codes that they can identify with and that do not betray them.[10] More recently, in her work "The Novelness of a Possible Poetics for Women" (1989), Castro-Klarén suggests a reexamination of Latin American literature: "The figure of Women and the subsequent problematics implied by its presence should cause a profound re-thinking of the possible history of Latin American thinking and its symbolic systems."[11] Perhaps a rethinking of the significant role that gender played in traditional texts in Latin America can chip away at the power structure expressed in binary terms of gender, which frequently allocates the powerful side of the hierarchal spectrum to the masculine.

Current theorizations of gender formulated by Judith Butler can provide an opening to a reexamination of "the history of Latin American thinking and its symbolic systems" as suggested by Castro-Klarén. Because Butler's depiction of gender as a "free floating artifice" or a social construct is not always directly related to the biological sexual body, we can thus perceive the feminine and masculine as being independent of male and female bodies that often transform and evolve according to different sociohistorical and political contexts.[12] If gender is not always directly associated with biological sex, as Butler concludes, can we not appreciate a rejuvenated analysis of masculinity and femininity in Latin American traditional texts, where the feminine is not always portrayed in a position of inferiority and passivity, but is constantly shifting and transforming within a complex power struggle during a time period characteristic of change and transitions? In the years following independence (or preceding, as in the case of Cuba) there arose new and improved gendered subjects within the narrative of the intelligentsia that surprisingly maintained both feminine and masculine characteristics in the authors' efforts to move their country into an age of progress and modernity. It is through these changes and transformations that we discover fissures and exceptions to traditionally accepted binary perceptions of gender. However, it is also significant to note that it is precisely because the writer employs binary conceptions of gender in his/her narrative that these fissures and contradictions arise.

By working with binary oppositions, I have found it extremely difficult to speak about gendered difference without repeating what I believe to be commonplace tropes utilized by the writers included in this work. In this way, I have felt it necessary to expand on traditional conceptions and theories related to gender during the nineteenth and early twentieth century in order to show the fissures and contradictions that gender troping often produces. It is not my goal to annihilate difference from narrative or theory or to position the feminine sphere over the masculine, only to disturb deleterious ideas attached to both feminine and masculine subjects throughout history, in the hopes of revealing the slippery consistency of gender and by that means disrupting traditional concepts of power.

History of Gender Troping

Gender troping has been a predominant tool used in the history of Latin America, especially during the discovery and independence eras, when the quest for the masculine position of power has been appropriated through the feminization of the Other.[13] Since the times of the discovery of America, the feminization of the Native American had been one of the primary sources of the discourse of hegemony utilized in the subjugation of the indigenous races in the New World. Because the indigenous people had no formal system of writing or weapons sophisticated enough to match those of the Spanish, many of the discoverers, including Christopher Columbus, portrayed them as "culturally virgin," ripe for the picking for conquest, colonization, slavery, or for the image of exoticism that they would provide in literary texts for the centuries to come.[14]

Gender became a means of not only defining the Amerindians during this period, but through a linguistic mode of emasculation they were described in many ways in opposition to the masculinized figures of the conquistadors. Descriptive phrases and adjectives such as *mansos* [gentle], *fácil de cristianizar* [easy to Christianize], and *generosos* [generous] refer to the passivity of the natives and to the facility to conform them according to the desire of those in power. Because the Indians were physically naked, Columbus perceived them to be deprived of all cultural property as they were characterized by the absence of customs, rites, and religion.[15] This passiveness, or absence of traits traditionally associated with civilization, exists in contrast to the active, male, courageous explorers and recalls aspects of femininity attributed to European women. The fact that they are described on several occasions as pacific peoples "sin fierro" [without iron] calls to mind the physiological nature of women who were described for their deficiency.[16] In the following passages from the *Diario del primer viaje,* Columbus accentuates their seemingly feminine behavior: "They were good people and did harm to no one" (November entry) and on December 24 he adds, "All display the most extraordinarily gentle behavior and have soft voices."[17] This process of textual emasculation not only arouses images portrayed in the myth of the golden age but also provided the crown with the opportunities of a spiritual and a mercantile conquest.[18]

Gender troping was also instrumental in imagining the formation of nations preceding and following the wars of independence. Although it is impossible and implausible to conceive of the independence of Latin America as a unified process, many of the budding nations shared similar characteristics that will be addressed here: fluctuations of power and identity, political unrest, and the rising prevalence of *caudillismo.* The nineteenth century in Latin America witnessed a series of changes and transformations as hegemonic powers were challenged, defied, and ultimately replaced. For many Latin American countries, independence from Spain in the earlier part of the century is denoted for its temporal flexibility with regard to social class, gender, and power and provided a stage for liberal reformists and utopist idealists who would later compete for a voice in these newly founded nations. A significant discrepancy of this era was that the heterogeneous masses of Latin American countries had to unify in order to fight Spain's powers of colonialism, but once these countries freed themselves of the motherland they had to compete separately for power and control in the government. In *El laberinto de soledad* (1950)[19] Octavio Paz argues that the elites of Mexico, who directed independence, wanted to free themselves from Spain because they felt subjugated by it; however, instead of adopting liberal ideas from France and the United States, they only intended to replace one feudal system for another:

> Entre nosotros [as opposed to the United States], en cambio, una vez consumada la Independencia las clases dirigentes se consolidan como las herederas del Viejo orden español. Rompen con España pero se muestran incapaces de crear una sociedad moderna. No podía ser de otro modo, ya que los grupos que encabezaron el movimiento de Independencia no constituían nuevas fuerzas sociales, sino la prolongación del sistema feudal. (109–10)
>
> [In effect, the United States is a novelty in the history of the nineteenth century, a society that grew and expanded naturally. Among ourselves, on the other hand, the ruling classes consolidated themselves, once Independence was achieved, as heirs of the old Spanish order. They broke with Spain but they proved incapable of creating a modern society. It could not have been otherwise, because the groups that headed the Independence movement did not represent new social forces, merely a prolongation of the feudal system.] (121)

Similarly, in Argentina, the *criollos* that led the independence movement utilized nativism in order to create a sense of unity among the people, providing promises of liberalism and equal-ity.[20] Although the *criollos* utilized the *caudillos, gauchos,* Indians, and blacks in their fight for independence, they never really intended them to be included in the voice of the nation.

After independence, Spanish America was left in a state of fragmentation and financial ruin, and Argentina was no exception. According to Tulio Halperín Donghi, the separate political units that emerged after independence were frequently denoted as sections.[21] In the 1820s, Buenos Aires was given the name "Las Provincias Unidas en Sudamérica" and underwent a series of struggles, civil wars, and a multitude of governors, until a provincial government was put in place headed by Martín Rodríguez, with Bernardino Rivadavia as chief minister.[22]

In 1825 *porteño* merchant and lawyer Bernardino Rivadavia was made head of the provisional national administration and given the title of president.[23] Rivadavia had traveled extensively in Europe and sought to organize the national image and interior of Buenos Aires based on the model of Western Europe. He made various radical reforms including decreasing the size of the army; stripping the army and the clergy of the *fuero;* implementing modernizing institutions such as universities and a stock exchange, and transferring control of many institutions such as hospitals and cemeteries from the church to the state.[24] Above all, he wanted to make Buenos Aires the center of economic and political control and sought to keep close economic ties with Europe by encouraging foreign trade, investment, and immigration.[25] In 1826 a rigorously centralized constitution was put in place whereby provincial governors were to be appointed as representatives of the national executive.[26] However, the predominantly Federalist contingency in the interior strongly opposed centralist ideas of government and was offended by Rivadavia's anticlerical moves. According to Bushnell, the anticlerical position of Rivadavia's Unitarians was so unpopular in Buenos Aires that it was viewed as the work of the Antichrist (124). When the opposition rose up against the new order that the Unitarians had conceived, they became disdainful of the people and "shut themselves up in a violent, anti-popular aristocratism."[27] This marked the initial rift between the enlightened progressive elite and the masses that would later serve as the benchmark for Domingo Faustino Sarmiento's paradigmatic dichotomy of civilization and barbarism.

A significant trend that became characteristic in Latin America following the wars of independence was *caudillismo.* John

Chasteen attests that the first *caudillos* became prominent during the wars of independence and carried this fame through peacetime politics, which he admits were not especially peaceful (125). As stated previously, the postindependence years in Latin America were characterized by their fragmented status, economic devastation, and political unrest. After the defeat of the republican governments led by the *criollos,* people often looked towards the military leaders, or *caudillos,* to restore order. Following Rivadavia's collapse in Argentina, Juan Manuel de Rosas insisted that he be given dictatorial powers in order to restore order and prosperity when he became governor of the province of Buenos Aires in 1829.[28] The *caudillo,* states Bushnell and Macaulay, "came to exercise power regionally or nationally through his ascendancy over a band of personal followers, the use of various kinds of patronage to forge ties of clientelism with the surrounding population, and where necessary, the use of brute force as well."[29] Juan Manuel de Rosas was one such leader who forged his union with the *estancieros,* or ranchers, until he gained a monopoly of both land and absolute power throughout Argentina.

Rosas, a Federalist, despised the Unitarians for their liberal ideas, and during his regime he utilized nationalistic discourse in order to turn the Argentine masses against the European-like Unitarians. Ironically, both Federalists and Unitarians used oppositional language during the Rosas regime as a means of eliminating the voice of the opposing Other. Epithets like "filthy, savage Unitarians" were used to denigrate the image of the Unitarians, thus polarizing them from the Catholic ethos of the nation. Similarly, Tulio Halperín Donghi states that the night watchmen of Buenos Aires preceded the hourly announcement of the time and the weather with the following defamations: "Long live the Holy Federation, Death to the savage, unclean, loathsome Unitarians."[30] The same mottoes were placed on top of all public and private documents, which consequently repudiated the Unitarians, categorizing them as the undesirable Other.[31] In addition, insignias that consisted of red ribbons were worn by Federalists, which visually distinguished them as the accepted subjects in a politically divided nation. Thus, on a linguistic and semiotic level, Rosas succeeded in emasculating the Unitarians, thereby effacing them from nationalist discourse. This ideology reflects the conceptualization of political identity where "identity is always purchased at the price of the exclusion of the Other, the repression or repudiation of nonidentity."[32]

However, in order to contest the suffocating hegemony of the Rosas regime, the Unitarians also used oppositional language in their texts in their portrayal of the Federalists as the irrational and primitive barbarians, linking them with the philosophical image of the feminine theorized by many popular nineteenth-century philosophers, including Immanuel Kant and Georg Wilhelm Friedrich Hegel. As I will demonstrate, in many significant nation-building texts formulated by the Latin American elite, the Other was defined with its similarities to the feminine and was thus intended to be excluded from public discourse.

Nineteenth-Century Philosophical Perceptions of Gender

Following independence, traditional concepts of authority, race, and class shifted, and it is not surprising that conceptualizations about gender many times became contradictory depending on the philosophical ideals and political perspective of the writer. According to Michael Aronna, gender played a pivotal role in defining Latin America within the scientific and philosophical theories about gender and race that culminated in the ideas of Immanuel Kant and Georg Wilhelm Friedrich Hegel in the nineteenth century. Kant utilized gender differences in order to establish a hierarchy of national character in his book *Observations on the Feeling of the Beautiful and Sublime.*[33] For Kant, women and all nonwhite peoples were limited to a sphere of sensory experience and therefore shared a propensity for immorality. He also argued that only a select minority of elite Caucasian men was capable of the civilizing qualities of reason.[34] Similarly, Hegel expounded on the immature status of Latin American countries for their perceived close relationship to nature. In *Lectures on the Philosophies of World History,* Hegel refers to the natives of South America and Mexico as "unenlightened children" known for their "mildness and passivity, their humility and obsequious submissiveness" towards Creoles and Europeans.[35] For both philosophers, the civilized man encompassed the esteemed quality of reason, while the immoral, weakened, and degenerative status of the nation was allocated to the space of the feminine. Both philosophers linked the violence and brutality of the Spaniards during the conquest and the atrocities of the Black Legend with the backwardness of Africa and the Middle Ages.[36] According to these presumptions, the Latin American *mestizo,* by association, was regarded as one of those inferior races described as uncivilized or immature, thus linking race to the degenerative perception of the feminine.[37]

The misogynist views of Arthur Schopenhauer and Friedrich Nietzsche also contributed to perceptions of gender that would later resonate in many Latin American national novels. These two nineteenth-century philosophers advocated the idea of chastity, or denying the will, as a means of strengthening the intellect in order to enhance self-healing and self-knowledge.[38] Because spiritual exhaustion was associated with illicit or excessive sexual activity, it is not surprising that Schopenhauer not only promoted the idea of chastity but also lived it.[39] Consequently, the masculine subject in many Latin American texts was often depicted as the man of reason, who exercised control of his will by repressing his sexual libido. Conversely, the uncontrollable desires and sexuality of women existed in opposition and many times were assigned to the weakened, degenerative, feminine status of the nation. Throughout the century, many writers utilized both conceptualizations of gender in order to promote their ideas and philosophy about the nation, oftentimes introducing in their writings a new national subject that would replace what they perceived as the current unacceptable political order. During the period following independence, which was characterized by constant changes and shifting ideologies, perceptions of gender held by intellectuals often differed from traditional conceptions of gender inherited from Catholicism and Spanish culture. Many times these contradictions surfaced in apparently homogeneous texts based on the paradigmatic construction of binary oppositions, producing ambiguous characters that defied traditional concepts of masculinity and femininity.

A classic use of Kant and Hegel's ideology by the Unitarians can be seen in the three guiding principles of the Argentine *Asociación de Mayo:* to look for the most fertile ideas in European theories; adapt those ideas to the country's needs; and discard the influence of contemporary Spanish literature (with the exception of some authors) by substituting texts of French and Italian thinkers.[40] The third principle is based mainly on Juan María

Gutiérrez's speech "Fisonomía del saber español" (Physiognomy of Spanish Knowledge), where he argues that the backwardness of Spanish culture had produced no illustrious individual or anything useful to man over the centuries.[41] One of the later and more prominent members of this group, Domingo Faustino Sarmiento, refers to Spain as the "backward daughter of Europe" and regrets that Argentina had not been colonized by a more civilized nation.[42]

The Generation of '37, also known as the *Asociación de Mayo* after the Argentine independence of May 1810, is the second generation of Unitarians that was formed by a young group of intellectual political exiles during the peak of Rosas's terrorism. According to Nicholas Shumway, the members of this group assigned themselves two major intellectual tasks: to identify the problems confronting their country and to devise a program that would bring Argentina into a new era of modernity (112). Although more liberal in their approach, the Men of '37 repeated former generations' errors by placing too much emphasis and faith in the redemptive power of European and US philosophies.[43] Shumway observes that the racist aspects of this intellectually based group, in many ways reflect the narrow-minded ideologies that had circulated in Europe for over two centuries, which can be seen in Sarmiento's well-known work *Civilización y barbarie: Vida de Don Facundo Quiroga* (144). In this work, Sarmiento reiterates Kant's and Hegel's xenophobic ideologies as he defines the racial aspects of Argentina as a compelling element contributing to the political failure of his country:

> A homogenous whole has resulted from the fusion of the [Spanish, African, and Indian] races. It is typified by love of idleness and incapacity for industry, except when education and the demands of a social position succeed in spurring it out of its customary crawl. To a great extent, this unfortunate outcome results from the incorporation of the native tribes through the process of colonization. The American aborigines live in idleness, and show themselves incapable, even under compulsion, of hard and prolonged labor. From this came the idea of introducing Negroes into America, which has produced such fatal results. But the Spanish race has not shown itself more energetic than the aborigines, when it has been left to its own instincts in the wilds of America.[44]

Shumway notes that this disdain for their country's racial factors reflects the ideas of all of the Men of the Generation of '37, despite their ultimate goals of uniting the polarized groups in their nation (37). Although they had initially set out to change the grave errors of the previous generation in their efforts to unite the Unitarians and the Federalists, the intellectual growth and development of this group was set against the backdrop of the Rosas' dictatorship (113). José Mármol's depiction of Rosas's supporters as "a people ignorant by education, vengeful by race, and impulsive by climate" (*Amalia* 44) and Juan Batista Alberdi's comment "All that is civilization on our soil is European" (*Bases* 239–41) reflect a strong belief in a European superiority that was both adopted by the Generation of '37 and incorporated into their future national plans.[45]

One of the principal objectives of this group was to define the social ills of Argentina and somehow explain the perilous condition of their country under the tyrannical rule of Juan Manuel de Rosas. During their first meeting, the group's founder, Esteban Echeverría, proclaims that Argentine history since independence was divided into two periods. While the first period "belonged to the sword," the second period is "a new dawn," inaugurated by "the forum of intelligence, where rigorous and profound reason proclaims a new era."[46] Inspired by popular European thinkers of their day, the Men of the Generation of '37 set out to cure the infirmed status of their nation after the wars of independence and designed a social and political plan that would transform this fractured country into a modern nation. As indicated in Echeverría's speech, the members of the group identify themselves as the beholders of the second period—those active men representative of the voice of reason and intelligence confronted with three significant obstacles inherent in the national makeup of their nation: the land, Spanish tradition, and race (145). Two of the more prominent members of the group, Sarmiento and Echeverría, wrote political treatises that have been instrumental in shaping the national identity in Argentina. Despite the apparent contradictions that surface in these texts with regard to gender, it is important to know that these writers identify themselves as the masculine voice of reason, assigned the crucial mission of incorporating the civilizing qualities of progress into a nation hindered by the brutal aspects of the land and the racial composition of their people.

In *Civilización y barbarie: Vida de Don Facundo Quiroga* (1845), Domingo Faustino Sarmiento adopts positivist notions of science in order to show the barbaric effect that the vast and indomitable nature of the land had in the formation of the *caudillista* tendencies prevalent in Argentina.[47] By explaining and categorizing these social elements within the concepts of civilization and barbarism, Sarmiento hoped to annihilate the *caudillo* type from his country. Doris Sommer notes that the gendering of both land and narrator in this text reflects a heterosexual coupling that would lead to the journey towards progress of Argentina. According to Sommer, the masculine, rational character of Sarmiento offers himself as a Mr. Right to the feminine, virgin lands of Argentina, forming a union that would lead his nation into an era of progress and reason.[48] However, one of the underlying contradictions in Sarmiento's essay is that the author equates the land, the Indians, and the *gauchos* with the irrational, uncontrollable forces of the feminized space of the land. Sarmiento, as a Romantic, is caught between his love of nature and his need to condemn it as one of the primary contributors to the formation of the barbaric nature of the *gaucho,* Juan Facundo Quiroga, who in this text is emblematic of Juan Manuel de Rosas.

Initially Sarmiento serves as the mediator between Argentina and Europe, explaining "a los ojos atónitos de la europa" [to the astonished eyes of Europe] the complexities of this new world of politics, that struggles between the progress associated with civilization and the rudimentary savage life that he defines as barbarism (10). Yet the text moves away from the narrative voice as impartial observer as his construction of the Other takes on a life of its own through his celebrated virile qualities. In chapter 2, Sarmiento systematically classifies the *gauchos* according to types—the *gaucho malo, the rastreador, the cantor,* and *the baqueano* [the Outlaw, the Track-Finder, the Minstrel, and the Path-Finder]. It is in this part of the text where the objective voice of the narrator begins to fuse with the romanticized image of the *gaucho,* known for his strong character. The initial individual tone of *yo* [I] in the work now changes to *nosotros* (we): "También nuestro pueblo es músico. Esta es una predisposición nacional que todos los vecinos le reconocen. . . . Esta es una preocupación que acusa nuestros hábitos nacionales" (42) [Music, too, is found among our people. It is a nacional taste recognized by all our neighbors] (29).[49] This becomes even more evident in chapter 5, which is dedicated to Quiroga. In this chapter Sarmiento explains and reinforces the myth surrounding Quiroga's name "Juan Quiroga Facundo de Tigre de los Llanos," thus celebrating the hypo-virile qualities he initially wishes to subvert. The protagonist's struggle of man against nature is highlighted during an encounter with a fierce tiger in his youth: "Esta escena horrible duraba ya dos horas mortales; la postura violenta del gaucho y la fascinación aterrante que ejercía sobre él la mirada sanguinaria, inmóvil del tigre, del que por una fuerza invencible de atracción no podría apartar los ojos" (74) [This horrible scene had lasted for nearly two mortal hours; the gaucho's constrained attitude, and the fearful fascination exercised over him by the fixed and bloodthirsty stare of the tiger, which irresistibly attracted and retained his own glances] (75). Facundo represents the epitome of manhood in this scene set against the brutal forces of nature. Many critics have noted that although he sets out to objectively construct a negative image of the Other, Sarmiento fuses with the text as a protagonist, showing fascination and awe for that which he intends to show as barbaric. It is ironic that the Other, which is traditionally assigned to the feminine, is characterized as the virile masculine figure of Facundo. Paradoxically, if the construction of the Other in this text is so typically male, its antithesis, the refined educated European, can be more appropriately defined within the concepts of the feminine, which is an unexpected twist that becomes even more evident in Echevarría's short story *El matadero.*

In *El matadero,* Echeverría also uses the hypo-masculinized figure of the Other in order to describe the barbaric nature of the Rosas regime. Echeverría's construction of masculinity, like Sarmiento's, is depicted in the incarnation of the barbaric Other, in this case in the violent, bloody setting of a slaughterhouse in Argentina during Lent. The floods and the violence of the "chusma" [mob] create a grotesque imagery depicting a sense of turmoil and loss of control. In this story the relationship between the sole Unitarian and Matasiete backed by the angry masses typifies the violent nature of the dictatorship. The role of women in this text exists in the background, but they undoubtedly contribute to the depravity of the followers of Rosas. Situated in the macabre scenario of the slaughter of fifty "novillos" [young bulls], the black and mulata women are assigned the role of "achuradoras" [scavengers]: "cuya fealdad trasuntaba las harpies de las fábulas" (316) [whose ugliness matched that of the fabled harpies] (9).

Race and class are instrumental in this work, serving as a stark contrast to the whiteness of the perceived civilizing qualities of

Europe, coveted by the Unitarians. The slaughter is followed by the sheer chaos of "sangre" [blood] and "tripas" [guts] being thrown about. The women, unlike those defined within the traditional concepts of femininity, or *marianismo*, are haggard, greedy, and unkempt and are seen slipping in pools of blood in their zealous attempt to grab at the intestines made available by the slaughter. Meanwhile, a young boy is beheaded without a care from the crowd. This savage imagery of carnage and confusion contributes to the barbaric nature of Matasiete, who is the leader of this bloody endeavor and representative of Rosas and his followers: "Simulacro en pequeño era éste del modo bárbaro con que se ventilan en nuestro país las cuestiones y los derechos individuales y sociales" (9) [It was a miniature version of the barbaric way individual and social issues and rights are aired in our country] (12).

The use of oppositions throughout the text works to highlight ideas of good and evil, enlightenment and oppression, civilization and barbarism, feminine and masculine, which are inverted during this oppressive regime. Juan Carlos Mercado points out that Matasiete's name is symbolic in the text because its meaning refers to "bully or braggart," and the elements *mata* [(he) kills] and *siete* [seven] refer to the fierce masculine nature of the butcher.[50] Similarly, the Unitarian is positioned in a submissive state of powerlessness as the angry mob begins to "desnudarlo" [unclothe him], thus increasing his status of vulnerability. This tormenting of the weaker Unitarian calls to mind José Piedra's essay "Nationalizing Sissies," where he explains the homoerotic nature between bullies and sissies during colonialism. Piedra states: "Whether it leads or not to an actual sexual takeover, in principle, bullying a sissy remains a misogynist, heterosexist, and xenophobic exercise, but one that could backfire against the enforcers of such prejudices."[51] This ideology can easily be applied to *El matadero* in the xenophobic actions and attitudes of the masses against both the Englishman and the Unitarian. The gendered positioning of the virile Federalist Matasiete hovering over the effeminate Unitarian serves as a symbolic portrayal of a nation at odds—a (feminized) bully depicted for his primal characteristics and excessive masculinity, who is ultimately responsible for the annihilation of a sissy, representative of the enlightened Unitarians and the (masculine) voice of reason. Gendered characteristics spill over in this early nineteenth-century text, due to the author's use of gendered oppositional codes in texts written during an increasingly changing political climate. Echeverría and Sarmiento sought to reappropriate the masculine position of power, yet in both texts they represent a passive, dominated positioning that clearly casts them into the feminine domain.

Sarmiento's *Facundo* and Echeverría's *El matadero* provide two early examples of gender troping in nineteenth-century narrative. I believe that this tendency becomes a more common trend that not only persists during the turn of the century but also intensifies due to the extensive scientific and philosophical explorations about gender that emerged during the fin de siècle in Europe. During the nineteenth century, the recently emancipated Spanish American countries looked towards most of Europe and the United States as models of civilization and progress and incorporated scientific findings in their nation-building strategies. In addition, many prominent writers, including Domingo Faustino Sarmiento and Esteban Echeverría, had traveled to and/or resided in Europe, where they discovered a profusion of literary trends and modalities that they could incorporate into their nations.[52] Echeverría returned from Paris in 1830 charged with the utopian prophesies of Claude-Henri Saint-Simon (1760–1825) and the Romantic ideals of Victor Hugo (1802–85).[53] Similarly, Sarmiento, armed with the basic tenets of positivism theorized by Auguste Comte (1798–1857), systematically categorized his country into a series of classifications and types so that he could proscribe the solution of education and immigration as a means of leading his country into an age of progress. Sarmiento, like Echeverría, used conceptualizations of gender in order to exclude the barbaric Other from the national spectrum in an effort to gain the coveted position of power through narrative.

In *The History of Sexuality* (1978), Michel Foucault traces back to the seventeenth-century confessional as the locus of the fascination, elaboration, and proliferation of discourses about sex that later became incorporated into institutions, such as government and capitalism, as a means of controlling the proletariat. This classification, codification, and policing of gender codes and stereotypes reached its peak in the nineteenth century and consequently polarized even more already dichotomous perceptions of gender. Foucault examines the ways in which sex was regulated through discourse, how that discourse was wielded into power, and how both were perceived as truth.[54] In *The Dialogic Imagination,* Mikhail Mikhailovich Bakhtin claims that there are no neutral words and forms: "Each word tastes of the context and contexts in which it has lived its socially charged life; all words and forms are populated by intentions."[55] Because power and knowledge were so intricately linked to gender and sexuality in the turn-of-the-century epistemological discourse of science, gendered discourse became a more frequently used trope employed in narrative concerning the nation.

In *The Descent of Man* (1871), Charles Darwin defined the superiority of man over women as due to natural differences.[56] And in *Principles of Sociology* (1896), Herbert Spencer further claimed that human development depended on the expenditure of fixed energy. Spencer argued that since women depleted their energy with the reproductive system, they were heavily handicapped and less intelligent.[57] Similarly, Patrick Geddes and J. Arthur Thompson postulated theories of sexual differentiation based on cell metabolism in *The Evolution of Sex* (1889).[58] Male cells were said to be katabolic, or active and energetic, whereas female cells were anabolic, or energy-conserving, passive, and life-supporting. They concluded that men were aggressive, competitive, and inventive, whereas women, like the ovum, were placid, altruistic, and nurturing.[59] These are just a few paradigmatic treatises that have proclaimed the superiority of men over women and have ostensibly contributed to the exclusion of women from nationalist discourse. However, the nineteenth-century scientific investigations of Jean-Martin Charcot, Cesare Lombroso, and research concerning the biological and physiological anomalies of the Hottentots, proved to be particularly deleterious to the image of women for their theories that highlighted the relationship between gender, race, and pathology. Many of these classifications described as deviant would be included in the discourse of degeneration and utilized by many Latin American writers anxious to advance their nations into an age of modernity.

Nineteenth-Century Perceptions of Women

In *The Lost Rib* (1985) Sharon Magnarelli argues that the result of the vast mythology surrounding woman is that throughout history she has been alternately praised and disparaged, exalted and idealized, worshipped or degraded: "In so many ways, then, women have always been personae, characters, literary creations, both inside and outside of fiction, continually fantasized, fabricated, and counterfeited. We have alternately believed them to be a great deal more or considerably less than what they are."[60] In the nineteenth century, woman falls victim to all of the previous categorizations because, on the one hand, the scientific distinction between normal and abnormal, pathological and healthy, and sanity and insanity was clearly demarcated by the medical experts of the day. On the other hand, the writers of the literary movements of naturalism, Romanticism, and *modernismo* in Latin America frequently utilized the image of the idealized woman in their works.[61]

During the nineteenth century, the image of woman was visually accessible in many venues, and her anatomy and varied representations were exhibited in order to scientifically mark the difference between the pathological and the sane. In 1882 Jean-Martin Charcot established a neurological clinic at the Salpêtrière Hospital in Paris where he visually exploited the female illness of hysteria. Hysteria, originally derived from the Greek word *uterus,* was considered an exclusively female illness, which soon became linked with madness. According to Didi-Huberman, the great image factory was the Salpêtrière Hospital, where the methodical and theoretical fabrication of hysteria became truly canonical.[62] Every Tuesday Charcot held lectures on hysteria in a huge amphitheater in the Salpêtrière to a curious audience including authors, journalists, actors, and actresses.[63] Women were on display and even told to pose according to the specific symptom that they were demonstrating so that Charcot could expound on the different manifestations of hysteria. Known for his use of visual investigations and lectures, Charcot contracted photographers to record the diverse imagery and poses believed to be related to the illness. The *Iconographie photographique de la Salpêtrière,* which encompassed a broad collection of visual imagery on hysteria, including poses, attacks, cries, *attitudes passionnelles,* crucifixions, and ecstasy, was published and available to the public in 1876, 1887, and 1880.[64] According to Elaine Showalter, hysteria became the illness in vogue during Charcot's residency at the Salpêtrière, showing a dramatic increase from only 1 percent in 1845, to 17.3 percent of

1. Charcot lecturing on hysteria at the Salpêtrière, etching after André Brouillet, 1887 (from the Wellcome Institute Library, London).

all diagnoses in 1883, at the height of his investigations on hysteria.[65]

Similarly, in Italy, Cesare Lombroso provided carefully detailed accounts of jaw size, arm span, and skull proportions in his book *The Female Offender* (1895), distinguishing the normal woman from the criminal. Lombroso's studies can be traced backed to earlier nineteenth century anthropoligical investigations held by A. J. B. Parent-Duchatelet (1836) and Pauline Tarnowsky (1889–93) who provided theorizations and categorizations of the degenerate characteristics of prostitutes. According to Dr. Lombroso, "The habitual criminal, a product of pathological and atavistic anomalies, stands midway between the lunatic and the savage, and represents a special type of the human race."[66] Among their detailed studies of the anatomy and behavior of criminal women, including prostitutes, Lombroso and his team reinforced myths of woman's relationship to the primitive, as well as scientifically defining the dichotomy between the virgin and the whore: "We also saw that women have many traits in common with children; that their moral sense is deficient, that they are revengeful, jealous, inclined to vengeances of a refined cruelty" (151). Lombroso

2. Augustine, "Extase," 1878 (from the New York Academy of Medicine).

labeled the criminal woman a "monster," contrasting her with her "normal sister" who is "kept in the paths of virtue by many causes, such as maternity, piety, weakness" (152). However, when these counterinfluences fail, and a woman commits a crime, Lombroso concluded that her wickedness "must have been enormous before it could triumph over so many obstacles" and thus exceeded that of any male criminal (152). Lombroso also led an intensive study on the male criminal (*The Criminal Man*) based on atavistic characteristics and biological anomalies; however, his investigations of normal versus abnormal women in *The Female Offender* reinforced already dichotomous conceptualizations of women.

Sexual anatomy also became the site for difference during the nineteenth century and was on display for visual interpretations and stereotyping. In his chapter titled "The Hottentot and the Prostitute: Toward an Iconography of Female Sexuality," Sander L. Gilman compares the iconic similarities between the prostitute and the Hottentot, thus establishing the common perception of the intrinsic relationship between pathology, race, and gender. According to Gilman, sexual anatomy is so important a part of the self-image that "sexually different" is tantamount to "pathological" and the Other is perceived to be impaired, sick, and diseased.[67] In 1814 Saartje Baartman, also called Sara Bartman, became the object of scientific and medical research in Europe, where she was put on display depicting her anatomical differences, thereby making her the icon of racial inferiority and black female sexuality.[68] Gilman states that the "Hottentot Venus," a photograph explicitly showing her difference, served as the emblem of black sexuality during the entire nineteenth century, a sexuality shown to be inherently different from that of the European. Sara's steatopygia, or protruding buttocks, proved to be a striking biological anomaly presented to the European audience.[69] Even after her death, Sara Bartman's sexual organs and brain were on display in the *Musee de l'Homme* in Paris, where they were available for observation until as recently as 1985. In addition to exploiting the anomalies of the female body, exhibitions of this type were used to mark the extreme difference between "primitive" and "civilized" societies.

In his book *Pathology and Difference* (1985), Gilman cites the resemblance of the iconic images of Zola's Nana with the pathological findings of the prostitute and her similarities between the

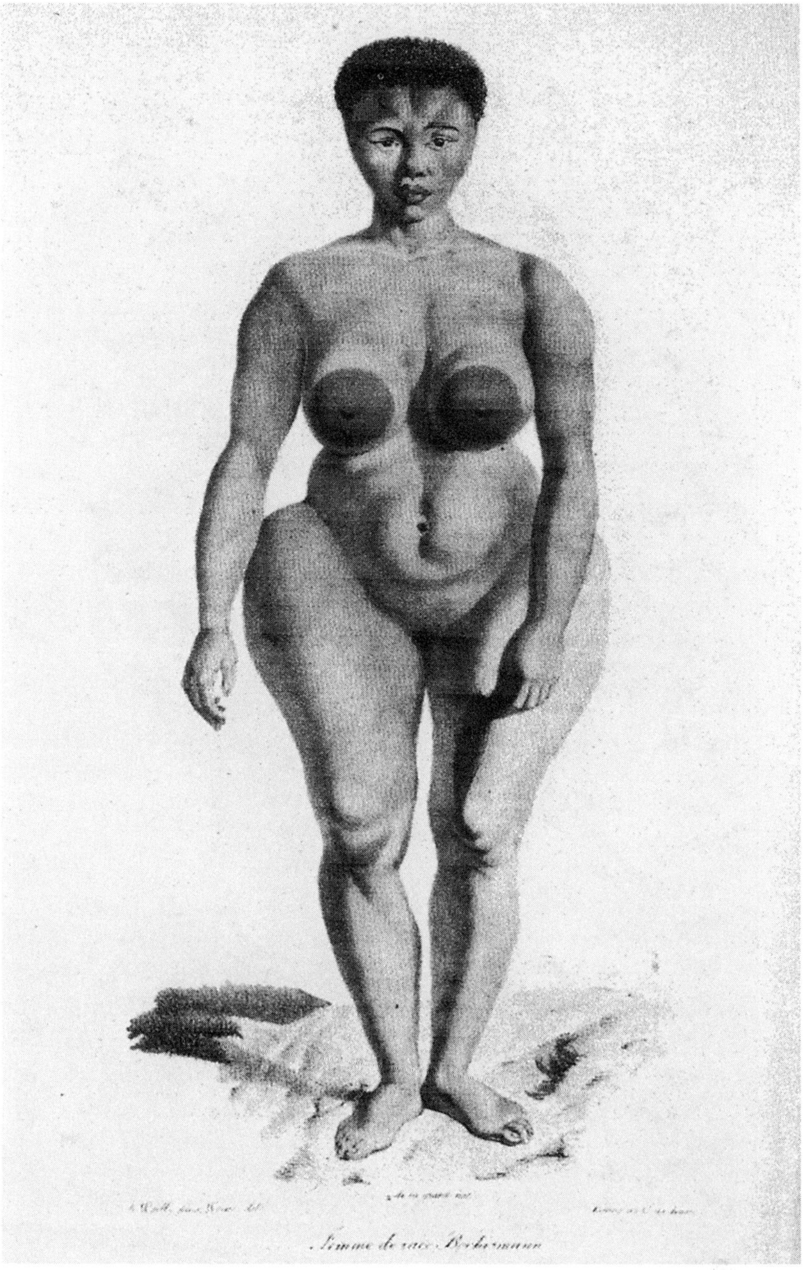

3. Saartje Baartman, the "Hottentot Venus" (from Geoffrey Saint-Hilaire and Frèdèric Cuvier, *Historie naturelle des mammifères avec des figures originales,* 1824).

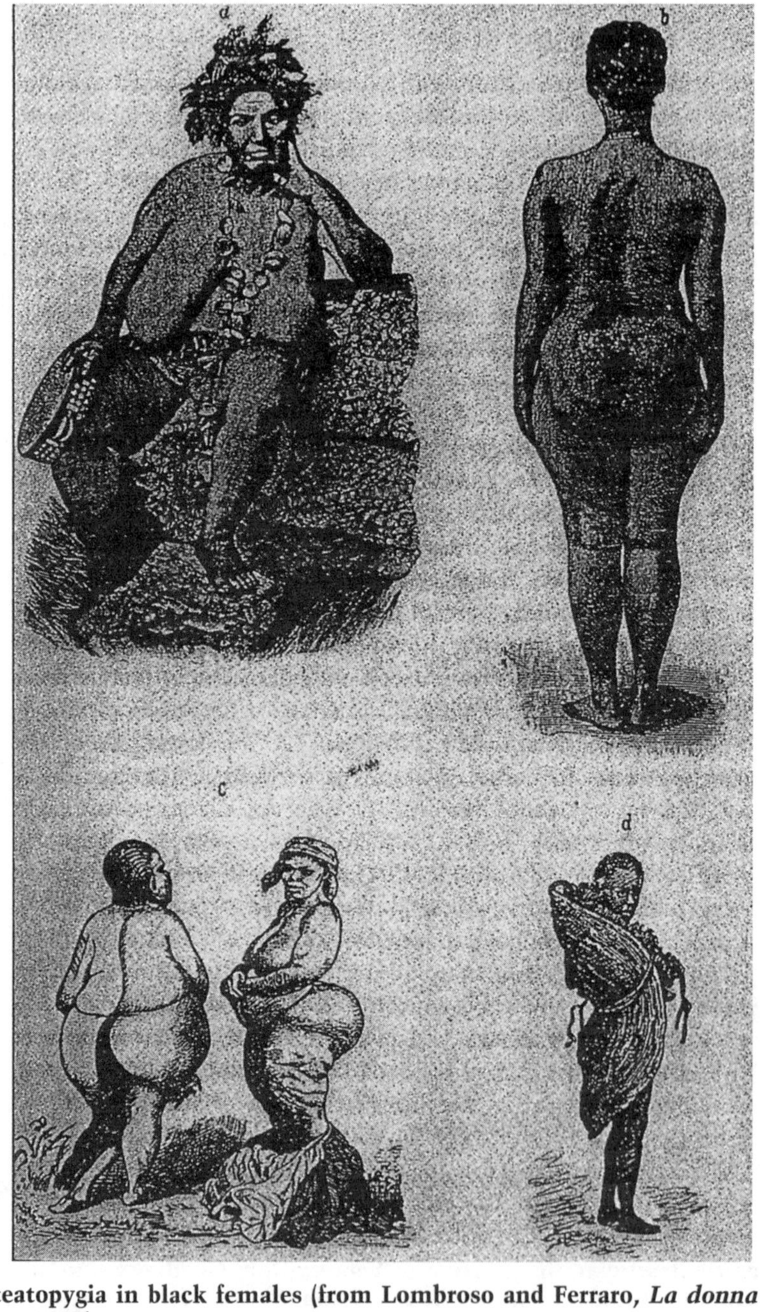

4. Steatopygia in black females (from Lombroso and Ferraro, *La donna deliquente* 1893).

Hottentots, thus providing a clear example that scientific postulations of femininity and pathology had infiltrated important literary works. The character Nana first appeared in 1877 in Emile Zola's naturalist novel *L'Assommoir,* and in this same year Edouard Manet painted Nana based on this image.[70] Surprisingly, Zola used Manet's painting when he wrote the novel *Nana* (1880), and the painting is included within the novel during the seduction of Count Muffet. When describing the seduction of Count Muffet in *Nana,* Zola expounds upon the "primitive" sexualized woman hidden beneath the masked surface of the desirable prostitute: "Nana was still smiling: but it was the smile of a maneater."[71] In this excerpt, Zola links the atavistic sexuality of Nana to the Amazon woman, which was believed to be primitive as well as destructive.[72]

However, it is in Manet's painting of Nana where Gilman points out the signs of pathology and difference. Manet's painting coincides with scientific studies of prostitutes as well as recalling perceived conceptions of degeneracy attributed to Hottentot women. First of all, she is depicted as being heavy even though being thin was in style.[73] She is also given the Darwin ear (the simplification of the convolutions of the ear shell and the absence of a lobe) and protruding buttocks, which were two characteristics that became significant of her degeneracy.[74] Zola concludes his novel when Nana contracts smallpox, a visually grotesque and agonizing disease that becomes emblematic of her true character.[75] According to Gilman, Nana reverts to the blackness of the earth, to the primitive, the world of disease. She, like Olympia, is "pre-eminently unclean":[76] "And it is this uncleanness, this disease, which forms the final link between two images of the woman, the black and the prostitute. For, just as the genitalia of the Hottentots were perceived as parallel to the diseased genitalia of the prostitute, so too the powerful idea of corruption links both images.[77] Nana is corrupted and corrupts through sexuality" (105). Emile Zola's *Nana* became the hallmark of naturalism in Europe, a literary movement that incorporated scientific studies and Darwinist ideas as a means of objectively examining the basest of social environments, which would then serve as a metaphor of nation. These scientific theories and investigations positing the "abnormal" woman as degenerative became influential to many Latin American writers who would link gender, race, and pathology to their nation's slow progression into

5. Edouard Manet, *Nana* (1877).

modernity. In fact, in *Pueblos enfermos,* Michael Aronna claims that the discourse of degeneration played a key role in the emergence of essays and letters in both Spain and Latin America, "which accounted for underdevelopment through psychological and medical explanations which found their nations to be too sick, immature, un-evolved and 'feminine' to possess the rational and moral qualities necessary for national progress" (21). In this work I will point out how the feminized Other is utilized in the narrative in order to promote a sense of nationalism and/or national healing.

In contrast to the pathological abnormal woman is the idealized woman in romantic novels and *modernista* poetry, which is another aspect of the feminine that will be instrumental in the novels discussed in this work. In her chapter "The Love Story: Reading the Writing in Jorge Isaac's *María*" (1985), Sharon Magnarelli describes the different roles of both male and female characters in the genre of the romantic novel. She states that on the one hand, men are physically stronger, better educated, more well-traveled, and thus more worldly and knowledgeable than women. Women, on the other hand, are the weak, passive recipients, dedicating their time to taking care of the man, concerning themselves with the home and religion: "Somewhat over simplified, it might be said that men in this novel go out and do things (are active) while the women sit home and wait" (27). Similarly, dichotomous roles of men and women can be seen in the philosophy of Auguste Comte, the founder of French positivism, in his *System of Positive Polity* (1852), where he reinforces altruistic qualities traditionally associated with "good" women: "Clearly, the essential duty and mission of woman is to save man from the corruption, to which he is exposed in his life of action and thought." In turn, the man's responsibility was to relieve "the loving" sex from any obstacles or anxiety that could interrupt those affections.[78] These idealist qualities attributed to women were utilized in many romantic novels and were considered antithetical to the pathological woman discussed earlier.

Similarly in *modernista* poetry, the idealized, often sexualized version of the woman is utilized in the poet's search for beauty and many times becomes emblematic of poetry itself. In the late nineteenth century, *modernistas* were frustrated with the rising accumulation of wealth by the bourgeois, utilitarianism, the survival of the fittest, and the positivist ideas of Comte.[79] Writers sought to fill the spiritual void left by positivism in their poetry and often used the image of woman as a means of escaping the harsh realities of the modern world. Cathy Jrade remarks: "Woman is more than the poet's Muse. She is the other that complements and completes, the one with whom the poet attains a vision of beauty, harmony, and artistic perfection that is simultaneously in tune with and supported by nature."[80] In "Copa con alas" from José Martí's *Versos libres,* the woman is the *copa con alas* [winged cup], or the poetic muse, and it is the poetic voice's union with this feminine image that becomes symbolic of the act of writing poetry. In the second stanza, the poetic voice grasps on to the feminine image of the muse that ascends into the heavens: "Una copa en los aires ascendía / y yo, en brazos no vistos reclinado / tras ella, asido de sus dulces bordes / Por el espacio azul me remontaba!" (17–20: 70) [A goblet rose into the air / And I, in unseen arms reclining / In its wake, seized by its fragrant rim, / And soaring through blue spaces!] (149).[81] It is through this trajectory, that the priestlike qualities of the poetic voice, just like the creative forces of the *herrero* [blacksmith] and the *joyador* [jeweler] deliver the divine message to the masses through poetry. Similarly, in Rubén Darío's classic poem "Sonatina," the poetic voice, like the knight in shining armor, arrives to save the distressed woman from her apathy with the mundane world of materialism and riches, reflecting the sentiments of *mal-del-siglo* held by most *modernistas.* The male poetic voice, thus, appropriates the visages of the idealized woman in order to reach a higher plane, which is represented in this case as the metafictional poetic process.

Historically, the image of motherhood has always been a highly exalted virtue throughout the Western world and in Latin America can best be defined referring to the concepts of *marianismo.* The term *marianismo* comes from the Virgin Mary and represents the ideal of true femininity that Hispanic women must live up to. Modesty, virtue, and sexual abstinence until marriage are some of the basic characteristics of *marianismo;* however, the sacred bond between mother and child can be regarded as one of its prominent features. The Mexican poet and feminist Rosario Castellanos speaks about one of the more significant characteristics of woman in the following passage: "The Mexican *woman* does not consider herself—nor do others consider her—to be a woman who has reached fulfillment if she has not produced children. . . . Love for one's child supplants or substitutes for all other kinds of love, which qualify as less perfect because they presuppose reciprocity" (9; emphasis in original).[82] Thus, motherhood, whose most significant trait is self-sacrifice, becomes a practice that is not only lived but also must be perceived by others in order to have a significant impact.

The image of motherhood has also been a compelling means of imagining the nation in Latin America. In her essay "Beyond Ethnocentrism: Gender, Power, and the Third-World Intelligentsia" (1988), Jean Franco argues that for many male writers confronted with the uncertainties of a postcolonial third world, the mother's body provided the only source of stability.[83] Franco notes the necessity of many Latin American writers to defend the motherland against the rise of imperialist threats from the outside: "In a society scarred by the violence and death that inevitably accompanied imperialist penetration . . . it is not surprising to observe a certain 'feminization of values'" (508). In her book *Talking Back* (1992), Debra Castillo also comments on the importance of the female body in maintaining the stability of national identity in Latin America. She argues that the image of woman is "the primordial site for the generation of discourse" that must "embody those unchanging, pristine values of permanence, privacy, immobility, and purity as the essential core of national identity."[84] Consequently, idealized images of altruistic women and self-abnegating mothers are held up as positive social bodies reflecting the ego/ethos of male-oriented nationalistic discourse.

This imagery serves as a stark contrast to the pathological women discussed previously and was also instrumental in imagining the nation. Aligned with the medical experts of their day, many writers throughout Latin America utilized the image of the female body in order to examine the social ills of their respective nations. It is no surprise that in *Between Civilization and Barbarism* (1982), Francine Masiello laments the inequity between the actual progress made by women writers in Argentina and the objectified, pathological portrayal of women in works written by men. She argues that the female body became a "metaphorical map upon which Argentine men, in a scientific mode, traced the ills of the past and offered a prognosis for the nation's future."[85] This critic points out that this unnerving focus on the reproductive and pathological status of the female body only reinforced a sense of the sexual inferiority of women (92). Among the many examples that Masiello offers, *Nelly* (1896) stands out for its metaphorical portrayal of the pathological body of the hysteric used in an endeavor to cleanse the infirmed status of the nation. In *Nelly,* Eduardo Holmberg, a Darwinian naturalist devoted to positivism, saw the female body and psyche as an outlet for disorder and chaos that needed to be controlled by science so that the family and nation could finally prosper (89). Among other novels that advocated the image of women for their national projections one may include the following: *María* (1867) by Jorge Isaacs, *La charca* (1894) by Zeno Gandía, *Juana Lucero* (1902) by Augusto D'Halmar, *Santa* (1903) by Federico Gamboa, and *Nacha Regules* (1918) by Manuel Gálvez. The novels that I have chosen for this study also reveal the manipulation of the feminine in their depiction of nation and their struggle for power: José Martí's *Amistad funesta,* Rómulo Gallegos's *Doña Bárbara,* and Miguel Ángel Asturias's *El Señor Presidente.*

These novels, however, also portray masculine subjects that are held up as positive models of nationhood. It should not be surprising (but often overlooked in feminist theory) that just as conceptions of femininity underwent a series of permutations according to the evolution of philosophical and scientific investigations, perceptions of what it meant to be masculine were also under scrutiny during the nineteenth century. The masculine subject, oftentimes a reflection of the alter ego of the writers included in this study, was strategically constructed in order to reflect the voice of reason in their nation's transition towards modernity and/or progress and many times was posited against the image of the pathological feminized Other.

The Formation of the Masculine National Subject

In my reading of mid-nineteenth- and early twentieth-century texts written by prominent writers in Latin America, I have noticed wide variations of gender, specifically with regard to the proposed male national subject. In *El matadero* by Esteban Echeverría, the Unitarian is characterized as more feminine in opposition to the highly masculinized characters associated with the *matadero.*[86] In the Cuban Gertrudis Gómez de Avellaneda's

Sab (1841), the androgynous nature of the mulatto's character works to blur not only sexual boundaries but also those of class and race. And in *Amalia* (1851), by the Argentine José Mármol, Doris Sommer notes that the delicate hands of the main protagonist, Daniel, are indicative of some of his feminine features: "The whiteness of his lovely hands could have made any coquette jealous."[87] In her book *Foundational Fictions,* Sommer argues that the members of the Asociación de Mayo were the second generation of Unitarians who were more willing to make peace between the parties in an effort to unite the nation, and she therefore attributes the unisex of Daniel as a means of unifying the polarities between the Unitarians and Federalists.[88] She further argues that the main protagonist of the Chilean Alberto Blest Gana's *Martín Rivas* seems to lack the traditional masculine traits traditionally attributed to men coming from the *campo* [country] and working in the mines. The androgynous virtuosity of Martín and the active and intelligent character of Leonor, states Sommer, "are intended to replace the conventional (oligarchic) habits with more flexible (bourgeois) relationships."[89] Remaining faithful to these dichotomies, one could deduce that all of the aforementioned characters are good and noble and can serve as exemplary models of the new national subject. Yet, ironically, all characters display feminine characteristics coupled with their biological, physiological, masculine makeup. Thus, the first contradiction in the dichotomy of gender is that feminine and masculine do not always exist in opposition but are many times intrinsically inherent within the biologically gendered body.

In his book *Difference and Pathology,* Sander L. Gilman argues that the perception of the Other as a threat to the individual's autonomy is a reflection of the loss of autonomy felt within the group. He states: "Group identity thereby serves as a means of defining the 'healthy,' that which belongs to the group and 'protects' those in it, as well as defining its antithesis as the outsider or the Other" (25). In other words, at the turn of the century it was extremely important to define the masculine subject in a way that was perceived to be healthy and progressive, thereby reflecting the ethos of the nation. In order to achieve this goal, it was often necessary to clearly distinguish the masculine subject from the feminine pathological Other without compromising the political objectives of the work. The importance given to scientific and philosophical discourse concerning gender in the nineteenth century, as well as the changing historical landscape of many Latin American countries during this period, made it extremely difficult to construct a traditional masculine subject; specifically because conceptualizations of what it meant to be masculine during this era were in flux, and also because many of the undesirable characteristics of the Other maintained masculine characteristics. The homosexual, the abnormal woman, and the hypo-masculinized subject are three categories that were often feminized and cast into the realm of Other and were consequently instrumental in disturbing the hierarchical binaries of gender in many Latin American texts. I believe that these considerations are important because they must have been instrumental in the formation of masculine subjects, at the same time being the very reason for the construction of the many ambiguously gendered subjects prevalent during this time period.

In his book *The Wilde Century* (1994), Alan Sinfield traces conceptualizations of masculinity and their relationship to femininity and homosexuality leading up to the period preceding the infamous trials of Oscar Wilde in 1896. He argues that although the polarity of masculine and feminine became more clear-cut in the eighteenth century, conceptualizations of what it meant to be feminine and masculine varied widely up until the end of the nineteenth century.[90] The eighteenth-century dandy, known for his idleness, refined habits, and elegance distinguished himself from the common working man: "To the people of the lower class, a noble—powdered, pomaded, refined—was both elegant and effeminate; but that bothered no one as long as the mode of attire remained faithful to the specific social condition which its wearer represented."[91] Because the aristocrat was expected to be effeminate, he was not accused of same-sex passion. Similarly, the eighteenth-century ideology of the cultivation of true feelings, or manly sentiments, as a basis of civilization would come under scrutiny in the nineteenth century, when the insistence that men be manly and women be domestic emerged as the dominant way of thinking.[92]

In her essay "Too Wilde for Comfort: Desire and Ideology in *fin-de-siècle* Latin America" (1992), Sylvia Molloy addresses the policing of gender codes at the end of the century, when budding nations were adopting from the outside, much of the "good" which was inevitably accompanied with the "bad."[93] She draws on Martí's impression and Darío's writings of Oscar Wilde's homosexuality as that of being particularly odd and even perverse. Likewise, José Enrique Rodó's censorship of Rubén Darío's "too soft" poetry and Martí's prologue to Juan Antonio Pérez Bonalde's "Niágara," which states there should not be feminine writers, are just two examples of the policing or keeping track of gender codes during this period when "US imperialism and the threat of the big stick penetration threatened the virility of Latin American men."[94] The thrust of US imperialism had already made its mark in Latin American countries in the late nineteenth century with its commercial interests in Central America and Mexico, its control of the Panama Canal Zone, as well as its interest in the annexation of Cuba prior to the Spanish-American War in 1898. Very much aware of the outside hegemonic forces of this rising power, Latin American intellectuals were conscious of the need to "beef up" their self-image in their narrative, as one can see in Rodó's critique of Darío's *modernista* verses: "Versos golosos, versos tentadores y finos, versos capaces de hacer languidecer a una legión de Esparta. . . . Si se tratase de ir a la Guerra, yo los proscribiría" [Inviting verses, tempting and delicate verses, verses capable of making a Spartan legion swoon. . . . If there were an oncoming war, I would ban them].[95] Consequently, the already negatively charged conceptions of femininity carried with it new shades of degeneracy when linked with the biological masculine body.

Similarly, in her essay "Politics of Posing" (1998), Molloy cites nineteenth-century Argentine psychiatrist, sociologist, and criminologist José Ingenieros's censorship of homosexuality, calling it only a posing or feigning of undesirable French and *modernista* behavior. According to Ingenieros, once the patient was convinced that he was not indeed homosexual, but only imitating "bad" behavior, the symptoms were easily curable. By labeling homosexuality a mere imitation of behavior or "posing," Ingenieros thus wiped this perceived degenerative, pathological behavior from "his" country.[96] According to Foucault, homosexuality, formerly perceived as aberrant behavior associated with sodomites and hermaphrodites, had now become a species in the nineteenth century (43). Molloy's essay recalls the phobia and disdain for homosexuality in the fin de siècle and the apparent disapproval of Latin American intelligentsia of feminine characteristics displayed by "normal" heterosexual men. According to Sinfield, effeminacy was not necessarily associated with homosexuality until the time of Oscar Wilde's trial, at which time a certain anxiety toward effeminacy in men's behavior ensued.

According to the scientific postulations of medical experts of the nineteenth century, prostitutes and victims of hysteria also displayed traits that were uncharacteristic of their gender. The prostitute, emblematic of the sexualized female in the nineteenth century, was perceived as the embodiment of all that is associated with sexuality, disease as well as passion.[97] Pauline Tarnowsky, a prominent St. Petersburg physician dedicated to the study of prostitution, claimed that the appearance of the prostitute and her sexual identity were preestablished in heredity. Of her many conclusions about prostitutes, one that is particularly poignant is that they become more "mannish" when they age: "But when they age, their 'strong jaws and cheek-bones, and their masculine aspect . . . hidden by adipose tissue, emerge, salient angles stand out, and the face grows virile, uglier than a man's . . . exhibits the full degenerate type which early grace had concealed."[98]

Similarly, according to nineteenth-century studies of hysteria, madness is said to occur by the acting out of traditional sex-roles or stereotypes. In *Women and Madness* (1973), Phyllis Chesler argues that in order for a woman to be healthy she must adjust and accept the behavioral norms for her sex even though these kinds of behavior are less socially desirable.[99] Many hysterics showed signs of desire for passion, which differed drastically from the acceptable codes of behavior of women. Consequently, many masculine subjects were portrayed to be very much in control of their faculties and did not respond to animalistic, primitive urges of passion, thereby distancing them from the image of the pathological woman, as well as abiding by Schopenhauer's theory of chastity.

However, the opposite side of the spectrum of this argument posed several problems as well. Depending on the historical context, many Latin American writers responded to negative constructions of hypo-masculinity that posed a threat to their political and social standing. In the years preceding and following independence in Latin America, the *machista* characteristics of the *caudillos* were lauded by the opposition and served as the necessary stronghold needed by the Creoles to win the wars of independence. After independence many *caudillista* leaders became powerful and popular, often resulting in their election as political figures in the postindependence years. Juan Manuel de Rosas is just one example, and for many Argentines he proved to be a cruel, despotic dictator who kept Argentina from the progress that they desired.[100]

When Rosas returned to power in 1835 he insinuated himself into every aspect of Argentine life. In addition to requiring that Argentine citizens wear the red insignia identifying themselves as Rosistas, he held elaborate public ceremonies, forced rallies, and held costume balls and military parades.[101] Through the dreaded *mazorca,* or the corrupt military police, he carried out acts of violence, torture, imprisonment, and murder.[102] It wasn't long before Rosas imposed a strict censorship on the many periodicals published by the Unitarians, which made it even more challenging for them to retaliate. Rosas's dictatorship, as well as all of the authoritarian institutions discussed in this work are portrayed as forceful and imposing, and can therefore be best described in terms of hegemonic masculinity. R. W. Connell defines hegemonic masculinity as the man's need to enforce the subordination of women and weaker men as the condition of sustaining his own masculinity. He argues that force and competence are, obviously enough, translations into the language of the body of the social relations that define men as holders of power, women as subordinate.[103]

In the gendered version of the paradigmatic dichotomy of civilization and barbarism, the writer contesting these *caudillo* types was initially posited as a masculine man of reason confronted with the feminine, barbaric forces of nature. Sarmiento and Echeverría strategically constructed the Other as the irrational, savage, and primitive subject who was allocated to the realm of the feminine for his association with nature and barbarism. However, in both *Facundo* and *El matadero* the antagonists are depicted for their hypo-virility, which by its very antithesis disturbs the presumed gendered position of the writer. By using gendered language in these texts, both writers disrupt traditional conceptualizations of patriarchal binary thought as the feminine is portrayed as the active hypo-masculine agent, whereas the presumed masculine subject is in a position of passivity, despite the fact that he is the beholder of reason.

The theories included in this introduction provide the foundation for the analysis of gender troping included in Martí's *Amistad funesta,* Rómulo Gallegos's *Doña Bárbara,* and Miguel Ángel

Asturias's *El Señor Presidente.* This study, which traverses the nationalist landscapes of Argentina, Cuba, Venezuela, and Guatemala, and ranges between the time periods of 1841and 1946, varies from country to country and responds to diverse and evolving conceptualizations of gender. Although each author's narrative style and concepts of gender vary from work to work, they are linked by the common strategy of employing gender codes in order to contest an overtly masculinist hegemonic political order. The utilization of gender troping in the quest for the coveted space of power results in the ambiguities of gender of both male and female protagonists, or in the latter case, of the narrative itself. In each text, the masculine subject is confronted with different variations of the feminized Other, and in this work I will investigate the diverse manifestations that gender takes in this struggle for power.

Part 1 of this work provides the historical backdrop to José Martí's *Amistad funesta,* highlighting the many chronicles and essays that he had written in which he employed gender troping as a means of resisting the hegemonic presence of the rising power of the imperialist United States, while laying the foundation of a new national [gendered] subject in Latin America. While part 1 provides an analysis of hegemonic forces external to the nation, part 2 looks within the body politic of Venezuela and Guatemala at the masculinist hegemonic dictatorships of Juan Vicente Gómez and Manuel Cabrera Estrada. In *Doña Bárbara* and *El Señor Presidente* both Gallegos and Asturias contest these hypermasculinized leaders, who govern in what David William Foster would term a hegemonic Western patriarchy.[104] Both writers seek to alter the ways in which the reader views traditional, contemporaneous conceptualizations of gender in order to expose the deleterious effects of the governing dictator and thereby open up a space in which they are able to reappropriate the (masculine) status of power.

In the introduction of Elaine Showalter's book *Speaking of Gender* (1989), Natalie Davis states that one of the aims of feminist theory is "to understand the significance of the sexes, the gender groups in the historical past" and to "discover the range of sex roles and sexual symbolism in different societies and periods, to find out what meaning they had and how they functioned to maintain the social order or to promote its change" (2). The writers included in this work used gender as a means to stabilize their position in an era of modernity and uncertainty, where threats of dictatorships and US imperialism compromised their very subjectivity. In an effort to contest these lurking powers, highly charged tropes of femininity and masculinity, as seen in *Paso de dos* and *El matadero,* were used in order to linguistically displace hegemonic institutions in an effort to reappropriate the coveted status of power. Thus, the passive, helpless image of the feminine subject positioned on the bottom of Cixous' hierarchal equation is by no means a renunciation of this gendered struggle for power, but a narrative ploy utilized to awaken their audience/readers to join in unison and react against oppressive hegemonic governments of this type, while at the same time offering alternate political ideologies that are more nurturing and accepting.

I
Walking the Tightrope: Negotiating Masculinity in an Age of Modernity

1

Feminizing the Other: Forging a National Identity in José Martí's Chronicles and Essays

During the years preceding and following independence, Latin American countries were faced with the project of defining themselves anew. Confronted with more powerful nations in Europe (excluding Spain) and the United States, it was important that each country defined itself on the same universal plane as these perceived modern nations. Many Latin American countries looked to France and England as the mecca of rationalization and culture; however, due to Cuba's proximity to the United States, Cubans also looked towards their northern neighbors as a model for progress. Revolutionary, writer, and intellectual José Martí (1853–95) became the mediator between his country and the metropolis New York City during his years of exile in the United States (1881–95). In *Escenas norteamericanas* and his other essays, he not only informed his fellow Latin Americans of the modernity of that great nation, but also constructed a sense of *Latinoamericanismo* from the place of exile.[1] As early as 1881 Martí reveals a sense of growing apprehension about the expansionist nature and imperialist drive of the United States, which he later refers to as the "seven-league giant" ("Nuestra América"). While most critics note that the apogee of Martí's anti-imperialist rhetoric is expressed in "Nuestra América" (1891), I argue that Martí's warnings of anti-imperialism begin as early as 1881 and are manifested in many of his earlier writings and in his only novel *Amistad funesta* (1885).

During the period preceding and following the publication of *Amistad funesta,* José Martí was living in New York as a political exile (1881–95) and wrote several essays subverting preconceived notions of the United States as the nation of progress and reason. Although Martí conceded that the United States was very advanced with regard to technology and admired the basic foundations of democracy, he argued that its materialist aspirations and lack of morality would soon lead to the demise of the nation. Martí used gendered speech in many of these essays in order to warn his compatriots of the dangers of the imperialist claims that the United States would inflict upon Cuba and Latin America if they were implemented during the expansionist years. I believe that in *Amistad funesta,* Martí uses the genre of the sentimental novel in order to portray the feminized, "hysteric" nature of the United States, thus warning Cuba to steer away from current proposed plans of annexation. The greed and irrationality of Lucía, which I argue can be linked to that of the United States, leads to the murder of Sol del Valle, who in the text is emblematic of the spirit of Latin America. While many critics claim that *Amistad funesta* is a didactic novel directed towards the good behavior of women, I believe that the novel is also symbolic of the political climate between the United States and Latin America between 1881 and 1885, and functions to reveal the deleterious character of this imposing nation in an era of industrialism and expansionism.

Gonzalo de Quesada y Aróstegui states that Martí wrote *Amistad funesta* shortly after his resignation from the independence project due to his disapproval of the *caudillista* tactics of Generals Antonio Maceo and Máximo Gómez.[2] During his temporary hiatus from the independence project, Martí became deeply involved in the US foreign policy in Latin America and the US elections of 1884 and wrote many essays expressing his growing apprehension of the "seven-league giant" that threatened the future progress of Latin American countries. Like Lucía's jealousy of anything that interfered with Juan's attention, the United States was threatened by England's interest in Central America and the rights to the Canal Zone and strove to exclude this formidable nation from any future plans in this region. The passionate and precipitous actions of James G. Blaine and other US officials between 1881 and 1885 resulted in rising problems for Latin American countries due to their meddling in boundary disputes between Guatemala and Mexico, Peru and Chile, as well as the many proposals of reciprocal trade treaties that were not always entirely beneficial to Latin American countries.

The purpose of chapter 1 is to highlight the use of gender troping in the popular essays, chronicles, and letters written by Martí between 1881 and 1894 and to examine US foreign relations with Latin America between 1881 and 1885, which would therefore posit the United States as an imminent threat to the identity and sovereignty of Latin America.[3] Based on these explorations, I will provide a gendered analysis of *Amistad funesta* in chapter 2 grounded on the fact that Martí utilizes the image of a pathological woman in order to reveal the hegemonic nature and trajectory of US foreign policy, which can be compared to that of a juggernaut whose destructive path could compromise future goals towards modernity and progress for Cuba and other Latin American nations in a period of national development and growth.[4] In his essays and in his only novel, Martí contests the imposing hegemonic presence of his northern neighbor and employs oppositional gender codes in order to displace preconceived notions of superiority and inferiority. As a result, the main characters of *Amistad funesta* move away from traditional codes of femininity and masculinity, thus revealing their more bigendered or androgynous characteristics.

During the postindependence years, while Latin American countries struggled to form a national identity, many were faced with negative stereotypes and depictions of their countries offered by well-known philosophers, travel writers, and prominent politicians of more powerful countries. José Martí, as a political exile, not only responded to these negative images, but also worked to displace perceptions of gender and power in his writings. Michael Aronna's exegesis of the discourse of degeneration in the Spanish and Latin American National essay shows how the philosophical ideologies of Immanuel Kant and Georg Wilhelm Friedrich Hegel were central to nineteenth-century discourse concerning progress, modernity, and the nation. Aronna concludes that a hegemonic, European modernity was personified as moral and mature, "while a subaltern European (Spain, Italy, Eastern Europe) and African, Asian, and Latin American premodernity was associated with immorality and childhood" (12). In *Philosophy of Nature,* Hegel supports these postulations arguing that Africa, Asia, and the Americas were considered to be immature due to their link with nature, a status that he proposed existed in opposition to reason.[5] Because both philosophers linked the violence and brutality of the Spaniards during the conquest with the backwardness of Africa and the Middle Ages, the Latin American *mestizo,* by association, was regarded as one of those inferior races described as uncivilized or immature, linking him to the feminine.[6]

As seen previously in the paradigmatic treatise *Facundo: civilización y barbarie,* Sarmiento links gender to race in order to lead Argentina into an era of modernization and progress. The racial and barbaric characteristics of Facundo and the *gauchos* are constructed in opposition to the rational civilized man, and in a plan of social whitening in Argentina, Sarmiento promoted the immigration of Europeans in order to "upgrade" or dilute the racial factors of his nation. In an age of Darwinism and positivism, many US officials shared similar views about race and gender. The overwhelming majority of the Protestant Anglo-Saxons reflected a homogeneous group that governed North America despite the influx of European, Asian and Latin American immigrants that entered the country during the nineteenth century. In "Engendering Critique," Beatrice Pita refers to the "concerted campaign [within the United States] to represent the Latin American countries as black or Indian, as violent, as childlike, and as *female*" (137; emphasis in the original).[7]

Travel writing also helped to shape attitudes about Latin America and its people and was largely responsible for the negative view towards many Latin Americans in the nineteenth century. After the independence years, many travelers, especially US, English, and French, came into Latin America and wrote about their impressions and experiences.[8] Alexander von Humboldt, one of the most recognized travel writers from Europe, arrived in Venezuela in 1799, when civil strikes and disorder were prevalent in a preindependence atmosphere. Therefore, some of his first impressions of Latin America were of discord and chaos.[9] Mary Louise Pratt argues that Humboldt had spent most of his time in the periphery of South American countries, touring the Amazon River or residing in mostly indigenous towns, such as Quito, Ecuador. Many of the impressions that were included in his avidly read books were therefore based on the mountain, plain, and jungle areas, described in their abundance and luxuriance.[10] According to Pratt, Humboldt's depiction of Latin America as the "new continent" as well as his construction of this primal world of nature as an unclaimed and timeless space recalls former mercantile voyeurism dating back to the first European inventors of America, including Columbus, Vespucci, and Raleigh, specifically for his portrayal of America described "in a discourse of accumulation, abundance, and innocence" (126). It was unquestionably the image of primal nature elaborated in the scientific views of Humboldt "that became codified in the European imaginary as the new ideology of the 'new continent.'"[11]

Negative perceptions of Latin America were also reflected in the impressions of many US government officials in the nineteenth century. The Mexican-American War of 1846–48 is testament to the unilateral and expansionist goals of the United States, which gained 525,000 square miles in its victory against Mexico. Otis A. Singletary argues that the question of annexation of Texas to the United States was just one of the components leading to the war. Feelings of anger and resentment towards the Mexican government had been culminating in the years prior to the war due to the intermittent attacks over border disputes following the revolt of the Texans, the political instability of the Mexican government, and failed diplomacy between the two nations.[12] US-Mexican relations were further jeopardized when President Polk sent his adviser John Slidell to discuss border disputes, the payment of outstanding claims owed to U.S. citizens, and the purchase of California.[13] Although the war was disputed among the political parties in the US government and considered by many to be an "unpopular war," Robert W. Johannsen points out that it stirred feelings of nationalism among the US soldiers who saw their initial victories as an indication of racial superiority and as proof of the value of the republican form of government of the United States: "Soldiers shared this belief as they perceived Mexicans as uncivilized, revealing that in their opinion the United States 'represented the highest stage of world civilization.'"[14]

In the Treaty of Guadalupe Hidalgo of 1848, which officially ended the Mexican-American War, Mexico ceded the territory currently known as Texas, California, Nevada, Utah, most of New Mexico and Arizona, and parts of Colorado and Wyoming, leaving the Mexicans disillusioned, financially broken, and resentful towards the United States. In return the United States agreed to pay fifteen million dollars and assumed the claims of its citizens against Mexico.[15] While the Treaty of Guadalupe Hidalgo promised citizenship to the inhabitants of the ceded territories, the United States at that time conferred full citizen rights to "free natural and proper thing to do . . . [trying] to conceal its own humble half-breed origins, unaware that when one man brands another as a bastard, it is always a sign of his own illegitimacy. There is no more certain announcement of a woman's sins than when she show contempt for sinners" (175). In this passage Martí compares these xenophobic aspects of the Yankee maniac with the excessive sinfulness of the woman who shows contempt for sinners. He asserts: "Too much faith in foreign virtue will weaken us in our formative years with an unmotivated and baneful distrust of what is ours" (175). In this sense, not only is the United States undergoing a process of emasculation in this essay, but those who follow in its footsteps are feminized as well.

Martí shifts concepts of superiority/inferiority and masculine/feminine in this essay by subverting preconceived virile qualities of the United States. He decries that the North American character has gone downhill since the winning of independence "and is today less human and virile" (176). The Spanish American character, on the other hand, "is in all ways superior, in spite of its confusion and fatigue, to what it was when it began to emerge from the disorganized mass of grasping clergy, unskilled ideologists and ignorant or savage Indians" (176). Although he admits to the original "disorganized" stage of Spanish America in its state of confusion and fatigue, he suggests that this is only a temporary status and that Latin America at this stage of development is still superior to that of the United States.

Martí ends his essay promising his readers that the newspaper *Patria* will publish articles, translated from the country's earliest journals demonstrating "two useful truths to Our America": "the crude, uneven and decadent character of the United States, and the continuous existence there of all the violence, discord, immorality and disorder blamed upon the peoples of Spanish America" (176). Thus, in this essay the perceived virile image of the United States is emasculated, highlighting the feminine characteristics of the uncontrollable, irrational subject, previously assigned to Latin America. This feminized image is pushed even more into the realm of the hysteric in "El Congreso de Washington," published in 1889.

In her article "Engendering Critique: Race, Class and Gender in Ruiz de Burton and Martí," Beatriz Pita shows how José Martí and nineteenth-century Mexican writer María Amparo Ruiz de Burton utilize gender codes in order to contest the hegemonic whites" only, thereby denying citizenship to those Indians who had formerly enjoyed rights under Mexican law.[16] According to Martha Menchaca, those classified as Mexican Indians were not entitled to exercise full political rights as they were denied the right to vote, practice law, marry Anglo-American women, or run for political offices (587). Therefore, by the mid-nineteenth century, US foreign policy had already exhibited a xenophobic exclusivity in its aggressive movement towards imperialism and expansionism.

This racial characterization of Latin Americans is also made evident during the closing years of the century with the United States's response to the Cuban Ten Year War (1868–78). President Grant's desire for expansionism led him to favor the recognition of the rebels' belligerency; however, Secretary of State Hamilton Fish persuaded Grant against this resolution due to the racial composition of the Cubans. Fish had visited Cuba and according to his biographer, Allen Nevins, had "placed a low estimate upon the intellectual and moral qualities of much of the population; he doubted the aptitude of this conglomerate of Indian, Negro and Spanish blood for self-government and thought . . . that evolution under Spanish tutelage might be better than revolution."[17] Benjamin concludes that the dominant North American view throughout the nineteenth century was that "for reasons of geography, racial composition, and cultural heritage, the island was incapable of self-government."[18] While many US politicians shared this negative view of Latin America, others, such as Secretary of State James G. Blaine, were eager to lay claim to Central America and the Caribbean for their strategic canal locations, as well as for the potential trade relations that Latin American countries could offer. In both cases, these countries were generally perceived to be underdeveloped, inferior nations by the rising imperialist presence of their North American neighbors.

José Martí as a political exile in New York was very much aware of these conceptualizations of Latin America, which were frequently published in prevalent periodicals. He became one of the chief defenders of the integrity of the Latin American soul, at the same time constructing a sense of the new modern man of Latin America—one who rises above the baseness of materialism and greed that progress had engendered. Surprisingly, gender plays a key role in both the depiction of Cuba and Latin America and in Martí's repudiation of this denigrating imperialist discourse.

Gender Troping in Martí's Essays and Chronicles

I will begin by examining the use of gender troping by José Martí in the late 1880s, and early 1890s during the time of his heightened anxiety towards the United States, as a means of pointing out the definitive use of gender in displacing or confronting a more hegemonic nation. These tropes, albeit not always as straightforward as in his earlier discourse, are indeed evident in Martí's previous essays related to the formation of the ideal [male] subject and the imposing threat of "the colossus." It is important to note that these later essays reflect the culmination of his deepest fears, which were the appropriation of Latin American nations by the insatiable appetite of the North, which he proposed would infect the young nations to the south with a materialistic and shallow character.

In "Nuestra América" (1891), as well as in many of his other anti-imperialist essays, Martí proposes the concept of a unified "Our America" in opposition to that Other America that fails to recognize it.[19] This is evident in "The Truth about the United States" (1894), where Martí's main objective is to belie the perceived virile, civilized nature of the United States. He begins the essay accentuating the virile qualities of the ancestors of its northern neighbors: "A nation of strapping young men from the North, bred over centuries to the sea and the snow and the virility aided by the defense of local freedom."[20] However, Martí introduces early on in the essay the disparity between the North and the South regions of the nation as well as the African American citizens who "from a frightful slavery and a sublime war have entered into the citizenship with those who bought and sold them" (173). Thus, according to Martí, the unity of the nation is indeed in jeopardy and it is only a matter of time before the democracy of the nation is dismantled: "The reasons for unity are weakening"; "The various localities are dividing and irritating national politics"; and "Democracy is being corrupted and diminished" (174). He compares this disparity in the development of the United States to "monsters," not nations, an image that I will later argue is utilized in *Amistad funesta* (174).

In the following passage Martí expresses his disapproval those who blindly fall into the trap of Yankee mania and abho those who blindly adopt the "subtle aristocracy" of ot nations, "publicly showing a preference for the fair skinned presence of the United States. Both see the United States as what Martí defines as a "civilización dañada"—"a damaged civilization, arguing that it is dangerous, in fact hazardous to one's political and economic health (both within the United States as well as without), to admire uncritically or to idealize a nation in decay" (130). Martí and Ruiz de Burton use the image of the juggernaut to reflect the "overwhelming and destructive force of corrupt governmental practices, US monopoly capitalism, and attendant imperialist designs."[21] In Martí's essay "El Congreso de Washington" (1889), he warns against the possibility of a second colonialism if Cuba were to ally with the United States, a country described as a "disdainful juggernaut, who moves forward squashing his servants' heads."[22] The uncontrollable image of the juggernaut recalls the irrational aspects of the feminized space denoted by Kant and Hegel. It is in this feminized "irrational image" constructed in 1889 that I will also trace back to Lucía Jerez, the main female protagonist in Martí's novel, written in 1885.

Pita notes that both Martí and Ruiz de Burton can only "couch the uneven power relations and desires of which they speak in gendered and sexualized terms" (137). In her article Pita refers to popular essays written by José Martí and points out that "Martí inverts the characterization, feminizes the United States and impugns its virility just as dominant US discourse has feminized Latin America into the role of subaltern female" (138). In many of his essays, including "Vindication of Cuba," "La verdad sobre los EEUU," and "Nuestra América," Martí builds up the virile qualities of the United States only so that he can subvert this commonly perceived power, which thereby opens up a space for the construction of the Latin American masculine subject.

According to John M. Kirk, by 1889 Martí was less concerned with his writings included in *Escenas norteamericanas* and concentrated heavily on the independence of Cuba.[23] However, talk of annexation of Cuba resurfaced, and on March 16, 1889, the *Philadelphia Manufacturer* published an article entitled "Do We Want Cuba?" (later printed in the *New York Evening Post*). In this article Cubans were referred to as an "effeminate" people, who had "a distaste of exertion," and were described as being "helpless" and "idle." Kirk notes that Martí was particularly concerned with the conclusion of the original article, which stated that "the only hope to make Cuba a worthwhile state was to Americanize it completely, filling it with 'people of our own race'" (qtd. in Kirk 284). In his six-page retaliation, entitled "Vindicación de Cuba," Martí displaced preconceived perceptions of femininity and masculinity and subverted the powerful stance of the United States. Kirk notes that Martí spoke avidly and openly against the United States now that it was seriously considering the idea of purchasing the island and of "americanizarla por completo" (284). Before this date, he also expressed his rising apprehension about the hegemonic presence of the United States in a letter written to Enrique Estrazulas, in which he states:

> Ahora que estoy fuera de mi, porque lo que desde años vengo temiendo y anunciando se viene encima, que es la política conquistadora de los Estados Unidos, que ya anuncian oficialmente por boca de Blaine y Harrison su deseo de tratar de mano alta a todos nuestros países, como dependencias naturales de éste, y de comprar a Cuba.[24]

> [I am now beside myself because what I have been fearing and predicting for years is finally happening: the policy of conquest announced officially by Blaine and Harris which conveys the desire of the United States to buy Cuba and deal arrogantly with all our countries as if they were their natural dependencies.][25]

In this letter Martí admits that for years, "desde años," he had been "fearing" and "predicting" his greatest fear, that Cuba and Latin America would become dependents of the United States—a fear that for him had seemed to come to fruition in the dates leading up to the Pan-American conference.[26]

While most critics focus on this period as the culmination of Martí's anti-imperialist rhetoric, I believe that in his earlier writings and in his only novel, *Amistad funesta,* Martí forms the foundation of his creation of a sense of Latin American identity through the use of an oppositional gendered discourse directed from and against the United States. I will support this theory by examining a series of chronicles and letters written before and shortly after the publication of his novel in which Martí utilizes gender tropes in order to displace preconceived notions of masculinity and femininity, thus marginalizing his more powerful rival, the United States.

While residing in the United States, Martí wrote for several periodicals and journals and continued to write prolifically be it in the form of essays, poetry, short stories, or correspondence.

Many critics note that at first Martí was duly impressed with the sense of freedom there was in this great country; however, as Susana Rotker has pointed out, as well as Philip S. Foner, Martí reveals a rising sense of anxiety about the United States that becomes evident in the early 1880s.[27] In "The (Political) Exile Gaze," Susana Rotker lists three significant stages in Martí's experience in the United States beginning with his arrival to the country in 1881, denoted by a sense of awe and admiration, and ending with, what Rotker terms, "his full radicalization," which refers to his goals of independence as well as maintaining Cuban sovereignty from the United States.[28] *Amistad funesta* (1885) was written during the second stage, when Martí gains a heightened critical perspective of his host nation and begins to see the inequity of US foreign relations, as well as noting the excesses of materialism in New York. In her analysis, Rotker highlights the evolution of Martí's gaze towards the United States from one of awe to one of apprehension and radical criticism.

In fact, in "Knights of Labor Strike" published in *La Nación* (Buenos Aires), September 15, 1882, Martí claims: "We are at the height of a struggle between capitalists and workers."[29] In this essay, he sets the dichotomy that will persist in his later works between the monster (the capitalists and industry) and the average working man whose wife and child "eat in the evening what the poor husband worked for in the morning" (243). Although there is still a tone of admiration for the United States in this essay, we begin to see the foundation of a critical perspective of the monster that is defined as the capitalist or industry versus the workers who rise up and strike against them. In an ideal union, the workers of the Knights of Labor, as well as those who were hired to replace them, would join together to resist the heartless capitalist.

In 1884 this capitalist monster becomes even more defined under the auspices of protectionism in his essay entitled "The Fruits of Protectionism," which Martí often expressed was a corrupt, evil system that resulted in the accumulating wealth of the rich. In this essay, Martí refers to the United States as a "colossal industrial nation," with factories described as "Herculean mills" that resembled "hollow mountains turned upside down."[30] He notes that because of protectionism, US economy is in a state of peril: "But the market was glutted, imports increased with the mad desire for luxury, the country needed no more domestic articles than it had, and what it would need would be far less than the factories produced."[31] This description is denoted for its uncontrollability, lack of boundaries and greed, and begins to show signs of the feminine perception of pathology as opposed to the logical masculine signs of reason. Although the illusion of pathological femininity is cast onto a mere system, and not men, Martí will later direct his invective to those who orchestrate and propagate this system, including those US officials dedicated to establishing trade relations with Latin America in order to dump surplus goods.

It is evident that Martí does not wish to eliminate the United States from future plans of progress and growth in the Americas, only to reveal the irrational essence or juggernaut that lies masked under the seductive face of modernity and progress and that has revealed itself in the actions of current politicians and elitists that had governed the country. These dangers are highlighted in his essays written between 1881 and 1885 as he points to the precipitous actions of US officials with regard to US foreign policy in Latin America (including previous treaties with Mexico following the Mexican-American War), its unilateral interest in the rights to control the Canal Zone and the incessant need for trade relations with Latin America in order to satisfy the basic concepts of protectionism in the United States. It is important to note that although Martí admired the basic concepts of the US constitution and democracy, the educational system and the advanced agricultural technology, his disdain towards the evils of protectionism ruled by the elite in the United States became the primary focus of many of his chronicles during the mid-1880s.

In his essay "'Definir, avisar, poner en guardia . . . ' Visión Martiana de Estados Unidos en *La América*," Pedro Pablo Rodríguez explores Martí's position that the core problem and downfall of the United States is protectionism. Because of protectionism there was a surplus of products in the United States and therefore it became necessary to develop trade relations with Latin America, which had become the motive for the foreign policy initiated by Secretary of State James G. Blaine in 1881 under President James A. Garfield. Although many of Blaine's attempts were thwarted upon the assassination of President Garfield, leading to his subsequent resignation, Blaine was elected as the presidential candidate for the Republican Party in the United States for 1884, and in his campaigns he advocated the importance of relations with Latin America. Martí became very involved in this campaign against Blaine and in several of his chronicles included in *Escenas norteamericanas* he urged the Democrats to rise in opposition against the Republicans.[32] Before examining further Martí's anti-imperialist essays, it will be helpful to look at the nature of US foreign policy between 1881 and 1885, which in many ways was motivated by the basic concepts of protectionism.

US-Foreign Relations, 1881–85

One cannot begin to embark on an analysis of US-foreign relations with Latin America between the time period of 1881 and 1890 without taking into consideration the enormous impact that Secretary of State James G. Blaine had during his short term in office. Blaine was one of the most charismatic, influential, and controversial political leaders of the late nineteenth century. He served as secretary of state under Garfield beginning in 1880 and until Garfield's assassination in 1881. David Healy claims that people either loved or hated Blaine and that historically he has been pictured as anything from absolute devil to virtual saint.[33] While former Secretary of State Hamilton Fish regarded Blaine as a mere demagogue and corruptionist, risking the nation's safety through adventurist foreign policies purely for personal profit and advancement, Lester Langley argued that "Blaine contributed more to the shaping of American foreign policy than any individual of his generation" and displayed "more intellectual creativity than any other late-nineteenth-century secretaries of state."[34] My next section will focus on Blaine's political policies and his foreign relations with Latin America during the brief period in which he was in office, as well as highlight Martí's disdain of the seductiveness of Blaine's charisma.

Blaine's political motives and his advocacy of protectionism served as an impetus to his foreign relations with Latin America. As a strong supporter of the Republican Party, he advocated the party's economic growth and industrialization. He favored a protective tariff to keep Great Britain's cheaper manufactured goods from flooding the American market, and he believed in business and businessmen, thus maintaining close ties with men of wealth.[35] Healy notes that both President Garfield as well as Blaine were interested in developing trade relations with Latin

America and were concerned about Great Britain's political penetration and interest in that region. Both men realized that Latin America sold the largest share of their exports to the US market but bought the majority of their manufactured goods from Europe. During his office as secretary of state, Blaine placed special emphasis on Latin America, showing a keen interest in the acquisition of canal rights in Central America and in establishing reciprocal treaties with those countries in order to dump surplus goods manufactured in the United States.[36] Healy claims that during his short term in office Blaine managed to take several precipitous actions, which resulted in negative consequences: "Within three months of taking office, he [Blaine] had strongly opposed European moves for a joint international guarantee of the neutrality of a future isthmian canal, given his support to a movement for the reconfederation of the Central American states into a single political unit, involved his government in a boundary dispute between Mexico and Guatemala, and launched a diplomatic intervention in a major South American war" (Healy 20). Healy is referring to some of the discrepancies in Blaine's foreign policy in Latin America.

David M. Pletcher refers to the years between 1881 and 1885 as "the awkward years" due to the inexperience of US diplomats and the muddling of foreign policy that took place during the terms of Garfield and Arthur.[37] He asserts that the outward pressure for new markets and the apparent European threats to American influence in Latin America and elsewhere stimulated an expansionist impulse in the United States that had never entirely disappeared since the days of manifest destiny (9–10). In the period leading up to "the awkward years," Great Britain had proven to be a considerable contender in the world economy, specifically because it still controlled most of the desirable markets (6). Both the United States and England eagerly sought the rights to the Canal Zone in Central America, and Blaine had tried to eliminate its rival from the picture. During his office he proposed a modification of the Clayton-Bulwer Treaty, which was a treaty signed between Great Britain and the United States in 1850 designed to prevent the monopoly or exclusive rights of either country to the Canal Zone. In his extensive correspondence with the British government, Blaine consistently tried to exclude England from their rights to the construction of a canal.[38]

In addition, both Blaine and President Garfield sought a secure political climate in Central America so that they could further their plans for trade relations and gain control of the isthmus. President Justo Rufino Barrios of Guatemala pursued the reconciliation of five countries in this region, and in 1881 he solicited the support from the US government concerning its boundary disputes with Mexico over Sonoscu of Chiapas. Although Blaine agreed to be a neutral arbitrator in the dispute, he was clearly on the side of Barrios and Guatemala. In his correspondence to Mexico, he revealed his favoritism, thus jeopardizing strong foreign relations with Mexico at the time. Blaine had left office before the matter could be resolved due to the assassination of President Garfield, and Mexico and Guatemala averted war by resolving their differences in 1882 without his interference.[39]

Blaine had also interfered in foreign relations between Peru and Chile in the War of the Pacific (1879–84). He had supported Peru against Chile, arguing that Chile's military aggression was encouraged by Great Britain. Blaine's intervention in the settlement treaties between the countries strongly influenced Chile's decision to accept money funded by the French Bonds Company, the Credit Industriel, instead of appropriating the valuable nitrate fields in Peru. Blaine was later accused of making this decision due to his personal interest and gain, and he resigned as secretary of state shortly after Garfield's assassination.[40]

In the years following Blaine's brief hiatus from the political scene, foreign policy leaders maintained their aggressive stance towards establishing reciprocal treaties with Latin America. According to Healy, the secretary of state under the Chester A. Arthur administration, Frederick Theodore Frelinghuysen, launched two Latin American diplomatic initiatives that were as ambitious and precipitous as Blaine's programs. First of all, in a project that overlooked the Clayton-Bulwer Treaty, Frelinghuysen convinced the federal government to buy out the Maritime Canal Company and take over the canal project. On December 1, 1884, the Frelinghuysen-Zaval Treaty was signed, stipulating that the United States would loan the Nicaraguan government four million dollars, to be repaid from canal profits. The canal would be jointly owned, and Nicaragua would retain civil jurisdiction in peacetime.[41]

Frelinghuysen also instigated an ambitious attempt to tie Caribbean trade to the United States through a network of bilateral tariff reciprocity treaties that were intended to cover Mexico, Central America, the West Indies, and northern South America.[42] The first treaty was signed with Mexico in 1883, but after that, Healy claims, progress became more difficult.[43] Soon after a treaty was negotiated with the Dominican Republic followed by El Salvador, Colombia, and Venezuela, and special negotiations with Spain resulted in reciprocal treaties with Cuba and Puerto Rico. However, as in the case of Blaine's administration, these treaties were proposed too late at the end of the presidential term and were not approved by the Senate.[44]

Blaine resurfaced into the political arena in 1884, when he was nominated for the presidency by the Republican Party. Although he largely disagreed with the political machinations of Frelinghuysen, Blaine was ready to promote a program of Latin American reciprocity treaties and even planned to employ the services of Frelinghuysen's star diplomat, John W. Foster, to do his negotiations.[45] José Martí became deeply involved in the 1884 US elections, and in his many writings, including *Escenas norteamericans,* he advocated for a bolder response by the Democratic Party to stand up to the Republicans. The aggressiveness of the Republican Party, under Blaine, would prove to be a real threat to the future sovereignty of Latin America, and Martí struggled to keep the Republicans out of office.

Escenas norteamericanas includes a plethora of writings from the metropolis New York City, directed to Latin American nations informing them of the activities of this modern nation in which Martí resided. The chronicles in this collection range from the Cuban patriot's impression of such trivialities as holidays, vacation spots, and biographical sketches to more serious topics related to protectionism, US foreign policy, and the elections. Many times Martí's deepest thoughts about US imperialism, the disparity of modernity, and his position as an outsider and political exile are couched within very unassuming essay topics. In his chronicle entitled "Las Pascuas," published on December 12, 1881, Martí provides an informative treatise about the hustle and bustle of the Christmas season in New York. Within this chronicle depicting the gaiety and festivities of the holidays, Martí introduces the opportunist activities of US officials and businessmen in Central America and the indecorous activities of Secretary of State Blaine. In the midst of a detailed description of riches, food, Tiffanys, and the generosity of Santa

Claus, Martí alludes to the "concepciones monstruosas" [monstruous conceptions] of a Peruvian company that maintains that the North Americans have the rights to all of the gold and riches of all of South America and "en pago de un crédito de aventurero, abra el Perú todas sus minas a los reclamantes avarientos, sus lechos de oro, sus vetas de plata, sus criaderos de guano; y, en prenda del contrato, sus puertos y ferrocarriles" [in payment for an adventurer's credit, Peru shall open up all of its mines to the avaricious claimants, their streaks of gold, their veins of silver, their sources of guano; and to guarantee the contract, their ports and railroads] (*Oc* 1416).

Martí then shifts to what must be a fabricated perception of a Christmas celebration in the White House, including the president, who sits at the head of the table, and Senator Hawley, who boastfully conjectures: "Y cuando hayamos tomado a Canadá y a México, y reinemos sin rivales sobre el continente, ¿qué especie de civilización vendremos a tener en el futuro?" [And when we have taken over Canada and Mexico, and we reign without rivals over the continent, what kind of civilization will we come to have in the future?] (*Oc,* 1416). Martí then focuses his attention on Secretary of State James Blaine, whom he portrays as one of the chief US *caudillos* on the Latin American stage during the time. His description of the former secretary of state positioned at the foot of the mountains ["púsose de pie en las montañas del Istmo"], with his arms spread wide, refusing European countries into the canal territory ["y abrió los brazos para impedir el paso a pueblo alguno de Europa"] is reminiscent of his covetous stance towards the rights to the canal during his term of office (*Oc* 1,417). According to Philip S. Foner, by the mid-1880s Blaine had come to represent for Martí all the evil and corruption in American politics. Martí attested that Blaine was a man who was "purchasable, who true to his character, buys and sells in the market of men," a man who sought "under the pretext of treaties of commerce and peace, the wealth [from other nations] of which the economic eras of the Republican Party had begun to deprive the [North American] nation."[46] In this and in many other of his essays Martí responded to these aggressive plans and warned his fellow Latin Americans that they were slowly yet systematically being taken over by their northern neighbor.

In an essay concerning Central America written in January 1885, Martí expresses that his deepest fear, that of the appropriation of Spanish American territory by the United States through a series of treaties, is indeed coming to pass:

> Ha celebrado [Cuba] con el gobierno norteamericano un tratado comercial, que de tan absoluta manera liga la existencia de la isla [Cuba] a los Estados Unidos, que es poco menos que el vertimiento de cada uno de estos países en el otro, lo que acaso vendrá a parar, con gran dolor de muchas almas latinas, en perder para la América Española la isla que hubiera debido ser su baluarte. (*Oc* 323)
>
> [[Cuba] has celebrated with the North American government a commercial treaty that so absolutely binds the existence of the island [Cuba] to the United States, that it is just a little less than the spilling out of each one of these countries into the other, which perhaps will result, to the deep sorrow of many a Latin soul, of having lost for Spanish America the Island that should have been their bastion.]

In this essay Martí condemns those Latin American "hombres activos" [active men] who are anxious to develop and modernize their countries "a costa aun de la libertad futura de la Nación" [even at the cost of the Nation's freedom in the future] by ceding their natural riches to their northern neighbor. He gives the example of Nicaragua, who has already signed a contract giving the United States the rights to territory where it had initially planned to build a canal (*Oc* 323). In these treaties Martí includes the one signed between Mexico and the United States, as well as another signed with Santo Domingo.

In this same essay Martí depicts his northern neighbor as the new *cacique* of the *hacienda* that will exercise its domain over all of the Antilles: "Y vendrán los Estados Unidos a ser, como que les tendrán toda su hacienda, los señores pacíficos y proveedores forzosos de todas las Antillas" [Because they will own all the property in the West Indies, the United States will become the pacific lords and inevitable providers of those nations] (*Oc* 323). In this passage Martí is careful to point out the "pacific" yet "inevitable" consequences of US interests in Latin America, and in his many essays he is devoted to unveiling the mask of aggression that covers the face of modernity in the United States. In a chronicle published in *La Nación* August 1885, he states: "Por violencia confesada, nada tomarán. Por violencia oculta, acaso. Por lo menos, se acercarán hacia todo aquello que desean. Al istmo lo desean" [Through self-acknowledged violence they will take nothing. Through concealed violence, perhaps. At the very least, they will move closer towards getting everything they want. And they want the isthmus] (*Oc* 329). In this excerpt Martí alludes to the covetous desires of the United States towards the isthmus and to the pacific manner in which the United States acquires the territory that it desires. This methodical means of pursuing something and acquiring it is manifested in the seductive, yet pathological behavior of Lucía Jerez in the novel and can be compared with her incessant need to control Juan. Yet Juan is also not inculpable of his actions, or lack of actions. His inability to stand up to Lucía or try to control her behavior results in the death of Sol del Valle, which I argue to be representative of the spirit of Latin America.

In a period when Cuba was still striving to gain its independence, it is surprising that one of Martí's primary preoccupations was the imminent threat of the colossus. Susan Rotker states: "The locus of power is displaced in his chronicles: the gaze focuses on New York (a familiar, yet threatening entity) rather [than] on the immediate colonial authority that Spain represented for Cuba."[47] One of Martí's principal objectives is to inform his readers of the nature of US imperialism so that when they would engage in economic relations with this powerful country, they would realize their own worth and not be blinded by star-dazzled eyes. In his essay regarding the proposed reciprocal treaty between the United States and Mexico, he celebrates the backbone that Mexico displayed for refusing the treaty that had been initially proposed. However, in the conclusion of this essay, he clearly states that Latin Americans should not decline the opportunity to establish trade relations with the United States. He argues that there must be a treaty between both countries, yet that the treaty proposed was not adequate: "Tratado debe haber; pero no aquél que se proponía, y yace en buena hora" [Treaty there should be, but not that which was proposed, and it will come in good time] (*Oc* 314).

Martí's principal objective was that Latin American nations know their neighbor and realize that the US will propose treaties that will meet their needs above others. In other words, I would argue that Martí wanted to reveal the irrational force of the juggernaut behind the seductive mask of modernity and progress, so that local national officials could, like Mexico, stand up to the colossal presence of their northern neighbor and make sound decisions that would benefit both sides. In an era when Latin Americans were being described as subalterns and inferior, Martí utilized gendered speech in order to reverse conceptualizations of authority and power, many times characterizing the United States as that subaltern (feminine) Other.

The Formation of the Ideal Masculine Subject in Martí's Discourse

It is important to note that conceptualizations of gender and their relationship to the rational man had shifted considerably by Martí's time from how they were portrayed in Sarmiento's works, in large part due to the displacement of the artist and the intellectual in an era of modernity, as well as the emergence of new forms of hegemony. In his book *Divergent Modernities* (2001), Ramos explores the writings and perspectives of José Martí as one of the first US Latinos who wrote about his experience of confronting modernity and the cultures of US imperialism. In the foreword to this invaluable book, José David Saldívar states that Ramos, like Habermas and Max Weber, describes cultural modernity as a period in which homogeneous worldviews of religion and metaphysics broke down and "scientific discourse, paradigms of morality and jurisprudence, and the production of art in turn became 'unevenly' institutionalized" (xiii–iv). Ramos contrasts the discourse of the emergence of Latin Americanism by "enlightened *letrados,*" such as Argentine Domingo F. Sarmiento and Chilean Andrés Bello, with the "divergent subalternity of Cuban journalist, revolutionary, and poet José Martí, who Ramos suggests, inaugurated 'the constitution of a new kind of intellectual subject for the Americas'" (xiv). Ramos notes that while Sarmiento employed rationalist discourse in order to control the barbaric element in his country, Martí found himself confronted with a sense of fragmentation and alienation characteristic of modern times (xxxix).

The dichotomy of virile men and feminine men in his construction of a utopian Latin American identity can be seen in Martí's prologue to Juan Antonio Pérez Bonalde's "Poema del Niágara" (1882), where he posits the natural man against those other men who "like women, weak women . . . are likely to exhaust the honey sweet wine that seasoned the festivals of Horace."[48] During this "age in ruins," men are like "certain damsels, who latch onto certain virtues only when they see them [either] praised by others."[49] These perceived virtues that Martí condemns in what he refers to as "feminized" men refer to the appropriation of ideologies and epistemologies that overlook the true nature of man and ignore the riches brought about by literature and aesthetic beauty.

In *Divergent Modernities* Ramos argues that Martí's prologue "reflects on the problems of production and interpretation of literary texts in an unstable society, prone to the fluctuation of values that until then, had guaranteed the coherence and social authority of writing" (xxxvi). The intellectual, as the guide to progress, found himself in a transitional position, due to the importance given to positivism and modernity, which discounted the aesthetic qualities of man celebrated in previous generations. In this prologue Martí claims that "spiritual liberty" is in jeopardy and that "the first task of man is to reconquer it": "Men must be freed from the ill governance of convention that suffocates or poisons their emotions . . . and burdens their mental capacity with a pernicious, foreign, cold, and false sense of wealth" (310). Thus, as early as 1882, Martí posits the spiritual against the material, utilizing the examples of virile men (the poets) against impotent men who are likened to "weak women." In the prologue to "Niágara," Martí admits that the task of moving beyond the mere appropriation of objective ideologies is indeed difficult during these times: "There is no more difficult task than this, of distinguishing the acquired, proficient aspects of our existence from the spontaneous and natural" (309). He further argues that "under the pretext of completing the human being" these ideologies interrupt the true formation of man and only manage to "tie him up" and "strap him down" (309).

A year later in an essay published in *La América* (1883) concerning the school system in Buenos Aires, Martí uses gender in the formation of the ideal masculine subject by belittling those Latin Americans who are seduced by the greatness of the United States and France, who like starry-eyed young lovers, do not know their own worth: "¡Tan enamorados que andamos de pueblos que tienen poca liga y ningún parentesco con los nuestros!" [So love-stricken we are with other countries that have little ties and no kinship to ours] (*Oc* 277). He later compares those seduced by more powerful nations to little girls in love in search for a lover: "Como niñas en estación de amor echan los ojos ansiosos por el aire azul en busca de gallardo novio, así vivimos suspensos de toda idea y grandeza ajena, que trae cuño de Francia o Norte América" [Like little girls in love who cast their anxious eyes towards the blue sky in search of a gallant suitor, we live hanging onto every grand idea born in France and North America] (*Oc* 277). In his prologue to "Niágara" Martí argues that man should transcend these impositions, and in the following passage he directs the new man to the peaks of the mountains, thus defying any diversions created by "the tempest" [the United States or Paris]. He claims: "There is no west for man's spirit; there is only the north, crowned with light" (308). Martí heralds the poet of his times, investing him with priestlike qualities for lifting "his generous hands toward the sky in the manner of prayer" and lowering them "cupped, like a sonorous amphora, now replete with vibrant stanzas, caressed by Olympian scintillations." He then decries that "the poem is in the man" and that "the poem is in nature," a nature that interestingly enough is compared with the elevated characteristics of women: "the mother with nourishing breasts, the wife who never stops loving . . . consoling woman who gives strength in life and preserves after death!" (310). Unlike many intellectuals of his day, Martí celebrates the positive feminine qualities of the individual, and in later essays he advocates the union of the feminine and masculine in the project of nation building.

As opposed to Sarmiento's rational subject, Martí posits modern man's dependence on utilitarianism and materialism as being feminized and barbaric, lying outside of the confines of reason. Martí's ideal man rises above such base aspirations and is represented for his closeness to nature and the elevation and development of his soul. According to Susana Rotker, Martí "combined liberal faith in progress, reason, good deeds, and the perfectibility of man . . . with Kantian discipline of will without reducing scientific methods to utilitarianism as Auguste Comte had done."[50] Thus, in an era when the effects of positivism had reached their culmination in the United States, Martí criticizes the many negative aspects that this philosophy had engendered.

In his essay "A Glance at the North American's Soul Today," Martí criticizes the current educational system in the United States that produces materialistic men: "And from the public school they go on to their jobs, to the spectacle of luxury and the desire of possessing it, the vanity of exhibiting it, and to the cruel and ignoble anguish of competing with their neighbors."[51] He argues that this system produces a "spiritual crudeness" that afflicts the expansive "delicate minds" of North American men and makes them suffer. He urges his Spanish American readers that they must "feed the lamp of light and reduce the beast." In this analogy Martí utilizes the metaphor of light in his reference to the real man and that of the beast to the feminized, underdeveloped spirit of the North American soul. I argue that this analogy is also used to a large extent in his novel, especially in reference to Sol del Valle, noted as the spiritual character, and Lucía, who is depicted for her irrationality throughout the novel.[52]

In "Nuestra América," which Ramos considers the culmination of Martí's ethico-political discourse, the Cuban writer posits the virility of the real man of Latin America against those "sissies" who are ashamed of their Indian past and who side with the North Americans.[53] While the sissies "drown their Indians in blood," the real man recognizes his heterogeneous past and incorporates it into the foundation of the emerging nation: "With our feet in the rosary, our heads white, and our bodies mottled in Indian and Creole, we came naked into the world of nations" (297). In this now canonical essay, Martí defends the integrity of the Latin American countries, where there is now being born "the real man." Martí defines the real man as holding "the prevailing temper of moderation" and balancing "the serene harmony of nature in a continent of light" with the "influx of critical readings, which in Europe have succeeded the readings of trial and error and fallaciousness under which the previous generation was steeped" (299). This chapter provides the synthesis of ideas expressed in previous critical essays, expressed in many ways in his novel, *Amistad funesta.* As has been seen, gender plays a pivotal role in the political discourse of Martí, and is used in his essays, poems, biographical sketches, as well as his only novel. As a political exile residing in the United States, Martí's gaze transforms from one of awe and amazement to the critical perspective from which he will construct a sense of identity for Latin Americans. His utilization of gender in this construction posits the United States as the feminized, materialistic Other living in the modern city par excellence against the spiritual, noble, virile construction of the male subject in the utopian projection of Latin America.

6. Frontispiece to the August Barthelemy translation of Fracastorius's Renaissance poem on syphilis (1840).

2
Unveiling the Mask of Modernity in *Amistad funesta*

THE COVER OF THE FRENCH TRANSLATION OF THE RENAISSANCE poem "Syphilis" by Hieronymus Fracastorius (1840), features a vignette of a masked woman with her handsome courtier kneeling in front of her. From the side angle, only the spectator could see that beneath the masked face of the beautiful woman lies the disease and corruption of the prostitute. The man kneeling before her, mesmerized by her beauty, is ignorant of the consequences of engaging intimately with the diseased woman and is thus portrayed as a potential victim of this masked evil.[1] This revealing image captures the essence of popular nineteenth-century ideologies that regard the pathology of woman as the decadent force that denigrates man's well-being, as well as that of nations. As stated previously, this image served as a metaphor for many Latin American writers who utilized the image of the pathological woman in order to explain the slow progression of their respective nations into an age of modernity.[2] These pathological traits are also manifested in the female protagonist of Martí's only novel, *Amistad funesta,* showing the imminent danger of the inevitable union between the betrothed couple, Juan and Lucía Jerez.

In his essay "'Definir, avisar, poner en guardia . . .': Visión Martiana de Estados Unidos en *La América,*" Pedro Pablo Rodríguez explores Martí's position as editor of the journal *La América* from early 1883 until July 1884.[3] During this time Rodríguez notes that Martí was able to escape censorship, which he found working with other Latin American editors regarding his opinions about the United States, and was therefore able to express more clearly his principal objective of the defense of Latin America (81).[4] Although these *crónicas* were written in the United

States, they were directed to a Latino audience and were read all over Latin America. In his 1883 essay entitled "Los propósitos de La América bajo sus nuevos propietarios," Martí incorporates the word *intimidad,* or intimacy, in his reference to the inevitable union that would take place between the United States and Latin America.[5] This word frequently refers to a romantic union between two people, which in the following passage is denoted for both its advantageous as well as harmful effects:

> Sabemos que venimos en el instante en que una empresa [the rapprochement between Anglo and Spanish America] de este orden debía venir. Hay provecho como hay peligro en la intimidad inevitable de las dos secciones del Continente Americano. . . . La intimidad se anuncia tan cercana, y acaso por algunos puntos tan arrolladora, que apenas hay el tiempo necesario para ponerse en pie, ver y decir.[6]

> We know that we come in the moment in which an enterprise [the rapprochement between Anglo and Latin America] of this order should have come. There are benefits as well as danger in the inevitable intimacy of the two sections of the American Continent. . . . The intimacy will be announced so soon, and perhaps by some aspects so overwhelming, that there is scarcely enough time necessary to stand up, look and speak out.

It is important to note that in this foreboding tone, Martí admits to the *provecho,* or benefits, gained by this union, but what is even more clear is his tone of warning that Latin Americans must "stand up, look and speak out" [ponerse en pie, ver y decir]. I believe that in *Amistad funesta,* Martí's objective is to reveal the mask of modernity of the United States, exposing the more pathological traits that hide beneath it. He utilizes the inevitable intimate union between Juan and Lucía as a warning to fellow Latin Americans of what could take place if they do not stand up and take notice of the possible consequences that could arise by entering into relations with this aggressive nation.[7] Therefore, the pathological depiction of Lucía in the novel reflects the precipitous conduct of US foreign policy between 1881 and 1885 as it unmasks the deleterious characteristics of modernity.

Amistad funesta was published under the pseudonym of Adelaida Baralt in the journal *El Latino-Americano* between May 15 and September 15, 1885, in New York. This *novela de entregas* has been widely considered a didactic novel, or a sentimental novel, available for the most part to a female audience, serving as a model of how good and proper women should not behave.[8] Lucía's audacious, bold behavior stands out as particularly peculiar compared to the more virtuous female protagonists in the novel, including Ana, Sol del Valle, and even Adela. As a result, her more masculine qualities have led to a variety of interpretations including: the creation of a feminist model (Olga Uribe), the reflection of Martí's wife (Manuel Pedro González), and the construction of a strong and active woman who will be prepared to fight for the independence of Cuba (Juan Carlos González Espitia).[9] My analysis of the novel complements those of recent critics who explore the various implications of the ambiguously gendered makeup of the main protagonists. I argue that Lucía reflects the discourse of degeneracy sparked by the profusion of scientific studies about gender and pathology during the nineteenth century. Furthermore, it is my thesis that the title, *Amistad funesta,* or dangerous or foreboding friendship, serves as a significant warning to the pending economic and political ties between the perceived spiritual Latin American countries and the materialist United States.

Despite the hybrid nature of the novel, many critics have often referred to its impressionistic style and its use of symbolic imagery.[10] The poetic language, the use of symbols and fleeting impressions throughout this work have been noted as some of the more distinct characteristics of this modernist *novelita.* In chapter 1 the narrator himself refers to the significance of the symbolic level in the novel, specifically in reference to the main protagonist's, Juan Jerez's, perception of women as symbols: "Y él, en la mujer, veía más el símbolo de las hermosuras ideadas que un ser real" [And he, in the woman, saw more the symbol of conceived beauties than a real being] (72).[11] In the next section I point out the many impressions and initial symbols introduced in chapter 1, which I argue reflect a materialistic essence of the United States during modern times, analogous to that shown by Martí in his many essays.

The Setting

As indicated by Martí in the prologue, the novel is said to take place in some country (not specified) in South America: "Y como el autor es persona trabajadora, recordó un suceso acontecido en la América del Sur en aquellos días, que pudiera ser base para la novela hispanoamericana que se deseaba" [And because the author is a diligent person, he recalled an event that took place in South America in those days, that could have been the basis of the Hispanic American novel that was desired] (*LJ* 36). Despite the presentation of the idyllic setting of magnolias, gaiety, and the innocence of the gathering of the three young women sitting on the porch, the reader notes that there are some significant deviations, which will later be instrumental in the development of the plot, as well as in the characters. The setting takes place in the surroundings of Lucía Jerez's home, which is described as having many of the amenities of the materialistic elements of the modern era: "los corredores de columnas de mármol" [the corridors of marble columns] (*LJ* 61) and "la verja dorada" [golden railing] (*LJ* 65). The reader notes a tone of dissatisfaction on the part of the narrator in the first line of the novel when he refers to the "frondosa magnolia" [lush magnolia] that is being pruned by the gardener, who is described as having hands that are too academic ["manos demasiado académicas"] (*LJ* 61). In an era when too much importance was given to the epistemological discourse of science, Martí argued in his many writings that modern intellectuals and scientists placed too much emphasis on the objective approach to nature and human beings and therefore ignored the development of the soul.[12] This perspective becomes one of the main themes in the novel as Martí accentuates the dangers of falling prey to the desires of materialism, as he advocates the need to strengthen the soul.

The narrator then reveals a multitude of impressions that will be instrumental in my analysis of the novel. The whiteness of the magnolias in the first paragraph is compared to the human soul, which is said to have "a great need for purity" (*LJ* 61). The big white flowers found on the magnolia tree are turned by Martí into a symbol of the aspirations of the ideal modern Latin American man towards purity and chastity in his search for an elevated spirit. Martí establishes the foreboding tone of the novel when he implies that even the purest of men can be tainted and misguided when confronted by outside sources: "Desde que lo blanco se oscurece, la desdicha empieza. La práctica y conciencia de todas las virtudes, la posesión de las mejores cualidades, la arrogancia de los más nobles sacrificios, no bastan a consolar el alma de un solo extravío," [From the moment that whiteness darkens, misfortune begins. The good practice and consciousness of all virtues, the possession of the best qualities, the arrogance of the noblest of sacrifices, does not suffice to protect the soul from one sole stray] (*LJ* 61). This stray/*extravío,* is reminiscent of the tempest in Martí's prologue to Bonalde's "Niágara" because it serves as an obstacle to man's endeavor to elevate his spirit and is said to darken the soul, leading it away from a state of purity. In this 1882 prologue Martí directs the new man to the peaks of the mountains, thus defying any diversions created by the tempest [the United States or Paris]: "The mountain ends in the peak; the culmination wave spun by the tempest and thrown toward the sky ends in the crest; so too, must human life end, at the height" (308). Thus, in the first paragraph of the novel, Martí establishes the polarities of darkness and light, materialism and the soul, as well as reveals the trajectory of the plot, which is the infection (by the tempest) of the aspirations of man in his endeavor to elevate his soul (high) by the materialistic (low) obstacles that will be manifested in the character of the protagonist Lucía Jerez.

The setting of the novel, introduced in the first paragraph through the home of Lucía Jerez, takes place in an indeterminate South American country that mirrors the celebrated progress of other modern cities, such as those found in the United States. Martí presents the atmosphere of the surroundings of Lucía's house as a place of gaiety, festivities, and countrified elegance. The impression that Martí offers in this first chapter is that of a city that is bustling and full of goods in an era of modernity. The lack of conjunctions in the sentences and the movement of the discourse denote a sense of excess and dynamism: "¡Los nietos! . . . Los maridos. . . . La abuela, como viene cargada de chucherías para los nietos, de los juguetes que fue reuniendo en la semana para traerlos a la gente menor hoy domingo, de los mazapanes recién hechos" [The grandchildren! . . . The husbands. . . . The grandmother, as she comes loaded down with presents for the grandchildren, with the toys that she was gathering during the week to bring to the little ones today, Sunday, and with the recently prepared marzipan cakes] (*LJ* 63). The employment of hyperbole, a style that Martí uses in his many writings about the excesses of the United States, creates a sense of the abundance of elements and goods denoted in this city. In *Divergent Moderni-*

ties, Julio Ramos examines the use of excess words in Martí's description of the city. In his analysis of "Coney Island," Ramos states: "The city appears as an impulse that overruns boundaries, formal limits—forever displacing and configuring them" (191). He attests that the collection of chronicles included in *Escenas norteamericanas* has to be read "as an immense urban cartography, harnessed at times with the very verbal, fragmented material of the city itself" (191). This quaint city, situated in an indeterminate country in South America, has apparently absorbed similar characteristics of the materialist essence of the United States as denoted by Martí in other essays.

One of Martí's main objectives in his many writings about Latin America and the United States is that the nations need to know each other. In his more skeptical writings about the possible aggressiveness of the United States towards Latin America, he advocates that the leaders of the different nations to the south know what they are dealing with so that they can make appropriate transactions and treaty agreements. In the "Washington Pan-American Congress," published in *La Nación* in 1889, Martí states: "Dangers must not be recognized only when they are upon us, but when they can be avoided."[13] He further argues that nations must not be marveled at for their "lofty virtues and rapacious talents" but must be scrutinized, for when one establishes relations with them "they bury their roots far below the surface."[14] He proclaims that only a "virile and unanimous response" can save the developing Latin American nations from the aggressive actions of a "powerful and ambitious neighbor."[15]

In *Amistad funesta,* Martí slowly unveils the sordidness and extreme problems that exist underneath this apparently well-constructed society, offering the reader a somewhat distorted mirror image of a country that has already adopted the materialistic essence of the United States (and France to a lesser extent).[16] While on the exterior everything appears to be progressive, happy, and festive, amidst the gaiety and splendor described in this modern city of Latin America exists the problem of the Indians, who like *gusanos* [worms] stand out in contrast to the jubilation of the other inhabitants: "Parecen gusanos prendidos a trechos en una guirnalda" [They look like worms attached here and there to a garland] (*LJ* 63). Martí employs the medical discourse of science so prevalent in the nineteenth century and applies it to the latent illness found in this booming city: "Los indios, en verdad, descalzos y mugrientos, en medio de tanta limpieza y luz, parecen llagas" [The Indians, in fact, barefoot and filthy, in the midst of such cleanliness and so much light, look like sores] (*LJ* 63). Within the sterility of the modern city the *indios* are blatantly ignored and stand out in contrast like an open wound. In this way the text reflects upon the indigenous element of the majority of Latin American countries, many of which ignore the plight of the Indians as they adopt the progressive ideas of Darwinism and positivism into their national agenda. The progressive nation of the United States, argued Martí, offered a clear example of this contemptuous neglect towards the Native Americans, which was a grave oversight he wanted to avoid in his utopian vision of Latin America.

Martí had written several essays about the problem of the Indian in the United States around the time of the publication of *Amistad funesta.* In the novel the social context of the city surrounding Lucía's home reflects the gross neglect of the Indians and can be linked to Martí's criticism in contemporaneous writings about the treatment of the Indians in the United States. In his letter to the director of *La Nación,* published October 25, 1885, Martí attacks the inept governmental system of North America, which limits the Indian's personality: "El indio es muerto; con este sistema vil que apaga su personalidad" [With this vile system that snuffs out his personality, the Indian is dead] (*Oc* 323).[17] Once again, employing the epistemological discourse of science, he compares man's right to exercise his individuality to the rotation and velocity of a wheel—"como con el rodar crece la velocidad de la rueda." The Indian, unable to express himself freely in the remoteness and isolation of the reservations, finds himself in a condition of rust and decay just like the stagnant wheel: "Como la rueda, se oxida y se pudre" (*Oc* 363).

Within the utopian project of the main protagonist, Juan Jerez, who encompasses almost all of the qualities of Martí's projection of the ideal man, the Indian is protected, liberated, and incorporated into the national image. In the novel Juan Jerez serves as a mediator between the modern world, with its excesses and prosperity, and the ideal construction of the Latin American nation, which will unfortunately fall prey to the tempest. It is important to note that Martí utilizes the opposition between the ideal masculine subject of Latin America confronted with the pathological woman in order to warn his compatriots of the deleterious consequences of the excesses of materialism and modernity, which according to his many writings during that period can be found in the United States.

In an essay written in 1886, Martí complains of the hypocritical self-interest of the North American people in their endeavor to gain success and riches: "Los hombres, a pesar de todas las apariencias, solo están unidos en este pueblo por los intereses, por el odio amoroso que se tienen entre sí los que regatean por un mismo premio" [In spite of all appearances, in this nation, men are only united by their interests, by the friendly contempt that they hold for each other as they haggle over the same prize] (*Oc* 375). The Cuban patriot sought to achieve a similar level of modernity and democracy in Latin America; however, in doing so, he strove to avoid the decadence of the soul, which was what he had observed to be an unnecessary condition of the North American experience: "Como que no hay alma suficiente en este pueblo gigantesco: y sin esta juntura maravillosa, todo se viene en los pueblos, con gran catástrofe, a tierra" (*Oc* 375) [In this nation there doesn't seem to be enough soul, that marvelous cohesive stuff without which everything in a nation comes crashing down catastrophically].[18] He decries that in order to rise above these base materialist aspects found in their northern neighbor, Latin Americans need to feed the soul and reduce the beast: "Es indispensable alimentar la luz, y achicar la bestia" (*Oc* 375). Martí's utopian image of Latin America is constructed from and against the image of the United States, whose negative materialist essence I argue is incarnated in the irrational, pathological image of Lucía.

The Latin American versus the North American Soul

In his many essays and chronicles written prior to and after *Amistad funesta,* Martí had established the dichotomy between the North American soul and the Latin American soul. In "Coney Island" he describes the hustle and bustle of the modern city from the perspective of an outsider. He posits the Latin American in a position of superiority to the North American as he expresses the former's pity towards the vacuous condition of spirit found in this modern nation: "These men [Latin Americans] are possessed by the anguish of solitude in the end; the nostalgia for a higher spiritual world that invades and inflicts them."[19] The famous line in this essay, "Such people [North Americans] eat quantity; we quality" (321), is indicative of the dichotomous conditions constructed in the discourse of Martí, a discourse that he utilizes in formulating what Ramos calls a superior sense of Latin Americanism—one that contrasts with the materialistic essence that he continuously points out with regard to North America (xxxvii).

In the prologue to "Niágara," Martí condemns those men who blindly adopt outside ideologies in order to appear more educated. These ideas are expressed in *Amistad funesta,* where many Latin American leaders are described for their weakness or "sterility" for their misguided decisions and bad management of the natural resources of their countries. Those governmental leaders, as well as many influential intellectuals are described in the novel as being "cargadas de ideas de Europa y Norteamérica" [charged with ideas from Europe and North America] and are thus considered "estéril entre nosotros por su mala dirección" [sterile among us because of their misguided direction] (*LJ* 70–71). The adjective *estéril* [sterile] denotes the lack of virility of those misguided political leaders who, impressed by European and North American ideologies and influence, fail to adequately lead their countries into an era of progress. Thus, masculinity, for Martí, is the ability to separate oneself from the blind appropriation of learned ideologies, as well as to behold a heightened level of spirituality that transcends the decadence of materialist acquisitions promulgated by modernity.

In *Amistad funesta,* the construction of the idyllic national subject is manifested in the character of Juan Jerez. Martí carefully establishes the dichotomous polarities of spirit versus materialism in his depiction of good and bad men in chapter 1. On page 72, the decadent vices of materialism blend with sexual indulgence as Martí notes the corruption of man due to his base desires of engaging in illicit pleasures. The indulgence in materialism and/or sexuality, according to the narrator, is not without its consequences, given that one must pay the highest price of all—"that of his own cleanliness" (*LJ* 72). These amorous flings, elegantly disguising base wants later infect the individual's life like an ulcer ["roen luego la vida como úlceras"] (*LJ* 72). Like the masked prostitute on the cover of the Renaissance poem

"Syphilis," the men who engage in these amorous escapades are unaware of the severe consequences caused by them. Juan Jerez, who is not a victim of the decadent misgivings of these men, looks with amazement at those self-loathing men and women who engage in such imprudent actions (*LJ* 73). In contrast, the narrator offers the image of the man accompanied by the good woman who stands by him and his child, which he claims is far greater than the petty satisfaction that the complicity of a whimsical lover provides for an honorable man ["Era mayor que las penosas satifacciones que la complicidad con una amante liviana produce a un hombre honrado"] (*LJ* 73). In this example, it is clearly man's engagement with women that rebukes him or qualifies him as being honorable, an act that is carried to fruition in the dénouement of the novel.

The opposition between good and bad women is reflected in previous works written by Martí, often highlighting the celebrated qualities held by educated women. In his essay "Graduation Day" (1884), he praises the dutiful woman who "will be transformed from a mere vessel of fragrant flesh into an urn of spirit against which men will always press their anxious lips!"[20] The contrasting metaphors of "copa de espíritu" [cup of spirit] versus "copa de carne" [cup of flesh] in this passage will be utilized in the novel in order to guide the reader away from the dangers of the flesh.

The Main Protagonists

Many critics refer to the autobiographical characteristics that stand out in the main male protagonist of Juan Jerez, and in many ways Juan reflects all of the attributes associated with Martí's projection of the ideal male subject.[21] Juan is noted for his relationship to nature as opposed to the progressive desires of positivism and accumulation of wealth: "Y así Juan Jerez, a quien la Naturaleza había puesto aquella coraza de luz" [And so Juan Jerez, to whom Nature had given that shield of light] (*LJ* 67). The use of light/*luz* is an image used throughout the novel, which reflects goodness and the elevation of the soul. Once again, Martí defines Juan's efforts and preoccupations during these modern times as being noble and virile, as he is said to be of a noble and viril heart: "de un corazón noble y viril" (*LJ* 68). Like the masculine subject of reason defined by Kant and Hegel, Juan is described as being an exceptional type ["de la raza selecta"], and because of his priestlike qualities ["un sacerdote de todos los hombres"], he does not fall prey to the materialistic aspirations characteristic of most men of his profession (*LJ* 30). Furthermore, his philanthropic activities towards the Indians in the novel clearly demarcate the difference between Juan's/Martí's utopian program in Latin America and the current treatment of Native Americans in North America.

In many ways Juan encompasses all of the qualities of the artist, the martyr, and the man of nature, all celebrated virtues that stand out in José Martí's narrative.[22] Like Martí, he is described as a genuine poet ["poeta genuino"] and possesses martyr-type qualities that can be associated with the dedication and selfless activities of this Cuban patriot (*LJ* 73). However, other critics have pointed to the failure of Juan as a model protagonist, specifically due to his weak demeanor, or what I will point out to be his more feminine characteristics. In the preface of the Spanish edition of *Lucía Jerez,* Manuel Pedro González states that, without realizing it, Martí created Juan in his own image, reflecting his alter ego, which he argues inadvertently compromises the novel and jeopardizes Juan's character. He claims that this identity weakens the novel and diminishes the character of Juan Jerez, who does not begin to measure up to his creator, but cannot be separated from him by the knowledgeable reader (*LJ* 42).[23]

In creating the pathological character of Lucía, Martí had no other choice but to contrast this monstrous, masculine character with the more docile, feminine characteristics of Juan. Juan's complete disinterest in sexuality may be perceived as reflecting the self-control of those of a higher intellect, as suggested by Nietzsche and Schopenhauer. For others, however, he could be considered as revealing an asexual behavior, which contrasts considerably with the *machista* culture prevalent in Latin America. Also, Juan's poetic-type behavior, albeit idyllic, seems somewhat "effeminate" in this late nineteenth-century text. While Lucía is manically crushing flowers due to her jealousy and anger, Juan is seen picking up flowers in order to save them from passers-by: "Y eres tan bueno que te he visto recoger las flores pisadas en las calles y ponerlas con mucho cuidado donde nadie las pise" [And you are so good that I have seen you pick up trampled flowers in the street and place them very carefully where nobody would step on them] (*LJ* 146). A final and very important example of Juan's passivity is his inability to stand up to, or change, Lucía's behavior. Because this is primarily a didactic treatise, showing the consequences of drinking from the "copa de carne" [cup of flesh] as opposed to the "copa de espíritu" [cup of spirit], Lucía's trajectory towards destruction must come to fruition. At the end of the novel, after Lucía kills Sol del Valle, the reader is unaware of Lucía's destiny, specifically because Juan never reacts to this heinous crime. Although in most ways Juan does reflect the ideal male subject of Latin America, his opposition to Lucía tips him a little too far into the feminine sphere to be an adequate male national role model during this era.

Anderson Imbert states that the disapproval that Martí felt for his novel was unjust and argues that because the author condemned *Amistad funesta* the critics followed suit: "Puesto que el autor condenaba *Amistad funesta* también ellos decidieron condenarla" (581). Juan's questionable gender may be one of the more striking features that possibly led to the failure of the novel as a political treatise, or even of being accepted by contemporary critics. Nevertheless, Juan's only significant flaw is the inability to resist the more masculine, forceful actions of Lucía, which in the text are constructed as hegemonic due to her insipid penetration into all aspects of his life.

Lucía Jerez

Enrique Anderson Imbert refers to Lucía as one of the best-depicted feminine creations found in nineteenth-century Spanish American novels (106). In the following passage he alludes to the pathology and to the aggressiveness of Lucía, which are characteristics that set her apart from any other female protagonist thus far portrayed in Latin American nineteenth-century literature: "She is one of those creatures passionately wanting to live more and more but which are, nevertheless, enveloped in an atmosphere of death, in conflict with themselves, vital, irrational, anguished paradoxical, and possessing a tragic feeling of life that relates them to Unamuno's creatures."[24] Lucía's passion to live, love, and control the man that she loved can thus be perceived as both admirable and manic.

Lucía is first introduced in the beginning of the novel during a Sunday gathering with Adela and the sickly Ana. As noted before, the symbolic level of the novel denotes the more profound psychic characteristics of the protagonists, and Lucía stands out for her deviance from normal, acceptable codes of femininity. Lucía's first indication of difference can be seen in her physical appearance, her preference for flowers and the shocking red color of her dress. While Adela is described as "delgada y locuaz" [thin and talkative] wearing a crème silk dress adorned with roses, the sickly, frail Ana wears a white dress accented with a blue flower fastened with threads of wheat: "una flor azul sujeta con unas hebras de trigo" (*LJ* 62). Adela's character is associated with the whimsical qualities of youth due to her desire to travel to Paris, whereas Ana, who wears "una flor azul" [a blue flower] is depicted for her artistic qualities, her maternal character, and her elevated soul.

From the onset, Lucía defies traditional concepts of the feminine as she is seen as active and energetic and wearing a red silk dress. In addition, Lucía stands out in contrast to both women as she does not adorn her "vestido de mayo" with flowers because, as the narrator notes, "No se conocía aún en los jardines la flor que a ella le gustaba: ¡la flor negra!" [It was still unknown in the gardens the flower that she liked: the black flower!] (*LJ* 62). Thus, from the very beginning of the novel, Lucía is depicted for her deviance from the other female characters; however, one cannot help but note a sense of defiance and agency in her strong character and her resistance to follow accepted codes of conduct for women.

Throughout the novel, Lucía's deviance from traditional codes of conduct can also be perceived as pathological according to contemporaneous studies of hysteria during the nineteenth century. In her book *The Female Malady,* Elaine Showalter refers to the period between 1870 and World War I as the golden age of hysteria because this recurring female malady had become the focus of English, American, French, and German physicians of the period. She states that hysteria was linked with the essence of the feminine in a number of ways: "Its vast, unstable repertoire of emotional and physical symptoms—fits, fainting, vomiting, choking, sobbing, laughing, paralysis—the rapid passage from one to another suggested the lability and capriciousness traditionally associated with the feminine nature" (129). In the introduction, we saw that hysteria had become the illness in vogue in the late nineteenth century popularized by Jean-Martin Charcot's vivid illustrations and scientific studies, which were available to the public. A closer examination of Lucía's character reveals her tendencies towards this disease, which in the novel culminates with the irrational act of the murder of Sol del Valle.

The many examples of Lucía's deviance from traditional codes of femininity can be seen throughout the novel. In chapter 1, she is depicted as being tall, which according to the narrator is a physical characteristic not typical for her years or her gender: "más de lo que sentaba a sus años y sexo" (*LJ* 81). Similarly, Lucía's rocking chair is described as pushing more towards the front than the back, as it changed position due to the energetic gestures of its owner: "como obediente a un gesto enérgico y contenido de su dueña" (*LJ* 65). F. C. Skey, who gave lectures on hysteria to students of St. Bartholomew's Hospital in 1866, noticed that hysterical girls were typically energetic and passionate, "exhibiting more than usual force and decision of character, of strong resolution, fearless of danger, bold riders, having plenty of what is termed *nerve.*"[25] Lucía's personality throughout the novel can be described as forceful, careless, and bold, thus defying traditional conceptions of her gender.

Showalter also notes that many specialists on hysteria referred to the biological explanation of hysteria that attributed unsatisfied sexual drives in adolescents and in young women to their hysteric outbreaks.[26] In chapter 3 of *Amistad funesta* Lucía entertains the idea of using her sexual prowess in order to keep Juan by her side: "¡Y esto ni se puede decir, esto que yo quisiera hacer! Si yo pudiera hacer esto, él sentiría todo lo que yo lo quiero, y no podría querer a más nadie" [And this cannot even be said, this thing that I would like to do! If I could do it, he would know how much I love him, and he could not love anyone else] (*LJ* 184). Although this novel was written under contract and one of the stipulations of writing was to avoid indecorous scenes that would provoke young minds, Martí manages to include "the unspoken" as a means of alluding to Lucía's deviance from traditional and acceptable codes of behavior for women.[27]

There are numerous indications in the novel that attest to the more virilelike qualities of Lucía, which stand out in their opposition to the traditional passive role of the female heroine. It is her selfishness, however, that aligns Lucía with the materialistic qualities of the United States described by Martí and places her within nineteenth-century conceptions of madness. In chapter 2, Lucía confesses to Juan that she is envious of anything or anyone that takes Juan's attention from her. In the following passage, her jealousy is depicted for its pathology with the expressions *I suffer* ["sufro"] and *I [would] die* ["Me muero"]: "Y odio un libro si lo lees, y un amigo si lo vas a ver, y una mujer si dicen si es bella y puedes verla tu. . . . Me muero de una envidia enorme por todo lo que tu puedas querer y lo que pueda quererte" [And I hate a book if you are reading it, and a friend if you are going to see him, and a woman if they say that she is pretty and you can see her. . . . I am dying of a deep envy towards everything that you may want and that may want you] (*LC* 146–47). According to nineteenth-century studies on hysteria, women suffering from this disorder abandoned traditional roles of self-sacrificing daughter or mother and demanded service and attention from others.[28] The previous passage exemplifies Lucía's manic need to control Juan by demanding his full attention.

While Lucía and Juan are presented as the inevitable ideal couple in the novel, Martí is careful to point out the foreboding characteristics of Lucía's personality. When the handsome couple entered the room, a shadow was cast upon Lucía's face revealing "sus dos ojos llameantes, como dos amenazas" [her two blazing eyes, like two threats] (*LJ* 81). Lucía's apparent beauty and youth are depicted in the novel as being deceiving. Underneath the veneer of beauty and class lies the pathology of an explosive and pathological woman: "Lucía, en quien las flores de la edad escondían la lava candente que como las vetas de metales preciosas en las minas le culebreaban en el pecho" [Lucía, in whom the flower of her youth hid the burning lava which, like the precious veins of metals in a mine, slithered through her chest] (*LJ* 75). The deceiving presence of Lucía, like the modern features of the United States, should not be overlooked for its pathological essence that lies beneath the glimmering exterior.

In her essay "'Esclava vencedora': La mujer en la obra literaria de José Martí," Jacqueline Cruz attests to Martí's misogynous view towards women, which has been curiously overlooked by most critics. Cruz claims that Martí differentiates between the modern woman and the traditional woman in *Versos sencillos* and in *Amistad funesta*—the former being associated with the modernity of the United States, and the latter, which is exalted in Martí's works, pertains to the Hispanic American society and/or its rural areas.[29] The voraciousness of Lucía's appetite in her relationship with Juan and her link to materialism can be compared to the materialist essence of the city of New York that Martí depicts in his many writings.

In the following passage from *Escenas norteamericanas* written shortly after *Amistad funesta* (October 1885), Martí warns his readers about the misgivings of a materialist-based society [the United States], advocating the need to study these people in order to avoid the same mistakes: "En lo que peca, en lo que yerra, en lo que tropieza, es necesario estudiar a este pueblo, para no tropezar como él" [In he who sins, in he who errs, in he who stumbles, it is necessary to study this nation, so that one does not stumble like them].[30] Martí admits that the United States is a great nation; however, one must look beyond the exterior in order to see the decadent immorality that it has engendered: "Cae en un pigmeismo moral, y un envenenamiento del juicio, en una culpable adoración de todo éxito" [It amounts to primitive morals, and a poisoning of judgment, in guilty adoration for all that is successful].[31] The poisoning of the mind can be perceived as a mental decay associated with the pathological status of the individual that is achieved in his or her endeavor to acquire material possessions.

Lucía's pathological profile is reflected throughout the novel and is manifested indirectly in Ana's artwork. In her paintings, two monstrous figures crushing flowers are featured, providing a glimpse of an unforeseen future. The first piece is set in the corner of the garden where the sky is very clear, giving the impression of calmness and tranquility. A young man, dressed in a gray (business) suit, looks at his hands in shock because he has just broken a lily ["acaba de romper un lirio"], which has left his hands stained with blood (*LJ* 91). This painting provokes a deeper analysis and urges the reader to attempt a symbolic reading of the painting and the text. As noted in the beginning of the novel, the white flower in this text represents the soul and, according to this reading, the soul has been compromised and even destroyed by the young man in the business suit.

The second painting, which is only formulated in Ana's mind, is more complex in that it reveals the dual nature of modernity and progress according to the many readings of José Martí. This painting will represent the modern city of Paris, which was widely perceived to be the mecca of culture and art. The young artist explains that she is going to paint a monster sitting on a hill, with the moonlight shining over his back, which allows her to trace (with lines of light) the prominent parts of the most famous buildings in Paris. Because of the contrast with the bright silhouette, the spectator will be able to see all the darkness of the monster's body with the head of a woman who will be devouring roses: "Toda la negrura de su cuerpo, el monstruo, con cabeza de mujer, estará devorando rosas" (*LJ* 92). The shadows created by the moonlight reveal the destructive identity of the monster with a woman's head, just as in a previous description of Lucía the shadows revealed her blazing eyes "como dos amenazas" [like two threats] (*LJ* 81).

In both paintings the flowers (man's soul) are victims of a horrible crime. In the first painting a business-type man is the culprit and, in the second, the image of a hybrid monster/woman devouring roses results in horror and chaos. The first painting could refer to the increased economic relations that Latin America had established with the United States as denoted by the businessman dressed in an elegant grey suit ["en un traje gris muy elegante"] so typical of New York City. The second painting, which takes place in Paris, suggests the many progressive ideologies originated in France that had been blindly adopted by leaders in Latin America.[32]

Ana clarifies the recurring theme of her paintings (and of the text) with her explanation of the two classifications of beasts in this world: "Una se viste de pieles, devora animales, y anda sobre garras; otra se viste de trajes elegantes, come animales y almas y anda sobre una sombrilla o un bastón" [One dresses in fur, devours animals, and walks on claws; the other dresses in elegant suits, eats animals and souls and walks about with a parasol or a walking stick] (*LJ* 92). This description is reminiscent of Martí's 1885 essay in which he described the United States' "pacific" yet "inevitable" means of appropriating Latin American territory. Ana, like Martí, is described as having the fortunate capacity of seeing pure, superhuman matters and the admirable outrage provoked by the battle of ferocious appetites that consumes the world: "y la hermosa indignación por la batalla de apetitos feroces en que se consume la tierra" (*LJ* 92). Like Martí, Ana gently urges her viewer to look beyond face value and see the monster that lies beneath the mask of civilization and modernity.

Throughout the novel, Lucía's manic habit of crushing small objects in fits of jealousy links her symbolically to the destructive forces of the perpetrators in both paintings. Lucía even expresses feelings of jealousy due to the attention that Juan is giving Ana during this lengthy explanation of the paintings by rolling a white handkerchief so vigorously that it appeared to be a serpent: "Y lo enrolló tanto y tanto, y lo desenrollaba con tal violencia, que, yendo rápidamente de una mano a la otra, el lindo pañuelo parecía una víbora" [And she rolled it up so so much, and then unraveled it in such a violent manner, that passing so rapidly from one hand to another, the pretty handkerchief seemed like a serpent] (*LC* 94). The *víbora,* or serpent, is a biblical reference to the fall of man due to Eve's manipulation of Adam. In her essay, Cruz notes that Martí utilizes the image of Eve in his dichotomous vision of women in *Versos sencillos,* as well as in *Amistad funesta,* depicting her as the one who seduces and dishonors the innocent male protagonist, who can be compared with Adam.[33]

Juan and Lucía

In his essay "Graduation Day" (1884), Martí states that just as in the model family, the combination of feminine and masculine qualities are necessary for the success of a nation: "Just as no child is born without father and mother, so there is no nation without happy communion between the virile and feminine elements of the spirit."[34] I believe that *Amistad funesta* hints at the possibility of a new paradigmatic couple between Juan and Lucía, reflecting the popular belief that a union with the United States would facilitate the progression of Latin American countries into an age of modernity. Due to the proximity between Cuba and the United States, as well as the deep economic relations they had established throughout the nineteenth century, the question of annexation was believed by many to be inevitable.[35] Similarly, the rising economic relations between North America and Latin American nations in the form of treaty negotiations and reciprocal trade treaties were indicative of the importance and inevitability of future deeper relations. From the very beginning of the novel, however, Lucía shows signs of excessive greed, immaturity, and agency, deeming her a dangerous counterpart to Juan. In addition, Lucía violates all of the qualities that Juan and Martí hold in high regard, specifically their respect for nature and the elevation of the soul. Thus, Lucía can be more adequately described as the tempest of Martí's prologue to "Niágara," due to her obstruction of Juan's aspirations for a healthy modernity, as proposed by Martí.

Throughout the text Lucía is portrayed as being an obstacle in the spiritual endeavors of Juan. Like Martí in his prologue to "Niágara," Juan aspires to the spiritual heights that can be reached by man in his quest to elevate his soul by separating himself from the base wants of materialism. In chapter 3, Juan uses the poem "Excélsior" by North American poet Henry Wadsworth Longfellow (1807–82) in his allusion to the great heights that he wants to achieve with Lucía at his side. "¡Más alto!" [Higher]—he cries, simulating the poetic voice of this inspirational poem. However, Lucía, not knowing that she is meant to accompany him, cries out: "Yo te quito la bandera de las manos. Tú te quedas conmigo. ¡Yo soy lo más alto!" [I will take the flag from your hands. You stay with me. I am the highest!] (*LJ* 143). The image of moving to a higher plane with the flag in hand alludes to José Martí's lifelong patriotic mission of achieving Cuba's independence from Spain and Latin American nations maintaining their own sovereignty. Lucía's incessant need to control every aspect of Juan's life is evident in her desire to thwart Juan's journey by taking the flag from his hand. In doing so, she forces Juan to choose between a spiritual ascension or a materialistic ascension, by offering herself as the only desired goal (¡Yo soy lo más alto! [I am the highest!]). Thus, this sporadic action, which threatens the integrity of the soul, can be interpreted as a subtle threat to Latin America if this union were to blindly take place.

Sol del Valle

Although Juan is committed to Lucía, Sol is presented as Lucía's rival due in part to her extreme beauty, but more so due to Lucía's uncontrollable jealousy. If Lucía is symbolic of the hysteric nature of the United States, Sol is emblematic of the muse of the modernist, the spirit of beauty and truth, the female Ariel, representing the elevated soul of Latin America. Throughout the text she is associated with light, purity, and the soul, whereas Lucía is linked to images of darkness, irrationality, and deviance. Like Cuba, Sol is presently monetarily poor, yet rich in the knowledge and appreciation of fine arts.[36] She has proven herself to be an exemplary student and holds the position of *profesora* at the institution from which she graduated. The home of Doña Andrea and Leonor (Sol) serves as a prime example of Martí's projected image of the elevated spirit of the *modernista* intellectuals of Spanish America during "estos tiempos negros":

> ¿Ni quien se niega, si los quiere bien, a que sus hijos brillantes e inteligentes, aprendan esas cosas de arte, el dibujar, el pintar, el tocar piano, que alegran tanto la casa, y elevan, si son bien comprendidas y caen en buena tierra, el carácter de quien las posee, esas cosas de arte que apenas hace un siglo eran todavía propiedad casi exclusiva de reinas y princesas? (*LJ* 111)

> [If they really love their brilliant and intelligent children, how could they deny them the opportunity to learn these matters of art, drawing, painting, playing the piano, that bring so much joy to the home, and elevate, if they are understood well and fall into the right hands, the character of he who possesses them, these matters of art that scarcely a century ago were exclusively reserved for queens and princesses?]

Sol del Valle is the poetic muse, ephemeral and free-floating. Martí refers to her as "una copa de nácar" recalling his famous poem "Copa con alas" that portrays the union of the poetic speaker with the female muse in a metafictional journey towards the creation of poetry. Although he later compares her beauty with "una copa de espíritu" [a cup of spirit] for some, others would consider her "una manzana apetitosa" [a juicy apple] (*LJ* 72). In this example, Martí alludes to the uncivilized male gaze as one that is oversexed, thus putting this gentle spirit in jeopardy. In the following passage, the omniscient narrator reiterates the covetous nature of men towards Sol: "Si hubiera un lente que permitiese a las mujeres ver, tales como les pasean por el cráneo los pensamientos de los hombres, y lo que les anda en el corazón, los querrían mucho menos" [If there were a lens that permitted that women see such things that pass through the minds of men, and what runs through their hearts, they would like them much less] (*LJ* 72). Lust, like the negative traits of materialism, poses an imminent threat to this young, innocent girl. Sol's elevated spirit and beauty, like that of Latin America, needed to be protected from the male gaze, or from the imperialist gaze of the colossus.

In order to protect her from her status of poverty, beauty, and youth, the director of the school introduced Sol to Lucía, hoping that she would take her under her wing and guide her into the proper social circles. Lucía displays signs of jealousy and irrationality throughout the novel, culminating with her complete loss of reason and control at the end of the novel. Lucía's failure to nurture and guide Sol in the high society of the day is due to her symptoms of hysteria, deeming her an unhealthy protector for the young Sol del Valle. Despite Lucía's recurring manic outbreaks, she had become an integral part in Sol's life since their encounter: "Lucía, ardiente y despótica, sumisa a veces sin causa aparente, y bella entonces como una rosa roja, ejercía . . . un poderoso influjo en el espíritu de Sol, tímido y nuevo" [Lucía, passionate and despotic, submissive at times without an apparent cause, and beautiful like a red rose . . . exerted a powerful influence on the timid and younger spirit of Sol] (*LJ* 157). Similarly, despite Martí's warnings, the United States had become a significant influence in the lives of many Cubans and Latin Americans during the nineteenth century.[37]

Sol and Lucía

Lucía and Sol's first encounter also serves as a prime example of Lucía's pathological behavior, as well as foreshadowing the climax of the novel. When Lucía first meets young Leonor, she accidentally pricks her with a thorn during their embrace (*LJ* 77). Some critics, such as Joan Torres-Pou, have alluded to the homoerotic nature of this encounter due to the fact that Sol appeared to experience joy when she was pricked by the thorn of a rose in her breast ["Le pareció sentir goce cuando se clavó en su seno la espina de la rosa"] (156).[38] Sol feels both pleasure and pain as a result of her minor flesh wound provoked by the thorn of a rose. This bittersweet union is indicative of the dual face of modernity described by Martí, which, on the one hand is described as pleasurable; on the other hand, its materialist essence is gently eating away at the soul, as represented by the destiny of Sol del Valle.

As in his early writings and the novel, Martí represents the base aspirations of materialism as that monstrous Other, which threatens the integrity of the soul. In *Amistad funesta,* Lucía is represented for her aberrant behavior, and her relationship with Sol is characterized by unhealthy, unseemly behavior in young women. In her analysis of the novel, Rosalinda Gayoso Wright explores the psychological implications pointing out Lucía's innumerable traits of neurosis. She claims that Lucía's hatred for Sol is not intentional and that she does try hard to combat her negative feelings. In her work Wright alludes to the controlling nature of Lucía, who consistently lavishes Sol with expensive gifts in order to dissuade her from loving Juan. She argues that the gifts that she presents to Sol are her way of minimizing her remorse for the overwhelming jealousy that she feels towards her and are also used as a means to manipulate her.[39] Similarly the materialist or economic amenities offered by the United States often served as an attractive consolation to the appropriation of territory and power in Latin America. These manipulative tendencies of Lucía toward Sol reflect Martí's fear of the insidious actions of the Unites States towards Latin America. In "El Tratado comercial entre los Estados Unidos y México" (1883), Martí speaks of the advantageous means that the United States has in this treaty and alludes to its effective way of implementing itself into the growth of cities. He argues that once the United States has established treaty relations, they have the control to dump surplus goods "de un mercado forzoso de sus industrias embarazadas por la sobra de productos no colocables" [from a forced market whose industries are pregnant from the surplus of products that cannot be placed] and raise cities "sin más autorización ni traba que las que les otorga el tratado, en un pueblo vecino" [without more authorization or objection than that which the treaty grants them in a nearby nation] (*Oc* 307). Thus, in exchange for the promise of the implementation of a modernized infrastructure and establishing trade relations with this progressive nation, Latin America, like Sol compromises its autonomy and runs the risk of infecting its soul.

Hysteria and the Pathologized Other

In Charcot's visual representations of hysterical women presented in the amphitheater at the Salpêtrière Hospital, the grand finale would be the performance of a full hysterical seizure.[40] The complete seizure involved a prolonged and elaborate convulsive attack that included three phases: the epileptoid phase, in which women lost consciousness and foamed at the mouth; clownism, which was eccentric physical contortions; and *attitudes passionnelles,* where women exhibited feelings of ecstasy and eroticism.[41] Martí included a similar finale in his novel by providing the various stages that Lucía went through in the events leading up to the murder of Sol. Lucía's behavior reflects *globus hystericus* or classic hysteria, which began with pain in the uterine area and an obstruction in the chest and throat. The seizure, associated with classic hysteria, consisted of alternate sobbing and laughing, convulsive movements of the body, heart palpitations, impaired hearing or vision, or unconsciousness. The fits were followed by exhaustion and rapid recovery.[42]

In chapter 3, Lucía is seen sitting before her mirror in her bedroom, where she considers her beauty as compared to her rival's, Sol del Valle.[43] In this scene with the mirror Lucía's insane jealousy of Sol leads to thoughts of masochism as she considers harming herself: "¿Me rasgaría las carnes: me abriría con las uñas las mejillas. Cara imbécil, ¿por qué no soy como ella?" [I would scratch out my flesh. I would rip my cheeks open with my nails: Stupid face, why am I not like her?] (*LJ* 183). Soon after, Lucía breaks out in a horrible crying fit, which surprisingly follows the symptoms of a hysterical attack:

> ¿Cómo no ha de quererla Juan? decía la infeliz, entre golpes de lágrimas, a los pocos momentos, siendo aquel llanto de Lucía extraño, porque no venía a raudal y de seguida, aliviando a la que lloraba, sino a borbotones e intervalos, sofocándola y exaltándola, parecido al agua que baja, tropezando entre peñas, por los torrentes. (*LJ* 185)
>
> [Why wouldn't Juan love her? said the wretch, between bouts of tears and crying that soon became strange, because it did not come in streams and all at once, soothing the one who cried, but gushing forth and in intervals, suffocating and exalting her, like water that descends through torrents, smashing against the rocks.]

Her intermittent fits of suffocation and exaltation resemble the classic symptoms of *globus hystericus,* where the choking sensation was said to be like a ball "rising in the esophagus, producing a feeling of choking or suffocation."[44] According to the ancients, this feeling was caused by the rising of the womb itself within the body.[45] The feelings of exaltation accompanied by the torrential excretion of fluids (tears) reflect the sensual or sexual aspects associated with the third phase of a classic hysterical attack, which is *attitudes passionnelles.*

Sol was the next to witness Lucía's hysteric behavior. After Lucía had shut herself up in her room for several days, Sol forced herself into her friend's room only to find her disheveled and tear stricken: "tan descompuesta que no le pareció que era ella, sino otra en su lugar" [so out of sorts that it did not seem to be her, but another in her place] (*LJ* 191). Lucía is described later as emitting *gemidos,* or sobs, from Ana's room. Ana had convinced her to embrace Sol, and Lucía, anxious to acquiesce, quickly changed her attitude about Sol by desperately trying to love her. She is described soon after as being very attentive towards Sol as she frantically helps her get dressed for the big dance. Absorbed in her new endeavor, Lucía becomes more preoccupied in Sol's appearance than her own: "Mírala, Ana, mírala" [Look at her, Ana, look at her]. In a jovial tone she cries "Yo me muero de celos" [I'm dying of jealousy] as she offers her a pearl bracelet (*LJ* 197). Her behavior is described as compulsive, as she displays a complete change in attitude towards Sol: "Toma; ¡te lo beso! ¡Qué bueno es querer!" [Take it; I will kiss it for you! How good it is to love!] (*LJ* 197). Her sudden altruistic behavior towards Sol could indicate a possibility for a renewed friendship, if it were not shown by a hysteric.

Women suffering from hysteria were said to lack maternal and altruistic characteristics attributed to traditional nineteenth-century women. Showalter states: "Since altruistic care and concern for others were regarded as especially natural in women, its absence struck doctors as unhealthy or insane egoism."[46] In the novel, Lucía was assigned the role of mentor for the young Sol del Valle and was therefore responsible for her well-being and her acceptance into society. Similarly, the proximity and economic advantages of the United States deemed it a leading nation that could guide Latin American nations into an age of modernity through reciprocal trade treaties and the implementation of a modernized infrastructure. Lucía, like the United States, pertained to the rising middle class that emerged in an age of industrialism and expansionism, whereas Sol, although highly educated and cultured, was a member of the lower economic class. Instead of a rational progression into the social circles, Lucía's precipitous actions and irrational behavior proved to be deleterious to Sol's position. Acting out a fit of enraged jealousy, Lucía throws pearls and expensive dresses at Sol, offering her items of material worth in exchange for her vow to leave Juan alone. By urging Sol to love Pedro, Lucía hopes to safeguard her prized possession, which is Juan. Her benevolence quickly turns to anger as she clearly tells Sol to keep away from Juan because she owns him: "Pero óyeme, a Juan no me lo quieras. Tú déjame a Juan para mí sola" [But listen to me, do not love Juan. You leave Juan for me alone] (*LJ* 198). Thus the spirit of Latin America is stifled by the covetous desires of Lucía and her need to possess Juan completely.

Juan, who represents the ideal man in Latin America, lacks one very important quality—a backbone. Like those Latin Americans who are mesmerized by the modernity and progress of the United States, Juan is ignorant of the pathological nature of the tempest and will therefore suffer from the negative implication of this illness. As noted in the novel, man loves a woman for the spirit that he believes that she beholds: "Ama a una mujer más por el espíritu que supone en ella" (*LJ* 188). Conversely, a woman without *ternura* [tenderness] is compared to a *vaso de carne* [cup of flesh] who like Lucía reveals in a single act her true nature: "cuando un acto claro e inesperado les revela que en aquella alma no existen la dulzura y superioridad con que la invistió su fantasía" [when a clear and unexpected act reveals to them that in that soul there does not exist the tenderness and superiority in which they had initially invested their fantasy] (*LJ* 188). Therefore, Lucía not only reflects the pathological traits of the United States brought upon by aggression and desire for materialism, through the character of Juan the reader is made aware of the false impressions that many Latin Americans hold of this modern nation.

In a letter to Manuel Mercado written in 1886, Martí expresses his anguish about remaining in New York due to the calculating nature of US businessmen. He expresses a great need to escape the city in order to "salvarme un poco de este contacto demasiado íntimo con los hombres de esta tierra, que no son, no, como los hombres en todas las demás" [to save myself a little from this too close contact with the men of this land, who are not, no, not like the men in the rest].[47] In the following passage he states that he is tied to New York due to the strategic position that it offers him, and then he compares this city with a cup of venom: "Todo me ata a New York, por lo menos durante algunos años de mi vida: todo me ata a esta copa de veneno" [Everthing ties me to New York, at least during these years of my life: everthing ties me to this cup of venom].[48] In his former writings Martí had revealed his dichotomous vision of women by utilizing the opposing images of *copa de carne* or *copa de espíritu/alas.* His reference to the United States as a *copa de veneno* in this letter, written shortly after the publication of *Amistad funesta,* not only reflects his feminization of this nation in terms of pathology, but also links this image to the perilous representation of Lucía in the novel.

Lucía and the United States

In "The (Political) Gaze," Susana Rotker states that Martí "builds a sort of collective ethos for Latin America from the place of exile, from and confronted by the continental giant" (65). As previously stated, she lists three significant stages in Martí's experience in the United States, beginning with his arrival to the country in 1881 and ending with what Rotker terms "his full radicalization," which refers to his goals of independence from Spain as well as Cuban sovereignty from the United States. During the second stage, between 1884 and 1892, Martí expresses his disdain for the "disadvantageous terms of the commercial treaty between Mexico and the United States which was more favorable for United States" and "gains definition when he perceives the possibility that US expansionists might end up purchasing Cuba from Spain" (69). *Amistad funesta* (1885) was written during this second period, after Martí had already formulated his discontent with the materialist aspirations and the expansionist endeavors of the United States. Martí uses the genre of the sentimental novel in order to portray the feminized, hysteric nature of the United States, thus warning Cuba to steer away from current proposed plans of annexation.[49] The greed and irrationality of Lucía, which can be linked to that of the United States, leads to the murder of Sol del Valle, who in the text is emblematic of the spirit of Latin America. Juan, who reveals the many attributes of the modern man of Latin America, refuses to see the irrational behavior of his betrothed until it is too late. His lack of initiative in the novel therefore results in the destruction of the Latin American soul. Similarly, his inability to foresee the consequences of Lucía's behavior is indeed a significant part of the problem at hand, which is representative of the many Latin American leaders who blindly established economic relations and reciprocal trade treaties with the United States, as pointed out by Martí in his writings.

During this period Martí was immersed in the North American lifestyle, culture, and politics, concentrating heavily on US foreign affairs. One of his chief antagonists, James G. Blaine, is the subject of many of his essays, specifically due to Blaine's blind-sighted relations with Latin America between 1881 and 1889. *Amistad funesta* was written shortly after the 1884 elections, when Blaine was the Republican candidate for the presidency of the United States. In his letter to *La Nación* dated July 6, 1885, Martí states how Latin America was a great preoccupation to the United States: "Nuestras tierras son ahora, precisamente, motivo de preocupación para los Estados Unidos" (*Oc* 327). Using the example of Mexico's relation with the United States, Martí points to the critical status of Central America due to former interventions instigated by Secretary of State Blaine. Martí then describes the United States using the image of a two-headed lion, strategically positioned to annex the countries of South America to the south, and/or Canada that lies to the north. In both cases the fierce image of a lion that swallows its adjacent territory belies any tone of rationality or control: "Donde se vio león con dos cabezas, mirando con la una, todo azorado, al norte, y la otra en la cola, abierta para tragarse al sur?" [Where a two-headed lion was seen, with one head, all flustered, looking to the north, and the other in the tail, open to swallow up the south?] (*Oc* 328). In chapter 1 of *Amistad funesta,* when the young group of friends sit down to enjoy a cup of hot cocoa, each of them has a differently designed cup, which according to many critics of the novel refers to their inherent characteristics. Whereas Juan had a cup displaying two eagles, denoting his honor and nobility, the handles of Lucía's cups were "dos pumas elásticos y fieros, en la opuesta colocación de dos enemigos que se acechan: descansaba sobre tres garras de puma, el león americano" [two agile and fierce pumas, positioned as two opposing enemies staring at each other: resting on three puma claws, the American lion] (*LJ* 85). Although Martí never specifically links Lucía to the United

States in *Amistad funesta,* the parallels between this work and the many essays that he wrote about the colossus are numerous and reflect very pressing issues that were of grave concern to the Cuban patriot.

Ambiguously Gendered Subjects

During Martí's residency in the United States, he wrote prolifically about his impressions of this great nation, its people, and its activities in foreign affairs. North America became the object of Martí's gaze, and in his many writings he employed the use of gender tropes in a strategic means of both disturbing and reversing traditional perceptions of power. Martí responded to popular perceptions of Latin America based on philosophical postulations, Darwinism, and the many periodicals by creating a superior sense of *Latinoamercanismo* that superseded other forms of power. In an effort to confront the hegemonic presence of the colossus, Martí sought to reverse the mechanisms of power, and by doing so he subverted traditional constructions of masculinity and femininity. However, by utilizing dichotomous perceptions of good women (Ana and Sol) confronted with bad women (Lucía and Adela) in his depiction of the dangers of excess materialism, Martí introduced a new type of female character into modern narrative.

Many critics have noted the transcendence of Lucía's character, whose sense of individuality and autonomy seems to escape the author(ity) of the author. In her essay "La mujer como invención de lo posible," Olga Uribe claims that Lucía is invested with a mysterious power that refuses to remain within the confines of the text and thus Martí generates a story "que se 'le escapa' al autor."[50] Furthermore, Juan Carlos González Espitia attributes Lucía's masculine qualities and her defiance towards nature as factors that result in the androgynous features of the main character: "Tal redefinición tiene como eje principal en el plano estético la androginización del personaje al convertirlo en un desdoblamiento del poder desencadenado de la naturaleza."[51] And to take it one step further, Keja Lys Valens refers to Doris Sommer's *Foundational Fictions* and argues that *Amistad funesta* is a national romance gone awry.[52] Through an analysis of Eve Sedgewick's homosocial relationships, Valens remarks on the feminine manifestations of the homosocial relations within the love triangle (two women and one man) and explores the lesbian love that exists between Lucía and Sol.

My analysis, like those of recent critics, stems from and points towards the questionable gendered characteristics of the main characters. Why would José Martí create such ambiguously gendered protagonists in a novel that seems to try to be a national romance? I have shown that Martí utilized gender codes for his purpose of denigrating the negative aspects of the imperialist nature of the colossus in his essays in order to warn his readers of the aggressive stance of US foreign policy at the end of the nineteenth century. In his essays and chronicles, he was dedicated to unveiling the mask of seduction, revealing the more pathological traits of this modern nation par excellence. This persuasive technique proved to be very effective in his endeavor to create a sense of Latin American national identity as well as to reverse traditional concepts of power in these writings. However, once he implements the use of gendered language as a persuasive tool into his novel, the results are surprisingly unexpected. In his novel, Martí disrupts dichotomous views of gender based on binary oppositions, with male as active and female as passive. Lucía succeeds in being a very strong and powerful female subject in this late nineteenth-century text and breaks the mold for female protagonists in genres of this type. In addition, with the exception of a significant flaw of not standing up to bullies, Juan proves to be an ideal national figure that embraces both feminine and masculine qualities, making him a unique male protagonist in Latin American narrative.

II

Loosening the Grips of Hegemony through Narrative: Gender Troping in *Doña Bárbara* and *El Señor Presidente*

According to Italian political theorist and activist Antonio Gramsci (1891–1937), the term *hegemony* describes how the domination of one group or class over others is achieved by a combination of political and ideological means. Although political force, or coercion, is always important, the role of ideology in winning the consent of the dominated classes may be even more significant. Gramsci argues that the balance between coercion and consent will vary from society to society, the latter being more prevalent in capitalist societies.[1] Hegemony is thus a complex and unyielding dynamic that will constantly be challenged by opposing groups in an unending struggle for power. Following the independence years in Latin America, gender played a significant role in the formation of nations and national identities and became instrumental in defining the ideal masculine subject, many times against an opposing hegemonic form of government. In many extreme forms of government, such as dictatorships and Fascism, the implementation of male domination over more feminized subjects signify common strategies of exerting power.[2] According to traditional gendered relations of power theorized by feminist critical thinkers, the male or masculine is denoted as the active agent, whereas the female or feminine is assigned the inactive, passive status. Within this binary gendered equation, the opposition of males in Latin American literary works is frequently portrayed "emasculating, feminizing and marginalizing the 'Other'" in order to (re)appropriate the masculine position of power.[3] Critics like Diana Taylor question if the opposition is not guilty of simply reversing concepts of power in this gendered dynamic of hegemony in the political arena.

In my investigation of how Latin American writers respond to hegemonic institutions, I think it is necessary to examine how their fictional characters and their forms of narrative are instrumental in revealing the power sources of a masculinist, hegemonic society. What are the mechanisms utilized by the authors to dismantle the pervasive force of existing hegemonic institutions in their endeavor to reappropriate the masculine status of power? My study focuses on the ways in which some authors in Latin America have disturbed concepts of gender and power in their texts to such a great extent that it is no longer viable to attribute the male position as the active status of power and the female to the passive role, as proposed by Hélène Cixous in her theory of the hierarchal nature of patriarchal thought.

Rómulo Gallegos's *Doña Bárbara* (1929) and Miguel Ángel Asturias's *El Señor Presidente* (1946) are two such novels that depart from a contestation to hypermasculinized oppressive leaders that govern in what David William Foster would term a hegemonic Western patriarchy. Both writers seek to alter the ways in which the reader views traditional, contemporaneous conceptualizations of gender in order to expose the deleterious effects of the governing dictator and thereby open up a space in which they are able to reappropriate the (masculine) status of power. My purpose in this unit is to examine the ways in which these authors use gender codes in their response to hegemonic institutions in their texts and to determine if said position of power can still be considered masculine.

In *Doña Bárbara,* Gallegos utilizes the concept of defamiliarization in order to expose the pathological status of the Venezuelan dictator General Juan Vicente Gómez (1908–35). Defamiliarization, a term introduced by Victor Shklovsky, refers to the constant tendency toward estrangement away from habitual responses to ordinary experience and/or ordinary language.[4] The characteristics of *machismo* that Gallegos attributes to Doña Bárbara in the novel denote the pathology and abnormality of this trait allocated to a woman, thereby making these atavistic characteristics transparent and thus easier for the reader to envision in the leader of their country. By displacing the vestiges of hypo-masculinity onto a woman, Gallegos shows more clearly how grotesque and inadequate this position is in an age of modernity and progress.

Gallegos introduces a new national male subject in his novel who shares both the intellectual qualities of the city combined with the latent *machismo* he beheld as a young boy growing up in the plains. These combined characteristics are not only necessary for survival in the *llanos,* but are also implemental in confronting the modern world denoted by imperialism and the prevalent trend of dictatorships in Latin America after independence. César Valverde defines the role of the male national subject in twentieth-century narrative in Latin America as being multidimensional. He claims that in the twentieth century the goal was to create male national subjects in rural settings that would revive a vanishing national spirit, fight against foreign economic and political intervention, neutralize the cultural hegemony of the "Northern giant," and portray the Latin character of the non-Anglo-Saxon cultures of this continent.[5]

The emergence of regional or *criollista* novels in the early twentieth century marked the shift in the importance given to North America and European countries as models of culture and progress. As the world witnessed the atrocities committed by those advanced nations during World War I, there arose a newfound interest in the peoples of the Americas and Africa. The focus of many Latin American writers during this period was to turn inward in their literary works, depicting the land and the social habits of the people as the central feature of the novel. In an effort to formulate a national identity, they depicted autochthonous characteristics of their country and in addition addressed the sociopolitical problems unique to their country and landscape. *Doña Bárbara*'s wide acceptance as a regional novel lauded for portraying the spirit of the *llano* often overlooks Gallegos's unique manner of contesting the oppressive force of the dictatorship of Juan Vicente Gómez. Critics discount his oversimplistic approach of reducing Venezuela's national conflicts to the dichotomous terms of Sarmiento's paradigmatic treatise of civilization versus barbarism.[6] A closer examination of how gender is utilized in the novel reveals a more complex approach than what is traditionally accepted.

In his chapter "The Crisis of Masculinity in Argentine Fiction, 1940–1960" (1997), David William Foster examines the use of Juan Domingo Perón's authoritarian masculinity as a significant feature of his cultural influence. Foster refers to the paternalistic authority created by Perón's masculinist image as general, president, and "Father of the Nation" as a model of hegemonic Western patriarchy.[7] This critic describes Perón as being "hypermasculine" in his implementation of a male authoritarianism and his use of militarism, oppression, and coercion in order to maintain his status of power. As stated in part 1 of this study, hypermasculinity, previously manifested in the *caudillista* form of governing in Latin America, was perceived as feminine for its exaggerated use of power and its link to barbarism.[8] In the novels discussed in these chapters, Gallegos's and Asturias's depiction of the dictators in their respective countries can be described as hypermasculine rulers who exert an authoritarian, patriarchal form of hegemony. Both writers employ visual representations of gender in their works as a means of renegotiating conceptualizations of gender, power, and nationality.

In *Doña Bárbara* Gallegos seeks to replace this feminized form of power incarnated in the *macho*-like woman with a new patriarchal order, which some critics argue resembles all too well the former patriarchal order of the Creole elitists.[9] The enlightened Santos Luzardo is inspired to civilize the feminine barbaric nature of the *llanos* [plains] while adopting the more masculine-gendered traits of his opponent, Doña Bárbara. In this endeavor Gallegos, unwittingly, supports Judith Butler's theory that gender is free-floating and can be altered or inverted presumably at will.[10] In his restructuring of gender codes within the text, Gallegos identifies the feminized barbaric traits in all of the inhabitants of Venezuela and uses his main protagonist, Santos Luzardo, as a prime example of maintaining these inherent characteristics. Instead of eliminating these traits from the national spectrum, Gallegos chooses to channel them into more productive endeavors. Thus, contrary to what most critics propose, Gallegos does not strive to annihilate barbarism, which is characteristic of Doña Bárbara and Gómez, but intends to incorporate its more positive aspects into the nurturing character of Santos Luzardo.

Miguel Ángel Asturias also addresses the complex relationship of power that exists between the dictator and his subjects in his novel *El Señor Presidente*. One of the more perplexing aspects of hegemony proposed by Gramsci is that those institutions described as being hegemonic are able to exert power over their subjects without force. Its influence is so insipid that it extends to all aspects of daily life, and the subjects are often unaware of the gravity of their subjugation.[11] Writers who challenge hegemonic institutions strive to expose the forcefulness and injustice of these institutions so that the people are free to act and/or react upon the oppressive governmental systems.

Whereas José Martí employed gender troping as a means of revealing the hegemonic nature of the imperialist United States before a deeper union were to take place; in *El Señor Presidente,* Asturias utilizes feminine imagery and feminine writing in order to expose the abusive power of the dictator in his country, while also providing a means of resistance against him. It is through language and writing that Asturias hopes to disturb the increasing hold of power that the dictator maintains over his subjects. The use of feminine writing, or *écriture féminine,* characteristic of this narrative, disrupts traditional forms of power located in and permeating language. Instead of reversing conceptions of gender and power, Asturias explodes traditional signs of authority and dominance that he suggests had originated in the violent behavior of pre-Columbian civilizations. By subverting the power of language, Asturias offers his readers an escape from the controlling role that language plays in maintaining the hegemony of a dictator.

In *Voice of the Masters: Writing and Authority in Modern Latin American Narrative* (1985), Roberto González Echevarría distinguishes between what he cites as the modern and postmodern tradition of dictator novels and traces the origin of the modern tradition in Latin America to Domingo Faustino Sarmiento's *Facundo* (65). The dictator novel originated as a means of contesting the oppressive power of the dictator, and different writers took diverse approaches to challenge this power. Both Gallegos and Asturias addressed the more veiled proponents of hegemony and sought to enlighten the readers to the extent to which they were oppressed by exposing the power sources of their respective leaders. The use of gender troping is utilized in both novels in order to achieve this means, albeit through very different approaches. In the following chapters I will show how both Rómulo Gallegos and Miguel Ángel Asturias utilize gender codes in order to contest the oppressive nature of a dictatorship, which is characterized by a masculinist form of hegemony, and in doing so create characters and narratives that transcend the boundaries of traditional codes of gender.

3

"Transgendering" and the Emergence of Ambiguously Constructed Subjects in *Doña Bárbara*

Disturbing Dichotomies

In the previous chapter we saw how José Martí employed the use of gender troping in order to contest the outside hegemonic forces of the United States, as well as to establish the formation of the new national male subject in his writings. A significant reason for the lack of widespread acceptance of *Lucía Jerez* by contemporaneous critics could be attributed to the feminine image of Juan Jerez, whose passive demeanor was utilized in order to construct the opposing pathological and more masculine image of Lucía. Feminine depictions of male protagonists had been a trend that had continued up until the end of the nineteenth century, one that had been sharply criticized by José Enrique Rodó for their lack of agency.[1] In an era of *caudillismo,* dictatorships, and the rising forces of imperialism by outside nations, there arose a tendency to "beef up" the image of the national protagonist, endowing him not only with the rationalist forces of reason as proposed by Kant and Hegel, but also the strength and force necessary to be able to stand up to external and internal hegemonic institutions of power. César Valverde notes that the prevalence in South America of uprisings, military coups, and diverse levels of social instability provoked the need to create strong masculine characters who could confront these imposing forces. Faced with the threat of national fragmentation and the penetration of established borders, novels like *Don Segundo Sombra* and *Doña Bárbara* look to create a strong Argentine and Venezuelan identity through strong, enterprising masculine characters.[2]

In Venezuela, Rómulo Gallegos, a prominent intellectual, politician, educator, and writer found himself stagnant within the perilous dictatorship of Juan Vicente Gómez, who ruled from 1908 until his death in 1935. Like Martí in *Lucía Jerez,* he utilized gender tropes in *Doña Bárbara* (1929) in order to visually portray the feminine forces of pathology and evil confronted with the rational position of the intellectual elites. By doing so, he also constructed a feminine character that would become emblematic of the *llanos,* or plains, serve as a central protagonist of this regional novel, and would indirectly be celebrated for the virulent characteristics found in the plainsmen of Venezuela. Doña Bárbara is known for her virile capacities of straddling a horse and being able to castrate a bull better than any of the *llaneros.* Even Gómez, whom she represented, enjoyed the novel immensely, and after finishing it said: "Este bachiller sí sabe cómo trabajan los hombres" [This scholar really knows how men work].[3]

The extreme *macho* nature of both Doña Barbara and the Venezuelan dictator was devoid of any of the (feminine) nurturing qualities that abounded in characters like Martí's Juan Jerez. I argue that one of Gallegos's main objectives in this novel is to expose the hegemonic masculinity characteristic of the Gómez dictatorship and to introduce into the national spectrum a more evolved masculine subject—one that embraces both traditional conceptualizations of manhood/*machismo* and the nurturing qualities traditionally associated with women. By adopting Sarmiento's paradigmatic treatise of civilization versus barbarism, this Venezuelan author created a novel that succeeded in polarizing themes of *ciudad/campo* [city/country], masculine/feminine, and rationality/irrationality, in order to reveal the deleterious and antiquated features of the reigning *caudillo.* As a result of gender troping, Gallegos also produced androgynous characters that refuse to fit neatly into dichotomous perceptions of gender in this or any era.

In *Doña Bárbara,* traditional paradigms and myths about women are manipulated and distorted in order to construct a highly masculinized version of Doña Bárbara who, in turn, becomes representative of the Other—the ugly face of barbarity.[4] Conversely, Santos Luzardo, the symbolically illuminated individual of the novel, is depicted for his moral superiority due to his intelligence and his association with the city. However, it is the city that strips him of his manhood. When Santos returns to Altamira in order to sell it, he changes almost instantly as he becomes aware of the barbaric atrocities committed by Doña Bárbara. Her infamy preceded her appearance in the novel as tales of black magic, stealing land, and being known by all as the Law of the Plain were casually communicated to Santos by the boatman during his journey to Altamira. Insulted by the brutal power that his adversary maintained, Santos becomes intent on civilizing the barbarity of the plains, thus bringing Venezuela into an age of modernity. From this point on, the reader sees the process of a gendered *bildungsroman* of Santos, who accrues layer upon layer of masculinity through his relationship with the land and his dealings with Doña Bárbara. Similarly, Doña Bárbara becomes more feminine through her encounters with Santos, as she is gradually divested of power and ultimately dissipates into the Venezuelan landscape.

According to many critics, *Doña Bárbara* can be analyzed as a reinscription of Sarmiento's *Facundo,* highlighting the oppositions between civilization and barbarism. Doris Sommer states: "However one reads it, *Doña Bárbara* respects a far more binary code than that of most nineteenth-century national novels."[5] She adds that the abstract and binary terms of civilization versus barbarism in Gallegos's novel are inherited from Sarmiento's *Facundo* (1845) and shows the parallels between both texts with regard to the land: "The untamed llano, then, takes on a woman's name as Gallegos's protagonist, just as the wild pampa took on the identity of an indomitable virgin for Sarmiento" (278). D. L. Shaw claims that "[Facundo] is the direct forerunner of Gallegos's *Doña Bárbara* and that education, the nineteenth-century solution for Latin America, led him back inevitably to Sarmiento, the great educator, and thus to the conflict of civilization and barbarism."[6] Many critics have dismissed the novel for its oversimplistic approach to resolving the national conflicts of Venezuela or Spanish America. Carlos J. Alonso has noted that Latin American writers have been even harsher than most critics in their analysis of this national novel. For example, Carlos Fuentes, in a sweeping evaluation of novels similar to *Doña Bárbara,* asserts that the Latin American *nueva novela* arose from "una conciencia de que la realidad no es ese dualismo simple, maniqueo, que nos presenta Ciro Alegría, Jorge Icaza, Rómulo Gallegos" [a consciousness from which reality is not that simple Manichean duality presented to us by Ciro Alegría, Jorge Icaza, Rómulo Gallegos].[7] Most traditional readings of the novel accept the predominant use of binary oppositions and fail to recognize the important role that gender plays in disturbing commonplace dichotomies of race, class, and gender.

The land, personified by the seductiveness of the hypermasculinized female persona, is just one of the contradictions in the paradigmatic construction of civilization versus barbarity. One can assume that the barbaric nature of *caudillismo* reflecting the paternalistic nature of the dictatorship of Juan Vicente Gómez is utilized in the construction of the barbaric Other. It is somewhat contradictory, yet not surprising, that this masculinized version of the Other is incarnated in the *macho*-like character of a woman, namely Doña Bárbara. However, the relationship between Santos and Doña Bárbara portrayed in the text betrays this binary conceptualization of gender. Throughout the novel, the reader notes the somewhat erotic relationship between the two protagonists. Doña Bárbara works her black magic in an attempt to win the heart of Santos. Similarly, the feminine, citified character of Santos also wants something from Doña Bárbara; yet it is not her love or her infamous sexuality—it is her masculinity that he desires. Using Judith Butler's theory, I will point out the slippery consistency of gender codes as they are simultaneously shifted and inverted in order to support the political objectives of Gallegos. According to Butler, gender is a free-floating artifice, whereby "*man* and *masculine* might just as easily signify a female body as a male one, and *woman* and *feminine* a male body as easily as a female one."[8] Through a reexamination of gender in an apparently homogenous text, one can find contradictions in the author's ideas about the dichotomous nature of gender, which in turn, forces the reader to question the function of binary oppositions located in the polarized paradigmatic construction of civilization and barbarism, good and evil, race and class.

Inverted Gender Codes

In the first chapter of *Doña Bárbara,* Gallegos establishes the antithesis of civilization and barbarity utilizing gender codes in order to depict concepts of good and evil. The title of this chapter, "¿Con quién vamos?" clearly demarcates the boundaries between God and the civilized man against Doña Bárbara, the plains, and her *hacienda,* El Miedo. However, the external features of the two main protagonists belie traditional concepts of gender according to the perspective of the rustic plainsmen. The femininelike characteristics of the main protagonist, Santos, contrast sharply with the strength and vigor of the hardworking boatmen: "insensibles al tórrido sol los broncineos cuerpos sudorosos, apenas cubiertos por unos mugrientos pantalones remangados a los muslos" (*DB* 17) [bronzed body bathed in sweat, apparently insensible to the torrid sun though but meagerly covered by dirty trousers tucked up above the knee] (3).[9] In contrast, Santos Luzardo is described as "un joven a quien la contextura vigorosa, sin ser atlética, y las facciones enérgicas y expresivas préstanle gallardía casi altanera"(*DB* 17) [a young man whose strong, though not athletic, stature and decided expressive features gave him an air of almost aristocratic hauteur] (4). Gallegos's description of Santos reflects former codes of masculinity according to male dominant critical discourse, which posited man and reason over nature. His lack of athletic qualities and his aristocratic demeanor denote his lack of virility as compared to the sweat and muscular physique of the boatman. His *hombría* [manhood] is further undermined when he takes a shot at, and misses, an alligator in the river.

Similarly, the racial aspects of Melquíades, Doña Bárbara's right-hand man, are clearly defined within the concepts of the barbaric Other, which consequently excludes him from the national makeup of Venezuela. He is described as pertaining to "an inferior race, cruel, gloomy, and entirely unlike the inhabitants of the Plain" (4) [un tipo de razas inferiores, crueles y sombrías, completamente diferente del de los pobladores de la llanura] (*DB* 18). The "suspicious" *patrón* informs the young city man that it was the black magic of Melquíades that prevented him from killing the alligator.[10] The henchman's knowledge of *brujería* [witchcraft] earns him the title of *brujeador* [sorcerer] in the novel, which polarizes him even more from the rational, enlightened depiction of Santos Luzardo. At the opening of the novel, it becomes evident that a seemingly feminine Santos is somewhat ill at ease in the vast plains of Venezuela as he is confronted with the fierce forces of nature.

After his experience with the boatmen en route to Altamira, Santos instinctively changes his former plans to expatriate. Captivated by the treacherous tales of Doña Bárbara, he decides to exercise his messianic powers and to save not only Altamira, but to implement the civilizing forces into the plains as well: "Luchar con doña Bárbara, criatura y personificación de los tiempos que corrían, no sería solamente salvar Altamira, sino contribuir a la destrucción de las fuerzas retardatorias de la prosperidad del Llano" (*DB* 17) [To struggle against Doña Barbara, symbol of the times, was not only to free Altamira, but to destroy the forces which were holding back the Plain] (29). Santos decides to throw himself into this task with the impulsiveness of the Cunavicheros combined with the ideals of a civilized man, which the former had been lacking (*DB* 17). *Cunavichero* refers to a rugged breed of men that can be traced back to Santos's ancestry. Although they had achieved a heritage of *caciques* in the plain, their submission to violence resulted in the separation of the family and the family curse.[11] The fight against Doña Bárbara thus transforms into a patriarchal mission to change the nature of Venezuela, instigated by a new and improved national subject.

In Gallegos's new, national male subject, the reader sees the synthesis of *ciudad/campo* [city/country] and follows Santos's subsequent taming of the (female) forces of barbarity as he simultaneously (re)appropriates the *macho* characteristics needed to survive in the *llanos* and Venezuela. The allegorical plight of Santos is significant on two levels: 1) his victory over Doña Bárbara represents the weakening of power of Gómez and other *caudillo* leaders in Venezuela; 2) the presentation of a new model of a ruling class, virile enough to stand up to bullies and nurturing enough to govern and educate the people, will be instrumental in elevating the masses to a superior status of nationhood. The predominant dichotomous struggle between good and evil is thus utilized in this regional novel to address pressing national conflicts and to improve the status of nationhood in Venezuela.

Nonetheless, Santos's city experience has softened him, giving him a refined, elegant appearance, which can be described as feminine. Carmelito, one of the peons hired by Antonio, had adopted the latter's loyalty towards the Luzardos and hoped that someday the owner would return and resolve the conflicts produced by Doña Bárbara. Carmelito's first impression of Santos, however, had clashed considerably with his idea of manhood, a trait that was necessary to combat the evil forces of barbarism. As soon as Santos stepped off the boat, Carmelito saw a more refined man whose smooth face and delicate skin revealed an aristocratic bearing, which Carmelito considered insolent (*DB* 49). The

Cunavichero heir was dressed in a tight-fitting coat with leggings, as well as a necktie, which the narrator playfully refers to as "a fine rag for this lonely country, where covering is plenty and everything else superfluous" (49–50) [que era demasiado trapo para llevar encima por aquellas soledades, donde con los de taparse basta y sobra trapo] (*DB* 49–50).

Among other things, Santos lacks one of the defining characteristics of manhood in the *llanos,* which is a mustache. Like the refined, elegant Unitarian in *El matadero,* he does not appear to be manly enough to overcome the *machista* forces of barbarism. A disappointed Carmelito murmurs: "¿Y éste es el hombre de quien tanto esperábamos?"(*DB* 50) [And this is the man we expected so much from?] (50). It is through the character of Carmelito in the novel that Santos must prove his manhood and gain acceptance of his fellow ranch hands, as well as his readers. The first impression of both the reader and the trepid ranch hand focuses on the feminine, citified, yet more intellectual, qualities of this young man.

Doña Bárbara is also introduced in this chapter and, conversely, she portrays almost all of the virile qualities associated with *machismo* and lacking in Santos. Marit Melhuus claims that *machismo* is assumed to be a male perogative and is directly associated with concepts of power: "Machismo, derived from the generic term macho, meaning male, is used synonymously with masculinity; it implies, above all, the ability to penetrate, and is associated with being active, closed, unyielding."[12] *Machismo* is oftentimes associated with violence, aggressiveness, and the ability to be in control, not only over women, but also over other men.[13] In addition, according to this concept, a man's manhood is enhanced by his ability to have sexual relations with as many women as he wants. The female protagonist, Doña Bárbara, is described according to these traits of *machismo* due to the supreme power that she holds in the plains as well as the ruthlessness that she displays toward her many lovers: "Ésa es una mujer que ha fustaneado a muchos hombres, y al que no trambuca con sus carantoñas lo compone con un bebedizo o se lo amarra a las pretines a hace con él lo que se le antoje, porque también es faculta en brujerías" (*DB* 23) [She's a woman who has pocketed heaps of men, and she never misses when she begins sweet-talking. She gives a man a love potion and ties him to her apron-strings, and then does what she likes with him, because she knows witchcraft] (11). Doña Bárbara, like the *machista* man, exercises her sexual prowess without any regard to her victims. She is not afraid to eliminate her enemies and lovers and is even said to have her own cemetery (*DB* 23). She is undoubtedly compared to the paternalistic dictatorship of Gómez, yet in this novel the forces of barbarism and the vastness of the lands are incarnated in the female body of Doña Bárbara.

According to Melhuus's definition of *machismo* and its relationship to masculinity, Doña Bárbara is the holder of power at the beginning of the novel. It is she who is the active subject and Santos, the passive one. While in Caracas, Santos had allowed his land to be taken over by Doña Bárbara and can thus be considered as the "penetrated" or passive subject: "Altamira, descuidado por su dueño, en manos de administradores fácilmente sobornables, fue la presa predilecta de su ambición [Doña Bárbara's] de dominio" (*DB* 45) [Altamira, neglected by its owner and in the hands of easily corrupted overseers, was the chosen prey of Doña Barbara's acquisitive ambition] (43). Doña Bárbara, the penetrator, was busy usurping the land of her opponent, by slyly changing boundary lines and writing up new deeds. She had contacts and dealings with the local officials and all of the people surrounding her, and she used them in order to acquire more land and power.

At the onset of the novel, gender codes appear to be inverted because while Santos is described for his feminine characteristics, Doña Bárbara is clearly defined as *macho* or *marimacho.* The text polarizes gendered conceptualizations of power, showing the inadequacy of the adopted forms of gender attributed to the two main protagonists. On the one hand, Santos Luzardo lacks the characteristics of manhood necessary to survive in the plains. His experience in the city is described as negative, depleting him of the attributes of what was perceived to be a man and a leader. He is described as a misanthrope ["se convirtió en un misántropo"] and as a result of his city life does not share nationalistic feelings for Venezuela ["al perder los sentimientos regionales había perdido también todo sentimiento de patria"] (*DB* 31, 33). In addition, he allows his land and his cattle to be appropriated by a woman, and branded as her own by the cow hands of El Miedo ["Además, dejaban que los cuatreros se metiesen a saco con ella y toleraban que los vecinos herrasen allí, como suyos"] (*DB* 33). The verbs *dejaban* [let] and *toleraban* [tolerated] can be attributed to the passive demeanor of a more open and yielding subject, which is the antithesis of what is perceived to be *macho*.

On the other hand, Doña Bárbara is the active agent early in the novel and is defined according to her similarities with the more hegemonic aspects of *machismo*. While investigating the plains life for his novel, Gallegos was presented with the inspiration for Doña Bárbara's character, which he described as "una mujer que era todo un hombre para jinetear caballos y enlazar cimarrones" [a woman that was all man riding horses and lassoing wild animals] (*DB* 10). Throughout the text Doña Bárbara is associated with masculine characteristics as she is labeled *marimacho, cacica, amazona,* and *andrógina*. Her propensity to take rather than to give places her in the category of the masculine realm ["más era hombruno tomar que femenino entregarse"], which is later reinforced by her complete lack of feminine characteristics ["carecía en absoluto de delicadezas femeniles"] (*DB* 47).

Doña Bárbara's history of being violated by a group of boatmen who killed her young lover is the motivating force behind her barbarism. She not only systematically repeats this act of aggression against men, but she carries out her violent acts of behavior better than any man. The introduction, thus, suggests a need for change in both protagonists, and it is through the process of transgendering that the text will be instrumental in restoring proper gender codes, thus inverting its current pathological depiction.

Juan Vicente Gómez

As already mentioned, the text also draws on some parallels between Doña Bárbara and Venezuelan dictator Juan Vicente Gómez. They both are *mestizos,* who come from indigenous and white parentage and are both nearly illiterate *caudillo* types who are very experienced in the *macho* activities of a cattle ranch. Gómez never married but is said to have fathered countless illegitimate children, while Doña Bárbara remained single and is known for her sexual prowess to the point of being named "la devoradora de hombres" [the devourer of men]. Although he made great strides in the stabilization of the economy and instigated modernizing projects such as railroads, highways, and public works, Gómez was a *caudillo* who ruled with oppressive force as a dictator between 1908 and 1935. In his essay "Cattle, Corruption, and Venezuelan State Formation during the Regime of Juan Vicente Gómez, 1908–35" (2003), Doug Yarrington examines the ways in which Gómez consolidated his power in Venezuela by appropriating the resources of Venezuela's long-established economy of land, livestock, and agriculture and forming alliances with the political elite: "Gómez orchestrated this process of appropriation by forming business partnerships with many of his state presidents and regional military commanders, the very men whose loyalty underwrote the centralization of political authority."[14]

Likewise, Doña Bárbara has exerted her influence over Mr. Danger, the judge magistrate, Santos's lawyer, and even the president of the republic. In the novel, she utilizes her womanly ways, black magic, and coercion in order to extend the boundaries of El Miedo and accumulate more wealth and power:

> Y entre uno y otro el lindero de El Miedo iba metiéndose por tierras altamireñas, mediante una simple mudanza de los postes, favorecida por la deliberada imprecisión y oscuridad de los términos con que los jueces comprados redactaban las sentencias y por la complicidad de los mayordomos de Luzardo, que se hacían de la vista gorda. (*DB* 45)

> [Lawsuits brought her league after league, and between one thing and another the boundary of El Miedo crept farther into Altamira by means of a simple change of boundary posts—this helped by the deliberate ambiguity and lack of precision the well-bribed judges wrote into their verdicts, and by the collective collusion of the Luzardo overseers who winked at it and let it pass.] (43)

Those who refuse to participate in her misgivings or take too much pride in possessing her are punished or mysteriously disappear: "haciendo desaparecer, de una manera misteriosa, a aquel hombre que podía jactarse de llamarla suya" (*DB* 45). Within this work Gallegos portrays the masculinist *caudillista* aspects of Doña Bárbara so that he can implicitly expose the illicit relations that Gómez had established in order to extend the hegemonic ties that consolidated his supreme power in the country.

Yarrington also compares the Gómez regime with sultanistic regimes, which he defines to be "extreme cases of patrimonial authority characterized by the concentration of discretionary authority in the hands of a ruler who advances state and personal power through a mixture of rewards and repression" (10). He argues that the consolidation of the Venezuelan national state was achieved through Gómez's international dealings with leading nations, such as the United States and England, and strengthened through the establishment of economic relations (specifically oil companies) with these countries. In the novel, Mr. Danger is representative of the obtrusive presence of US industry in Latin America. His manipulation of Lorenzo by providing him with alcohol in order to appropriate his land provides a simplistic explanation of the deleterious external influence of US imperialism, especially following the Spanish-American War of 1898. One of Santos's accomplishments in the novel is to remove the threat of Mr. Danger (imperialism) from the plains. Thus, the antithetical depictions of the characters in the text are representative of the more superficial polemics of the nation under the control of a patriarchal dictator who has consolidated his power through his dealings with key players both within and outside of the country.

In addition, Doña Bárbara's sexuality and seductive powers in the novel are instrumental in exposing the unnatural shift of power between Gómez and the elites on the national level, as well as highlighting the victory of barbarism over civilization. She can be compared to the Greek mythological character Medusa, who was believed to be so hideous, anyone who looked at her turned to stone, thus losing their human qualities. While Doña Bárbara was extremely attractive to men, her overly seductive forces and her nickname "la devoradora de hombres" relate to the fear of loss of manhood in the novel. According to R. W. Connell, Freud's theorization of the fear of castration that takes place during the formation of the masculine subject corresponds to the threat of the loss of sexual identity.[15] In the novel the seductive and alluring forces of nature, personified in this ambiguously gendered character of Doña Bárbara, are responsible for the complete emasculation of Santos's cousin and Marisela's father, Lorenzo Barquero, who is referred to as "ex hombre" after his dealings with her (*DB* 35). Despite his success in Caracas as a star student of law and speech, Lorenzo was lured back to the land, where his relationship with Doña Bárbara and the barbaric forces of nature pushed him into an abyss of alcoholism, placing him in the degenerative state of bestiality: "un organismo devorado por los vicios más ruines, una voluntad abolida, un espíritu en regresión bestial" (*DB* 43). Deprived of his land, his dignity, and his prestige, Lorenzo was cast into the lawless territory of Chusmita to live out his existence.[16] During his first encounter with Santos, Lorenzo warns his relative of the rising force of barbarism that will overcome him: "Ya te veré caer entre sus brazos y enloquecer por una caricia suya" (*DB* 103) [I'll soon see you falling in her arms and going mad for her caresses] (121). Like Gómez, who ruled with authoritative political oppression, Doña Bárbara succeeded in debasing her subjects to an emasculated status of bestiality and victimization.

Hybrid Subjects

From the very beginning of the text, the reader notes the dualistic nature of Santos's personality, where he is both repulsed and attracted to the plains and the wild, liberating forces of nature: "como si en su espíritu combatieron dos sentimientos contrarios acerca de las cosas que lo rodean" (*DB* 8) [as though indicating a conflict of emotions concerning his affairs] (4). This novel, being regionalist, pays homage to the land of Venezuela, thus creating an autochthonous text original to Spanish America. The land, as in Sarmiento's text, is both alluring and repulsive and needs to be controlled and recoded within the concepts of the law.

Both Doña Bárbara and Santos had previously displayed gender codes related to their biological sex in their youth. Santos nostalgically remembers the plains before he moves to the city as a young boy, and Doña Bárbara is described with her maidenly coyness and her love for Asdúbral before she was savagely raped by a gang of boatmen. While Santos retains the dualistic aspects of *ciudad/campo,* masculine/feminine, Doña Bárbara's femininity has been annihilated and substituted by her deep disdain for men: "Inhibida la sensualidad por la pasión de la codicia y atrofiadas hasta las últimas fibras femeniles de su ser por los hábitos del marimacho" (*DB* 29) [Her appetites were strangled by her greed, and the last fibers of femininity in her being were atrophied by the habits of the virago] (45). In addition, she maintains very masculine characteristics including her ability to toss a lasso and bring down a bull out in the open as well as her most skillful cowboy (45). Armed with the black magic learned from the Indian tribe with whom she lived, Doña Bárbara dedicates her life to avenging her perpetrators and victimizes her male lovers in order to increase her power. Doña Bárbara is also a *mestiza,* a product of a rape between a white man and an Indian woman. She originated from a violent union, achieved her masculine status as a result of violent sexuality, and perpetuates this cyclical infliction of violence through her male victims.

Gender Swapping

As stated earlier, Gallegos adopts the dichotomous model of civilization and barbarity in order to gain order in a country suffering under the perils of a dictatorship. However, the transference of gender codes in the novel disturbs traditional conceptions of masculine/feminine, good/evil, and civilization/barbarism and thus opens up the text to further interpretations. The linguistic signs throughout the text, such as *Santos* [saint] and *[Luz]ardo* [light/reason] at Altamira [high looks/looking upward] versus Doña Bárbara, feminized barbarism at El Miedo [fear], are clearly antithetical—referring to good versus evil, city versus country, order versus chaos, and civilization versus barbarism. The following equations, which reflect the inverted codes of gender typify the conceptions portrayed by Gallegos with regard to this work:

> [hypo-masculinized] woman = Doña Bárbara = barbarism = plains = dictatorship = irrationality/degeneration
> [feminine] man = Santos = civilization = city = progress = reason

I believe that Gallegos is aware that his proposed national subject needs to reappropriate some traditional codes of masculinity, and it is in the novel where this gendered *bildungsroman* takes place. However, it is in this process where gender codes become messy and blurred, thus subverting traditional paradigms of the dichotomous nature of gender.

According to French feminist theory and the tenets of poststructualism, sexual difference is constructed through the acquisition of language. The speaking subject is said to separate from the mother's body and enter into the symbolic phallogocentric universe of the father, which according to Lacanian theory, is based on the control of the phallus and logos. The entry into the symbolic world of the law of the father is linked to the acquisition of language.[17] In *Doña Bàrbara,* Santos is representative of the symbolic world for his knowledge of the official language as well as his knowledge of the concepts of law. Being a lawyer, he becomes intent on rewriting the plains of Venezuela, recoding them within the symbolic language of law. He is there to reestablish boundaries and to fence his property, thus providing order and closure to the vast feminized space of the plain. In this context gendered codes are once more flipped; Santos is enigmatic of the law of the land based on the phallus and logos, whereas Doña Bárbara occupies the feminine presymbolic space of lack of boundaries, difference, and the proper language to defend the rights of her land.[18]

The text presumes to be even more normalized if one examines the concepts of madness explicated in Elaine Showalter's *The Female Malady.* According to nineteenth-century theories of madness, a woman is perceived to be mad when she steps outside of the traditional roles of femininity (146). As discussed earlier, Doña Bárbara is the very antithesis of femininity in that she encompasses most of the characteristics of *machismo.* In addition, she has no maternal instincts with regard to her daughter, Marisela, which is one of the main tenets of femininity in Hispanic culture according to *marianismo:* "Ni aun la maternidad aplacó el rencor de la devoradora de hombres; por lo contrario, se le exasperó más: un hijo en sus entrañas era para ella una victoria del macho, una nueva violencia sufrida" (*DB* 43) [Not even motherhood could squelch the ogress' hatred. On the contrary, it deepened that hatred. A child in the womb was for her another victory for the male, a new injury undergone] (40). Thus, based on Freudian and Darwinian theories of madness, Doña Bárbara is the incarnation of madness and uncontrollability and represents a deviant status of femininity.[19]

Within these concepts of gender, Santos is the active agent and Doña Bárbara is the illegitimate Other. However, the civilizing codes of law and language are futile in the feminized *machista* space of the land, which Doña Bárbara represents. Santos becomes aware of this fact due to his failure to establish clear boundaries according to the law. The only way to combat his opponent is by accruing some of the *machista* characteristics of the *llano,* which he had shed upon his move to the city as a young boy. Valverde asserts that a very mannered Santos transforms into a more masculine subject, who is dangerously similar to Doña Bárbara. He further argues that it is only when he appropriates this primordial masculinity that he can reach his objectives (145). As seen in chapter 1, part 1, Santos does have latent masculine characteristics that need to be awakened and rejuvenated. In this sense, Santos has to live up to Doña Bárbara's masculine feats in order to reach his coming of age with regard to masculinity. It is against her that Santos tests his manhood, and each time that he makes progress, she seems to lose her masculinist essence, which in this case is representative of power.

An example of this transfer of gender is seen in chapter 8, part 1, when Santos tames the horse, showing one of the first real signs of masculinity in the text. Melhuus claims that the construction of *machismo* has men as its reference group: "It is in the eyes of other men that a man's manhood is confirmed, but it is through women that it is reflected and enacted" (241). In this chapter Santos proves himself to the other plainsmen by displaying the domineering act of taming a wild horse. Carmelito, who had previously questioned Santos's masculinity, was now duly impressed with this *macho* practice of the *llaneros.*

As Santos accrues masculinist codes, however, Doña Bárbara seems to shed them, and it is through her gendered transformation that his manhood is both constructed and reflected. In chapter 9, part 1, upon hearing about the taming of the horse, Doña Bárbara begins to dress in a more feminine manner than usual: "Ya no llevaba aquella sencilla bata blanca . . . sino otra, que nunca le había visto usar Balbino, descotada y sin mangas y adornada con cintas y encajes" (*DB* 90) [She was not dressed in the simple white frock . . . but had replaced it with another Balbino had never seen her wear, low necked, sleeveless, and adorned with ribbons and lace] (104). In this chapter, Doña Bárbara also asks the Mondragón brothers to move back their house, which served as boundary stakes that she had previously used to gradually accumulate land from Altamira. And finally, when questioned by Balbino about exterminating the troublesome Santos Luzardo, she states: "Dios libre al que se atreva contra Santos Luzardo. Ese hombre me pertenece" (*DB* 93) [God help the man that dares to do anything to Santos Luzardo. That man belongs to me] (107). At this point, a more feminine Doña Bárbara claims her stakes in this man and becomes intent on winning his affection. It is also at this point where she begins to lose her sense of power.

R. W. Connell recognizes the social organization of sport in the reproduction of hegemonic masculinity. He states: "What it means to be masculine is, quite literally, to embody force, to embody competence. . . . Force and competence are, obviously enough, translations into the language of the body of the social relations which define men as holders of power, women as subordinate."[20] Another significant example of the transference of gender is seen in chapter 4 of part 2, entitled "El Rodeo," where Santos lassos a bull and castrates him. Throughout this chapter, Doña Bárbara displays aspects of femininity as Santos reclaims his masculinity. Through his participation and mastery of the favorite sport of the plains, he thereby posits Doña Bárbara as his subordinate, revealing the expertise that he had fostered as a boy: "Con una rápida maniobra de jinete experimentado hurtó el encontronazo, cortándole el terreno al toro, y lanzó la soga por encima del anca del caballo" (*DB* 170) [With the rapid movement of the experienced horseman, he rushed forward, cutting off the charging bull, and flung his lasso over the rump of the horse] (215). As Santos regains his masculinity, however, he becomes aware that he must fight against the barbaric forces that reside within him. The hovering threat of his violent parentage signals his inherent tendency to return to the *cacique* nature of his ancestors. This is an overwhelming force that he must learn to overcome as an ideal masculine subject on the national spectrum.

As Santos becomes more *cacique*-like, Doña Bárbara displays more passive femininity uncharacteristic of her former nature. Earlier in chapter 4 of part 2, Santos notices the unusual, feminine qualities of Doña Bárbara, which he could not resist admiring: "No podía escapársele a Santos que la feminidad que ahora ostentaba tenía por objeto producirle una impresión agradable" (*DB* 163) [It could not escape Santos that her show of femininity had the sole object of making an agreeable impression on him] (205). Once again, it seems that as Doña Bárbara adopts feminine aspects in the text, it opens up a space in which Santos is able to retrieve his masculinity, as if they were both unable to display codes of *machismo* at the same time.

Gender codes become slippery in this aspect of the text because we must ask ourselves: Does Santos take on the *macho* aspects of Doña Bárbara, which have previously been coded as barbaric? Or does he take from the feminized space of Doña Bárbara, in which case he would become more feminized or barbaric? Obviously it is the former. However, gender codes have become so inverted, twisted, and subverted that the reader must ask him/herself: What does Santos Luzardo now represent? Was not the *macho* feminine space of Doña Bárbara representative of the exaggerated paternalistic dictatorship of Gómez? Why would Santos want to adopt these barbaric characteristics? Did he take all of the masculinity away from Doña Bárbara because she does mysteriously disappear? Or does he just take what he needs to make a well-rounded new national subject that combines the educated refinement of the city with the brutal force of the *llano*? I would argue for the latter, in which case one could deduce that the new national subject needs to reappropriate characteristics of his masculinity or *machismo* in order to move into an era of modernity. The land needs to be recoded in terms of the symbolic, and the national subject needs the *cojones* to be able to do it.

This leads me to ask: Can one take gender off and on like a hat or a coat? My analysis gives credence to the ideology of Judith Butler, who refers to gender as a free-floating artifice. Gender, she argues, is perceived in terms of performance, or drag, which is made evident in the process of the exchange of gendered characteristics in the text or what I refer to in the title of this chapter as "transgendering." Jonathan Alexander notes that the term *transgender[ing]* has come to be a "catch all" category used to define those who "play with" or "transgress" gender norms, and he points out that the aims of many self-identified trans-activists and -theorists are to create cracks in the monolithic structure of gender identity.[21] Although this term typically refers to those who personally live in conflict with their biological sex, Gallegos employs the process of "transgendering" in this early twentieth-century regional novel in order to visibly alter the gendered makeup of Santos and Doña Bárbara, thereby marking a shift in power at the national level. The shifting of gender codes is repeated in the text until Santos achieves the desired doses of masculine and feminine characteristics, thereby producing an ambiguously gendered national subject.

Furthermore, although Santos commits himself to the task of civilizing Marisela in the text, his relations with the masculinized qualities of Doña Bárbara can be compared to Eve Sedgwick's analysis of male homosocial desire.[22] The carefully constructed gendered relationship between both protagonists mirrors the homosocial bonds of persons of the same sex, or in this case, gender; for at one point in the novel they indubitably have to share equal quantities of masculinity and femininity. In addition, through the homosocial masculine activities of riding a bull, using a rifle, and taming a horse, Santos pits himself against his rival, Doña Bárbara, in order to achieve the status of manhood in terms the plains recognizes.

Be that as it may, a significant contradiction in the premise of Gallegos's work, which González Echevarría makes explicit in his essay "Doña Bárbara Writes the Plain," is that the symbolic order, associated with language and the law is invalidated by the manner in which Santos Luzardo's ancestors appropriated the land. Santos's main objective throughout the novel is to civilize the barbaric space of the land, to put up boundaries and to encode the land within the symbolic order. Threatened by the usurping activities of Doña Bárbara, Santos is intent on getting back what is rightfully his. Yet in chapter 10 of part 1, the narrator clearly states that this land was acquiesced by violence—the violence of Santos's ancestors over the aboriginal inhabitants who occupied it: "Hombre de presa, El Cunavichero les arrebató a los indígenas aquella propiedad de derecho natural, y como ellos trataron de defenderla, los exterminó a sangre y fuego" (*DB* 93) [The man of prey despoiled the aboriginal settlers of their just domain and when they tried to defend it, exterminated them with fire and sword] (108). Therefore, the validity of the civilized law of Santos is no more convincing than the law of the plain relegated to Doña Bárbara. One would have to question the statute of limitations within the codes of law or even question the legitimacy of the symbolic order in this text. Nevertheless, a seemingly homogeneous text based on clear binary oppositions with regard to civilization, barbarism, gender, race, and class seems to unravel before our very eyes.

When speaking of poststructualism and psychoanalysis in her book *Speaking of Gender,* Elaine Showalter concludes the following: "Thus to deconstruct language is to deconstruct gender; to subvert the symbolic order is to subvert sexual difference" (2). In the case of *Doña Bárbara,* the deconstruction of gender disturbs the binary nature of language, thus subverting the hierarchalization of patriarchal binary thought located in the symbolic order. Therefore, analyzing this novel through Judith Butler's theory of gender as a free-floating artifice can be considered a valid approximation to this text, one that challenges or subverts a closed analysis based on the paradigmatic construct of binary oppositions.

Masculinities Movement: The Evolution of Masculinity on the National Level

Although it would be anachronistic and illogical to argue that Gallegos was working within the concepts of queer theory by proposing an androgynous and hybrid national subject, I do believe that his objectives in the text reflect current motives of the masculinities movement that emerged in the 1960s as a response to feminist theory. R. W. Connell argues that the political premise of masculinist theory is to highlight the significance of social alliances and to promote gender reform.[23] He proposes that there is a possibility for hegemony to be positive, in accordance with Gramsci's original concept of the term in class relations "and it is quite conceivable that a certain hegemony could be constructed for masculinities that are less toxic, more cooperative and peaceable, than the current editions" (476). Present-day studies in this field examine the formation of masculinity, place it in historical context, and assay its intellectual and political consequences.[24] Much of masculinist theory has been directed towards the evolution of manhood based on antiquated gender roles and stereotypes and promotes more equity within gender relations. In order to accomplish these goals it is necessary to confront the dominance of hegemonic masculinity, which is implicit in the institutionalism of current predominant ideologies, as well as most governmental institutions within a patriarchal society.[25] I argue that one of Gallegos's main objectives in *Doña Bárbara* is to expose the hegemonic masculinity characteristic of the Gómez dictatorship and to introduce into the national spectrum a more evolved masculine subject. This new national subject embraces both traditional conceptualizations of manhood/*machismo* typical of the Venezuelan *llanos* and the nurturing qualities traditionally associated with women.

Furthermore, in his essay "A Whole New World: Remaking Masculinity in the Context of the Environmental Movement" (1990), Connell argues that in order to alter current conceptualizations of the masculine subject within a patriarchal society it is necessary to address both the personal and collective social groups: "Within that [patriarchal] framework, struggles for hegemony among men have two major sources: (1) the formation of different patterns of motivation or commitment in personal life (e.g., heterosexual versus homosexual, libertarian versus controlled) and (2) the formation of conflicting interests at the social level (e.g., capitalists versus gentry, bureaucrats versus militarists)."[26] In *Doña Bárbara,* Gallegos expresses both the personal and the collective through Santos's relationship with Marisela and the allegorical depiction of her mother as the reigning dictator. Santos's role as educator and nurturer within his relationship with Marisela serves as the representation of the evolution of the masculine subject within the (personal) family unit, which can then be applied to a wider conceptualization of gender at the national level. The evolution of Santos's character as both nurturer and *machista* can be interpreted as ambiguously gendered with regard to traditional conceptualizations of masculinity in Spanish America during this era.[27] The role of ambiguity in the novel thus transcends a closed reading based on binary oppositions and plays a key role in a deeper understanding of Gallegos's more liberal concepts of nation.

The Role of Ambiguity

Most critics would agree that Gallegos, like his contemporaries, utilized the pathological image of a woman in order to visually portray the degenerative aspects of his country, specifically referring to the ruling dictator, Juan Vicente Gómez. Within the text, Doña Bárbara's presence at El Miedo is a direct correlative to Gómez's rule in Venezuela. Skurski notes in her article that Gómez constructed an image of the national community based on the model of "an orderly and productive cattle hacienda under his patriarchal rule" (618), and Yarrington asserts that it is through the economic transactions of cattle that Gómez first appropriated his power.[28] Similarly, the *llano,* as noted by Doris Sommer, was the breeding ground where *caudillos* would raise their personal armies, which would periodically threaten civilization in the capital (280). Thus, the symbolic allusions of the dialectic construction of civilization versus barbarism are overwhelming and cannot be ignored. Yet the ambiguities produced in the text seem to surface despite the neatly constructed schema and thus provoke a closer more complex reading of the novel, revealing Gallegos's endeavor to confront the forces of hegemony under the reigning dictator.

According to Julie Skurski, ambiguity is an effective means of promoting a new type of authority in Gallegos's text. She claims that the shifting categories interact with the normative framework in a movement of reciprocal construction. Instead of fixing the unambiguous categories or deconstructing the categories by the indeterminacy of meaning, a new authority is constituted through the negotiation of ambiguity (622). Following this line of thought, I argue that the shifting categories of gender in the novel loosen the hegemonic hold of Doña Bárbara/Gómez over the *llano*/nation in order to open up a space in which a new authority can be negotiated. Gallegos, therefore, utilized his novel as a means of exposing and subverting the current status of a *machista* hegemony representative of the dictatorship of Gómez and sought to replace this oppressive leader with what Connell would term a more positive hegemony, or what the text refers to as a "buen cacicazgo" (*DB* 163).

Gallegos's use of the symbolic depiction of the hypo-masculinized *cacica* in the novel exposes and thus seeks to weaken the hegemonic hold that Gómez has over his people. Doña Bárbara's manipulation of Lorenzo, Balbino, her ranch hands, and several judges reveals the network of economic relations that she had established throughout the years in order to consolidate her power in the *llanos.* Like Gómez, she employs the practice of profiteering in her dealings with her workers, as well as her economic transactions with governmental officials.[29] Yarrington recognizes the important role that profiteering played in the formation of the state and state-society relationships under the Gómez regime. In similar sultanistic regimes, leaders such as Rafael Trujillo (1930–61) and Anastasio Somoza García (1896–1956) used their political power to establish business empires and personal fortunes (14–15). Similarly, through Doña Bárbara's transactions with key governmental officials, she succeeds in rewriting the plains within the codes of her law. Through the transference of gender codes in the novel it becomes evident that her hegemonic hold over her subjects is gradually weakened until she eventually disappears.

It has also been noted that Gómez's exertion of hegemony was achieved through his psychological hold on the Venezuelan people. Yarrington argues that Gómez was one of the first twentieth-century Latin American rulers to establish an effective reign of terror, as he managed to convince the people that they were under constant surveillance. Some even attributed to Gómez omniscient powers as a *brujo* [sorcerer].[30] The fear of the regime was further instilled by the stories of brutality seeping out of its prisons.[31] Doña Bárbara also maintained an enigmatic hold over the *llaneros,* as she was believed to be an expert in the skills of *brujería:* "Ella se creía realmente asistida de potencias sobrenaturales y a menudo hablaba de un 'Socio' que la había librado de la muerte una noche" (*DB* 46) [She really believed herself endowed with supernatural powers, and often spoke of a 'Partner,' who had saved her life one night] (44). It was widely believed that she had made a pact with the devil, *el socio,* whom she often consulted to assist her in carrying out her diabolical plans. Similar confabulations of her disposing of men at a whim and having her own cemetery contributed to the mythical qualities of her persona. Thus, mythical perceptions of both *caciques* contribute to the hegemonic nature of power that they maintain over their subjects. The text subverts the validity of these assumptions through the dubious tone of the narrator's comments. The use of phrases such as *fantasía llanera* [fantasy of the plains] and *se creía* [it was believed] in the previous passage challenges the veracity of such beliefs, thereby loosening the hold that language plays in maintaining this insipid type of hegemony, which has its roots in the mythical qualities of the *cacica.*

In addition, Doña Bárbara exhibits her knowledge of supernatural powers in chapter 6 of part 1, as she lifts a glass of water in order to see the image of the newly arrived Santos Luzardo: "El doctor Luzardo, que ha querido dejarse ver" (*DB* 68) [It's only Dr. Luzardo allowing himself to be seen] (74). While Balbino is impressed by her acts of *brujería,* Melquíades reveals the fallacies of these powers with his following mental notes: "Perro no come perro. Que te lo crea Balbino. Todo eso te lo dijo el peón" (*DB* 68) [Dog don't eat dog. Balbino can believe you. But the peon told you all that] (75). The narrator further discounts her skills at witchcraft, accusing her of concocting schemes like this in order to augment the sense of fear felt by those around her: "Era, en efecto, una de las innumerables trácalas de que solía valerse doña Bárbara para administrar su fama de bruja y el temor que con ello inspiraba a los demás" (*DB* 69). The narrative reveals the duplicity of the supernatural powers of *la cacica,* which in turn subverts the myth-making strategy utilized by both Doña Bárbara and Gómez to maintain their hegemonic hold over the people.

It appears that Gallegos, like Martí, has feminized his more powerful opponent in order to gain the masculine status of power. Yet, one of the many contradictions that arise in this formula is his approval of the feminized *macho* features of his opponent, Doña Bárbara, which produces ambiguous messages in the novel. Doris Sommer claims that Gallegos reveals a deep admiration for the dictator, which thereby weakens his argument in the novel and even aligns him with the positivist ideology that Gómez's political image had assumed.[32] Similarly, Ernest A. Johnson, Jr., reflects upon the overall complex impression of the novel due to the fact that Doña Bárbara and the *llanura* are only "semibárbara."[33] The narrative reveals both positive and negative aspects of *la cacica,* and at some points the narrator even seems to show compassion for her.[34] In addition, the gendered characteristics that Doña Bárbara portrayed were not appropriate for her biological sex, yet by divesting them from her, and incorporating them into the masculine national subject, Gallegos recognizes the dual aspects of the plains and validates some of its characteristics. This overwhelming fact disturbs the dichotomous nature that the text assumes and produces dubiously conveyed meanings.

In "Ambiguities of Authenticity" (1994), Skurski argues that in his novel Gallegos is providing a synthesis of methods and races in order to promote a new type of national unity. She proposes that Gallegos pertained to a more moderate group of elitists, who instead of divorcing themselves from the people, strove to unite with the masses, offering education as a way of consolidating and uplifting the nation. The ambiguous status of elitist national identity in the postindependence period resulted from their inability to relate to the Indian race and their failure to embrace the mother country, Spain.[35] While the upper elites distanced themselves from the masses, the moderate elites sought to consolidate the nation's people: "The quest for national identity did not entail validating Venezuela's cultural origins, but rather forging a synthesis of elite reason and popular energy through the taming of the nation's social and physical terrain. The discourse of authenticity posited a distinct Latin American path to civilization marked by the ascendancy of spiritual and telluric forces, guided by reason, over mere rationalist determinism" (Skurski 1994, 613). Thus the shift in Santos's position from a distant elitist on the verge of expatriating in the beginning of the novel to the renewed leader who reconciles with the land and people of the nation functions on yet another symbolic level of consolidating the nation with the elites.

Similarly, Santos's marriage to Marisela provides a model for the racial amalgamation of the moderate elites and the *mestizos,* which Skurski argues follows the ideological goals of unification initially proposed by Simón Bolívar. Bolívar's address to Congress in Angostura in 1819 reflects the formulation of national ideology, which is expressed in the novel: "All our moral powers will not suffice to save our infant republic from this chaos unless we fuse the mass of the people, the government, the legislation, and the national spirit into a single united body. Unity, unity, unity must be our motto in all things. The blood of our citizens is varied: let it be mixed for the sake of unity."[36] Skurski argues that the mythic battle between Bolívar and Gómez is woven through the novel in the spirit of the two leaders. She claims that because Gómez had already governed in Venezuela for twenty-one years by the time the novel was written, he had come to embody the defeat of the Bolivarian promise to elevate the *pueblo* (617). The novel thus reinstates the Bolivarian promise through the legal union and future offspring of Santos and Marisela.

The taming of the nation's social and physical terrain, as proposed by the moderate elites, is represented in the text in Santos's civilizing project of educating Marisela. In chapter 2 of part 2, Santos equates Marisela to the more positive aspects of the plains and plains people: "viendo en Marisela una personalidad del alma de la raza, abierta como el paisaje a toda acción mejoradora" (*DB* 149) [seeing Marisela as a personification of the soul of the Plainsman, open as the prairie and improved by every experience] (185). Her domestication and education in the text allude to the proposed governing style of Santos, which challenges the more coercive style of *la cacica* and Gómez.[37] Santos's loving and gentle means of inculcating his student results in the appearance of *ternura* [tenderness] within Marisela.[38] This trait, which is mirrored in his student, proves to be the redeeming characteristic that saves Santos from sinking into the abyss of barbarity, as did his ancestors before him. These newly acquired feelings of affection become instrumental in monitoring the exertion of power that Santos displays in his return to a *buen cacicazgo* (*DB* 273).

Santos does not officially regain his masculinity and his control over the *llanos*/Doña Bárbara until he resorts to taking more violent action against his opponents. In the chapter entitled "La hora del hombre," the narrator associates the real man with his ability to take control and to use violence if necessary. In this chapter Santos burns down the house of the Mondragón brothers and even shoots one of the brothers in the leg for not complying with his requests. Upon doing so, he puts himself at risk of being overcome by the barbarity of the land: "a riesgo de convertirse en víctima de la violencia enseñoreada de aquella tierra" (*DB* 273). The narrative appears to be contradictory at this point because previously acts of violence were directly associated with the unacceptable feminized forces of barbarism. Gallegos seems to deem the violent nature of *machismo* as a necessary attribute in order to confront the hegemonic status of Doña Bárbara and Gómez; yet at the same time he warns against the danger of exerting too much power. These ambiguously coded meanings are reflected in a speech that Gallegos gave in July 1948, when he recognized the positive forces that barbarism had in the formation of the nations of Spanish America.

Gauging *Machismo*

During the inauguration of the statue of Simón Bolívar, Gallegos praised the insightfulness of this national leader for knowing when to step aside. He quotes Bolívar, who claimed that although he was glorified in war he would be a dangerous citizen in government: "Un hombre como yo es un ciudadano peligroso en un gobierno popular, es una amenaza inmediata a la sobernía nacional" [A man like me is a dangerous citizen in a popular government; he is an immediate threat to national sovereignty].[39] Gallegos urges the viewers to look not at the sword that Bolívar holds in one hand, "sino en el símbolo de leyes prudentes que la otra mano sostiene" [but in the symbol of prudent laws held in the other hand] (4). He recognizes the rarity of such heroes who put the well-being of their nation over their personal needs and states: "No abundan en la historia hombres de acción con tanta conciencia de sí mismos y tanta responsabilidad de su destino" [There are few men of action throughout history so conscious of themselves and so responsible of their destiny] (4). Using the model of the father within the family, Gallegos celebrates national heroes such as George Washington and José de San Martín, who also knew when to put down the sword:

> Como el buen padre de la familia se sienta a compartirlo en la mesa cordial, colgado el sable de la misión cumplida, recobra el sitio del ciudadano para presidir el trabajo de los que van a asegurar en la paz la obra fecunda de la guerra. (5)
>
> [As the good head of the family sits to share a meal at a friendly table, having put away the sword of the mission accomplished, he regains the place of citizen to preside over the work of those who are going to secure in times of peace the fertile efforts of war.]

Thus, Gallegos's national novel represents the new generation of peaceful governors whose primary responsibility was to resume the nation's procedures without having to exert violence, oppression, or coercion. Based on this analysis, the novel reveals that taking in too much of the seductive forces of barbarism is synonymous with losing all sense of manhood, like Lorenzo's and Santos's former ancestors; however, at the same time the text suggests that it was necessary to take in just enough in order to remain impenetrable, thereby maintaining an appropriate dose of masculinity.

In many of his essays, Gallegos promotes the need for change, not only in national heroes, but in all of the (male) citizens of the country. In "El mundo es del justo" (1941), Gallegos points to the "messianic complex of his countrymen," who look for heroes like Bolívar to rescue them from the degenerative status of the nation. Gallegos was aware that this "venezolanísimo sentimiento," as he calls it, was reflected in the unanimous outcome of the elections that brought him to the presidency in 1948 (qtd. Crow 36).[40] At the conclusion of this essay, he rebukes popular beliefs for the need of a messiah, instead calling for change in all people of Venezuela:

> Es tiempo ya de que le allanemos los caminos—no al mesías que en ninguna escritura nos está prometido—sino al hombre responsable que en cada uno de nosotros reside. . . . La unánime dignidad ciudadana que componga la grande y majestuosa dignidad de la patria.
>
> [It is time now that we clear the way—not for the Messiah who was not promised to us in any writings—but for the responsible man which resides in each of us. . . . The unanimous citizen's dignity that makes up the grand and majestic dignity of the nation.][41]

These patriotic feelings of dignity are achieved, claims Gallegos, through respect for the law, limitations within the law, and the recognition of civic duties: "respeto a la ley, limitación dentro del derecho, superación ante el deber."[42]

During the independence years the nation celebrated the *caudillista* heroes who were responsible for leading Spanish America out of the grips of colonialism. Yet the strong arm of the military men as leaders of nations proved to be too heavy a dose of *machismo,* resulting in the degenerative status of the nation under the (feminized) barbaric figure of leaders such as Gómez.[43] The novel addresses the seductive forces of power inherent in the masculine subject that threatens to emasculate the novel's hero, thus positing him, not as a messianic hero, but as a model figure for the nation to be able to control excessive acts of violence.

When Santos feels that he has violated the basic concepts of the law by shooting Melquíades in self-defense, he is at once at risk of falling into the abyss of barbarism and therefore losing his (sexual) identity. It is Marisela who assures him that someone standing to his right was responsible for the mortal bullet, which thereby relieved Santos from being devoured by the seductive forces of the land. Thus, Marisela's display of *ternura* [tenderness] in the novel posits her as an indispensable counterpart to the masculine national subject.[44] It is through his relationship with her that Santos maintains his ties with his feminine and spiritual side and thus his link to civilization.[45] Valverde asserts that the only way for Santos to defeat Doña Bárbara and Mr. Danger is to resort to violence, but he realizes that he has gone too far (146). This critic concludes that because of his loving and maternal attitude towards Marisela, who in turn saves him from the destructive hands of her mother, Santos is presented with a masculinity that balances civilization, *machismo,* and maternal features (146). This maternal attitude that Santos displays in his relationships with Marisela in the novel is paramount to the consolidation of a new masculinity on the private level. Within the evolved patriarchal schema of the novel, Santos as the national male figure embraces traditional feminine characteristics of nurturing and gentleness, which is then mirrored in his female counterpart and, ultimately, in the nation.

Skurski attests that Santos Luzardo's formation as a truly masculine leader, ruled by rationality, "requires that he develop a spiritual, feminine side" (623). It is this spiritual, feminine side that makes Santos such a unique masculine figure, one that has indeed evolved significantly from a former era. While he accrues nationalistic traits of *machismo,* his feminine side serves as a necessary constant in the proposed evolved masculine subject. In addition, the blatant symbolism in the novel makes an easy transition for the application on the national level, thus promoting the evolution of gender in the political spectrum. The private gendered qualities of Santos are imposed onto a collective national level, thus altering traditional roles of masculinity, based on *machismo,* that had become all too common after independence. Like Bolívar, a former educated *caudillo,* Santos must struggle with the pathological (feminized) urges of barbarity while he nurtures the more (feminine) intellectual, nurturing aspects of governing. The novel then serves as a model of gendered *bildungsroman,* which once achieved, gauges the appropriate amount of gender and power that is acceptable in a progressive nation.

In conclusion, I would like to respond to popular criticism of the text. In "Doña Bárbara; un cuento de hadas" (1970), André S. Michalski claims that Gallegos's depiction of Santos is one of little density, reaching an almost allegorical entity (qtd. in Shaw 58). In addition, in her efforts to discount Santos's accreditations as a hero, Sharon Magnarelli refers to the similarities between Lorenzo and Santos in that they are both described as misanthropes.[46] And finally, D. L. Shaw suggests that Santos's acts of resorting to violence strip the rhetoric of its implications and "all that he has done is replace a bad cacicazgo by a good one" (58).

First of all, I believe that one of the main objectives of Gallegos is to visually portray the gendered evolution of Santos in the novel, so that it could be used as a model for the collective project of the nation. Santos's initial description as a misanthrope who is on the verge of expatriating would immediately disqualify his position as a national hero of a regional novel. On the contrary, Gallegos presents antithetical representations of masculinities during this time: those who retreat into a citified intellectualism and divorce themselves from the national makeup of the country and those who indulge too much in the barbaric lifestyle, typified by the emasculated Lorenzo or the lineage of *caciques* in the Cunavichero clan. It is through Santos's journey from one end of the gendered spectrum to a space teetering precipitously in the middle that Gallegos strives to reform the masculine subject, thereby consolidating concepts of race, class, civilization, and barbarism. I must concur that Shaw's conclusion that the novel replaces a bad *cacicazgo* system for a good one is indeed valid; however, one must recognize that the fusion of traditional concepts of civilization and barbarism, masculine and feminine, national and borrowed provides a more benevolent governing style, which can be considered a positive hegemony, as proposed by Connell.

Gallegos's seemingly simplistic portrayal of inappropriately constructed gendered bodies served as a visual and literal reference of the need to alter acceptable modes of masculinity that equated violence with manhood, at both the personal and collective levels. As an educator, he knew that an effective means of appealing to the masses was to provide a clear model of dichotomous constructions, which could then be easily absorbed into the national spectrum. While many critics continue to point out the flaws that exist in this dichotomous construction that echoes all too clearly Sarmiento's progressive endeavor to dilute or upgrade the races, in Gallegos's text these ambiguously constructed meanings reflect a more complex understanding of the national makeup and its need for change. John A. Crow claims that Gallegos realized that the evil of the military dictatorship did not lie in Gómez exclusively, but in the realities of Venezuelan life (35).[47] Instead of simply replacing a bad *cacicazgo* for a good one, his plan was designed to alter the ways in which all Venezuelan men perceived themselves as both leaders of families and of nations. In many of his essays Gallegos promotes the need to move beyond the violent nature characteristic of many of the national heroes and turn instead to the law-abiding conduct and nurturing qualities that nations must adopt in their trajectory towards growth and progress.

4

Écriture feminine and Feminine Imagery in *El Señor Presidente*

A New Type of Narrative: Resisting Hegemonic Patriarchy

Upon the publication of Domingo Faustino Sarmiento's *Facundo* (1845), the dichotomy of civilization and barbarism became instrumental in the construction of a national identity in Spanish America and marked a large part of the literary production throughout the century. The nineteenth-century novel was characterized by the epistemological discourse of science that adopted hygiene, public medicine, sanitation, and criminology in the production of subjects "both clean of mind and body and free of all traces of barbarism."[1] Ideas of progress and reason were conveyed through rational and objective modes of thinking and applied to nation-building projects within the novel, as well as within the essay and other genres. This positivist ideology defined more clearly the opposition between self and Other, and the image of the woman was cast into the sphere of the irrational that not only objectified her, but also excluded her from authoritative discourse. Unfortunately for women, many of these images carried over into early twentieth-century texts.

Throughout the nineteenth century, shifts within this paradigmatic construction were achieved in Latin America as new subjects and voices competed for recognition. In *Sab* (1841), Gertrudis Gómez de Avellaneda challenges the patriarchal institutionalization of the slave plantation in Cuba by introducing a mulatto slave as a central protagonist. Through the trials and tribulations of this hybrid subject, Avellaneda draws out parallel circumstances of women who suffer similar perils. Similarly, *Aves sin Nido* (1889) portrays the corruption of a patriarchal order in the mountains of Peru whose deleterious nature pervades every aspect of society. Through a traditional objective narrative, Clorinda Matto de Turner gently and strategically validates the indigenous voice without disturbing dominant authoritative discourse or the established patriarchal system of nineteenth-century Peru.

In the mid-twentieth century, Miguel Ángel Asturias introduces a new type of narrative in his depiction of the Guatemalan dictatorship of Manuel Estrada Cabrera (1898–1920). *El Señor Presidente* (1946) marks a rupture from the objective eye of realism by its innovative play with language and its appropriation of pre-Columbian civilizations, which, in turn, function to displace a hegemonic patriarchal authority, characterized in this text by the corruption of a dictatorship. In Asturias's novel the subjective world associated with the feminine challenges a paternal authoritative order, which is represented in the novel as oppressive. In this chapter I will point out how Asturias employs feminine images and feminine writing in order to reveal the deficiencies of the extreme patriarchal nature of the dictatorship, as well as to displace traditional paradigms of conceptualizations based on binary oppositions. In his novel he begins with the medium of language as a means of exposing and dismantling the hegemonic hold that the dictator has over his subjects. In order to challenge and subvert patriarchal ideology, which is the very foundation of the political structure of dictatorships, he dissects the image of the mythical power of the president in order to show its sources and weaknesses.

In *El Señor Presidente,* Asturias incorporates the concept of myth in order to encompass pre-Columbian as well as present-day realities that contribute to the vicious cycle of violence that is incarnated in the image of a dictator whose power is perpetuated by the fear and actions of the people under him. The novel, which at one time was named *Tohil,* after the Mayan god of fire, is symbolic of the unquestionable violence and power that dominated Spanish America even before the conquest. El Señor Presidente is the ultimate symbol of patriarchy, and his rule is marked by violence, disjuncture, and betrayal. Asturias addresses the mythical qualities of dictators in "El Señor Presidente como mito," which have their roots in the tribal functions of primitive societies with such gods as Tohil, Quetzalcoatl, and Huitzilopochtli. He argues that dictators inherit these mythical aspects from primitive societies, and they have continued to surface and thrive throughout Spanish American history. Tohil, like the illusive presence of dictators, survives eternally in history because of his mythical qualities. One of the objectives that Asturias cites in this article is "buscar por aquí las raíces de estos regímenes de terror y sangre, y desraizarlos" [to search for the roots of these regimens of blood and terror and unearth them] (Asturias 425).[2]

Miguel Ángel Asturias's resistance to the dictatorship of Manuel Estrada Cabrera can be traced back to his university days at law school at the University of San Carlos, when he participated in activities that led to the overthrow of Estrada Cabrera's twenty-two-year oppressive regime. His integral role in the formation of the student-based organization *El Estudiante* was instrumental in condemning the political rule of Estrada Cabrera as he solicited the involvement of the people.[3] Although the opposition succeeded in removing the dictator from power in 1920, Guatemala failed to achieve long-term peace in the country due to the installation of the subsequent dictatorial regime of General Jorge Ubico (1933–44).[4] Asturias withdrew from the activist political struggle after the fall of Estrada Cabrera but continued to fight for social reform in his country. In January 1922 he joined the moderate socialist weekly *Claridad* and later worked with poet Miguel Angel Osorio to establish the *Universidad Popular,* whose goal was to educate the Indian, the *mestizo,* and the poor.[5] Due to the tense political climate of the country, Asturias left the following year for London, where he planned to study economics but instead continued on to Paris, where he would live for the next ten years.

In Paris Asturias attended the lectures of Professor Georges Raynaud at the Sorbonne concerning the study of Mayan religion and soon became one of his more devout disciples. His interest in Mayan tradition and the *Popul Vuh* is reflected in the stories of *Leyendas de Guatemala* (1930) and his novel *Hombres de maíz* (1949). In *Leyendas de Guatemala* Asturias introduces the oral legends of the indigenous culture into the canonical milieu of Western literature. This book of short stories was translated into French and circulated throughout Europe with a foreword by the prestigious French poet Paul Valery. Similarly, *Hombres de maíz* highlights the matrilineal connection of the Indians and addresses the imminent threat that progress and the presence of foreign industry posed on the survival of their agriculturally based culture. The novel's language and narrative structure challenge traditional historiography based on an objective linear narrative and reflect more widely the essence of Mayan culture, which is based on oral tradition. This somewhat untraditional approach is evident in his renowned novel *El Señor Presidente,* in which I argue he addresses the abuse of a patriarchal order that has gone awry. The initial chapters of *El Señor Presidente* reveal Asturias's manipulation of gender codes that are utilized to expose the pathological status of the Guatemalan state under Estrada Cabrera, as well as emphasize the critical need for change. The absence of the maternal image, or mother, marks the desperate status of many of the characters in the novel who live under the paternalistic rule of the dictator.

Absent Mothers and Distorted Father Images

In chapter 1 of *El Señor Presidente,* the word *mother,* or *madre,* serves as the catalyst for pushing the character known as el Pelele into a frenzied outburst of desperation within the dismal setting of the beggars' dwelling surrounding the cathedral steps in an unnamed city. Tormented by fellow paupers and townspeople, el Pelele, the town idiot, no sooner falls off to sleep, when some mischief seeker whispers in his ear that painful word, *mother,* setting him off on yet another mad tirade that is enacted in an already absurd, chaotic world.[6] The chapter closes as the beggars curl up like worms, "se encogieron como gusanos," as they hear the taps of military shoes approaching the church steps, reminding them of the fateful oppression in which they live (*ESP* 10). At this point a mischievous military colonel approaches the idiot, eager to see him fly into his predictable fit of madness. This time the ominous word was too painful to bear and el Pelele flung himself at his offender, scratching out his eyes and attacking him incessantly until the colonel lay motionless: "Le hizo pedazos la nariz a dentelladas y le golpeó las partes con las rodillas hasta dejarlo inerte" (*ESP* 11) [(He) thrust his fingers into his eyes, tore at his nose with his teeth and jabbed his private parts with his knees, till he fell to the ground motionless].[7] El Pelele, "enloquecido bajo la acción de espantoso paroxismo" [in a paroxysm of mad terror], flees and escapes into the shadows (*ESP* 11). Teresa McKenna argues that el Pelele may not realize what he is running away from, "but he does run in search of something, his mother."[8] She claims that the image of the flight is regressive and signifies "an attempt to return to the security of the womb."[9] Ironically the regression to (the comfort of) the mother's womb becomes a recurring theme in the novel, one that stands in stark contrast to the paternal military regime of the president.

According to Cedomil Goic, no other work in Hispanic American narrative or in any contemporary novel represents to such an extraordinary and disturbing degree the maleficent and ominous presence of absolute human power and its annihilating influence.[10] Amidst the macabre setting of poverty, madness, and the inane motive for the murder of Colonel José Parrales Sonriente presented in the first chapter, the complete and utter lack of a maternal presence proves to be the instigating force that drives the narrative forward. What follows is a nightmarish, disjunctured presentation of reality that succeeds in capturing the essence of daily life within the paternal and oppressive regime of Guatemalan dictator Manuel Estrada Cabrera.

In his study of the literary manifestations of the figure of the dictator in Latin American literature, Roberto González Echevarría asserts that literary texts reflect the emergence and evolution of the dictator in history. He clarifies that in the writers' endeavor to question the ultimate authority of the dictator, "reflection does not mean copy or reproduction, much less scientific analysis; in literature, more often than not, reflection means, distortion."[11] In the carnivalesque depiction of the authoritarian state of a dictatorship in *El Señor Presidente,* the patriarchal image of the dictator is magnified, scrutinized, and distorted, thus refracting the multiple fragmented facets of his omniscient power, which was traditionally perceived to be monolithic. In the following speech within the novel, the celebrated image of the father and protector of the nation loses a significant sense of value, particularly because a woman popularly known as *Lengua de Vaca* recites it. She cries: "¡Viva el Presidente Constitucional de la República, Jefe del Partido Liberal, benemérito de la Patria, Protector de la mujer desválida, del niño y de la instrucción!" (*ESP* 90) [Long live the Constitutional President of the Republic, Benefactor of his Country, Head of the great Liberal Party, and Liberal-hearted Protector of Studious Youth!] (97). The words *patria* and *Protector* denote the loving nature of a father as the head of the family, which is symbolic of the benevolence of the ruler of the nation. This meaning is shattered, shortly thereafter, when a young drummer boy in the band falls down a flight of stairs producing a noise that resembles too closely the mortal sounds of a recent assassination attempt on the president. The innocent young boy is incarcerated and condemned to severe punishment, thus providing a parody of the national image of a loving father over his country. Similarly, the setting of the steps of the church, a patriarchal institution that traditionally provides shelter for the homeless and needy, offers a further parodic symbolization of the illogical sense of abuse, representative of a nation under this kind of paternalistic leader.

Within the novel, Asturias presents a distorted image of the patriarchal figure of the dictator in order to expose the hegemonic control that he holds over his subjects. The juxtaposition of the motherless setting of the church steps with the abusive actions of the father within the patriarchal order of a dictatorship is orchestrated in order to reveal the pathological condition of the nation under a dictatorship. By exploiting the means in which he maintains hegemonic control over the people, Asturias succeeds in revealing the complicated web of support in which the dictator's power relies. In this chapter I will show how his use of a subversive narrative challenging the dominant power structure of the dictator can be compared to the revolutionary modern writings with which French critic Hélène Cixous challenges patriarchal culture.

Écriture feminine

In "The Laugh of the Medusa" (1976), Hélène Cixous introduces the concept of feminine writing as a revolutionary means of challenging a masculine rhetorical structure based on binary oppositions and encourages women writers to release themselves from linguistic constraints imposed on them by the patriarchal order.[12] According to Cixous, feminine writing, or *écriture feminine,* is derived from Jacques Derrida's analysis of writing as *différance.*[13] For Cixous, feminine texts are those that "strive in the direction of difference, struggle to undermine the dominant phallogocentric logic, split open the closure of binary opposition and revel in the pleasures of open-ended textuality."[14] Cixous equates the voice in feminine writing with its relation to the preoedipus stage, or the time before the child is separated from the mother and has not entered into the phallogocentric universe of the father.

According to Jaques Lacan and his theory of psychoanalysis, the symbolic order is based on the control of the phallus and logos, and the entry into the symbolic world of the law of the father is linked to the acquisition of language. Upon his/her entrance into the symbolic order, the speaking subject internalizes the rules of patriarchy and the law through language. The speaking subject in Lacanian theory is said to be gendered because men and women enter the symbolic order in different ways. While the male easily identifies himself as a phallic *I*, the female is noted for her absence and negativity.[15] Cixous argues that because the symbolic order is centered on the phallus, the mother's body is not represented in language. She encourages (women) writers to write from their body and offers the example of writing in white ink, or mother's milk.[16]

One of Cixous' most suggestive theories is her hierarchical nature of patriarchal binary thought, which she argues is intricately embedded in the patriarchal order. Oppositions such as passive/active and masculine/feminine reach their significance only in opposition to the other. Cixous argues that within the patriarchal order the feminine is always allocated the passive, powerless side of the spectrum.[17] Through feminine writing she searches for a space in which hierarchal differences are erased, allowing the writer the freedom to move beyond the linguistic limits and confines located in patriarchal thought.

Cixous terms this writing *écriture feminine,* or feminine writing, but she is careful not to exclude men from this writing process.[18] In *Castration* she warns that great care must be taken in working on feminine writing to not get trapped by names: "To be signed by a woman's name doesn't necessarily make a piece of writing feminine. It could quite well be masculine writing, and conversely, the fact that a piece of writing is signed with a man's name does not in itself exclude femininity."[19] She affirms that although it is rare, you can sometimes find femininity in writings signed by men.[20] Although French feminist Hélène Cixous and Guatemalan Nobel Prize winner Miguel Ángel Asturias may not seem to be a likely pair, both writers share similar objectives in their endeavor to disturb the gendered power relations located in Western patriarchy. Both speak from outside the margins of power and representation and use their writings as a form of resistance in hopes of altering an oppressive form of patriarchy that threatens their identity.[21] The objective of my work is to read through Asturias's novel according to Cixous' analysis of feminine writing and to demonstrate his unique position as a male Latin American writer who posits the feminine space as a means of contesting and resisting a male-dominated hegemonic order. In this way he is validating the need for the implementation of a feminine order that either works with or supersedes current modes of male dominance found in patriarchal institutions, such as those characteristic of dictatorships.

In her book *Disappearing Acts,* Diana Taylor argues that whether it was a liberal agenda or a *machista*/barbaric form of government, the struggle for power from Juan Manuel de Rosas (1829–32, 1835–52) to the military junta (1976–83) in Argentina was about gender. She states that both forms of government can be considered patriarchal, but that the barbarian, or *macho,* model envisions a society basically free of women: "The 'barbarian' model, like the military model that grows from it, sees male identity (if not biological existence) as produced through a hierarchal, quasi-generational, all-male system. The soldier-male trains and produces other soldiers."[22] She argues that this version of nation explicitly distances itself from the family in that it considers the soldier-male (and not the family) the nucleus of the state.[23] The paternalistic nature of the dictatorship in Asturias's novel reflects the barbarian model of the state, described by Diana Taylor, in its suppression of the nurturing qualities associated with the presymbolic order and its relationship to the mother's body. The physical abuse inflicted upon the subalterns throughout the text signifies the force and status of a male-oriented system that threatens the feminine order. The military model in the text is supported and carried out by the law and can thus be considered as an exaggerated or distorted representation of the symbolic order.

In *El Señor Presidente,* Asturias utilizes feminine imagery and subversive writing as a means of resisting the intrusive paternalistic nature of the dictatorship. In this novel he alters the binary nature of language within the patriarchal setting of a nation under a dictatorship, thus displacing preconceived notions of power and authority. His depiction of the patriarchal figure of the dictator is utilized in order to alter the nation's passive status of resignation and acceptance of the hegemonic presence of a militarily imposed authority in the country. By employing feminine images related to the presymbolic order, Asturias reveals the exaggerated exertion of power of the president, and by incorporating this revelation in a subversive narrative, he is challenging the very legitimacy of authority located in patriarchal thought.

The Intricate Relation of Power Maintained through Language: The Dictator and the Subaltern

In her article "Hegemony in *El Señor Presidente:* A Psychoanalytic Perspective" (1977), Teresa McKenna claims that *El Señor Presidente* is primarily a novel about domination, which can be considered as hegemonic because it is manifested through a complex pattern of human relations and perpetuated through language (99). In the following passage quoted in *Conversaciones con Miguel Ángel Asturias* (1976), Asturias uses the metaphorical depiction of the poison of an enormous spider in order to relate the intricate web of power that dictators establish with their subalterns: "Dictatorship is like the poison of an enormous spider. It embraces all social classes, perverts them, buys them, frightens them, transforms them from men into purely mechanical beings, or into great fanatics, or terrible opportunists."[24] The overbearing hegemonic presence and actions of the dictator pervade all aspects of daily life, resulting in the emasculation of its subjects, who are deprived of both a voice and an identity within this order. In the novel, the subaltern is absorbed into the linguistic system of the dictator, revealing that one of the principal means of maintaining the intricate relationship between the dictator and the subaltern is through language. Furthermore, those who refuse to accept it and reproduce it are eliminated.

Throughout *El Señor Presidente* this image of power is manifested and reiterated in the various metaphors employed by Asturias. In chapter 2, following the murder of General José Parrales Sonriente, all of the beggars were called down to the police station for questioning and severely tortured for revealing what they actually saw—the truth. The torturers did not stop until they produced the "desired truth" from their victims, emphasizing the significant role that language plays in the continuation of the power of the dictator. All of the beggars changed their testimony to the desired one, except for Mosco, a legless blind man, who was later murdered for refusing to conform to the illogical linguistic system of the dictator. Paradoxically, the blind man was never a valid witness in the first place due to his lack of sight.

However, the metaphor of the spider and the fly implemented in chapter 32 highlights the unique relationship between the president and his right-hand man, Miguel Cara de Ángel. Within the novel, Miguel represents the hapless condition of the subaltern because whether he is on his good side as the favorite, or his bad, as Camila's husband, he is generally considered to be a pawn in the intricate discourse of the dictator. In her analysis of the novel Luisa Elena Flores embarks upon the following metaphor in order to reveal the dialogical mechanisms of power between the president and the subaltern: "*The President* is a work that portrays a dictatorship that metaphorically can be compared with a spider's web in which one can find the dictator in the center waiting for subalterns who fall into his trap like flies."[25] In her work she explores the changes in the discursive style of Miguel throughout the text from one of adulation to one of disinterest in chapter 32 that marks his rupture from the narrative discourse of the president. The all-knowing president had previously discovered from his sources that Miguel Cara de Ángel had married Camila in a romantic endeavor to save her from the grips of death. The dictator was angry because Camila is the daughter of the general that he was trying to kill. Miguel had therefore betrayed him by marrying into the family of the enemy and had thus compromised his allegiance to the dictator.

It is at this juncture that an inebriated and angry president asks his former favorite if he was familiar with the fly game as he maniacally proceeds to catch a loose fly in the room: "Miguel, ¿Tú conoces el juego de la mosca?" (*ESP* 207). The president continued to direct his narrative towards Miguel, spilling out words ["palabras"] that resembled vehicles on a slippery floor ["como vehículos en piso resbaloso"], which were followed by a gushing of orange-colored vomit ["chorro de caldo anaranjado"]. This parody of the intrusive narrative of the president refers to a deeper relationship of power attributed to the fly and the spider, to which the president had previously alluded. In his analysis of the novel, "Dictadura de la muerte en *El Señor Presidente,*" Orlando Muni refers to the metaphorical implications of the relationship between the fly and the vomit, signaling the dual lesson that it offers for Miguel: "It makes him understand that his role is to receive orders in the same way in which he received the vomit. Furthermore, he realizes that for the President, he represents a mere fly trapped in the web of his power."[26] Asturias combines the authoritarian rhetoric of power with the encompassing web of the spider in order to best exemplify the intricate relationship between the president and the subaltern in the text. His distortion of this rhetoric depicted in the emission of the vomit of a leader drunk with power further parodies the absurd extent of control that the president maintains. While Flores concludes that the ultimate death of Miguel is representative of the hopeless situation of the subaltern, I argue that the text offers a form of resistance against this power in the implementation of a subversive narrative that contributes to the dissolution of binary oppositions located in the text.

The first example of fissured binary oppositions that I would like to point out in Asturias's novel is evident in the expected opposition between the president and Miguel Cara de Ángel, due to the fact that they become rivals in the text. Flores begins her analysis with a description of the two protagonists, focusing on the metaphorical implications of their appearance. On the one hand, the president's physical description and cadaverlike appearance is associated with death precisely because his typical attire was one that appeared to be of the "deepest mourning." He wore black shoes, a black suit, a black tie, and a black hat which he never took off (*ESP* 37). On the other hand, Cara de Ángel is outwardly perceived for his similarities with an angel, as seen by the woodcutter's reaction to him: "Él que hablaba era un ángel" (*ESP* 25) [The man who had spoken was an angel] (26). He is described as having slender hands in which he holds a thin cane, and he wears a broad-brimmed hat that "looked like a dove" (26) [parecía una paloma] (*ESP* 25). Furthermore, his association with Camila and the love that he expresses towards her are reflective of life, love, and nurturing. However, the description of Cara de Ángel is ambiguous, referring to both feminine and masculine characteristics, life and death, angel and Satan. He is described as having a complexion of golden marble, fair hair, a small mouth, and an almost feminine appearance, in strong contrast with the manly expression of his black eyes: ["tez de dorado mármol, cabellos rubios, boca pequeña y aire de mujer en violento contraste con la negrura de sus ojos varoniles"] (*ESP* 25). Flores notes that the dichotomous aspects of Cara de Ángel are depicted by the phrase "bello y malo como Satán" [beautiful and wicked like Satan]. She argues that this phrase refers to the somewhat contradictory qualities of this protagonist, who is physically beautiful, but at the same time morally marked for his evil doings (20). Monica Zapata also alludes to the synthesis of oppositions depicted in the favorite and comments on the evolution of this protagonist, who attempts to do good deeds in order to redeem himself of former crimes.[27]

Other critics address some of the conflicting struggles within the text, which provide the basis for the plot. Richard J. Callan attests that the novel reveals a "reenactment of the archetypal struggle between fertility and destruction,"[28] whereas Teresa McKenna claims that "in Asturias' fictional system, the hegemonic state polarizes the society, pitting those with the president against those opposed to him" (99). This binary struggle for power revealed in the relationship between Miguel and the president is not so clear, however. Miguel Cara de Ángel straddles both sides of the authoritarian narrative of the president, and many specialists of the novel, including Flores and Muni, would agree that on both sides he is perceived to be a pawn in the latter's intricate web of power. I would argue, however, that like this dubiously constructed character, Asturias's narrative transcends the confines of oppositions located in the symbolic order and offers a discourse of resistance that many critics have overlooked. Oppositions such as life/death, sanity/insanity, and president/subaltern are dissolved, opening up new spaces for resistance and renewed meanings. The implementation of a subversive narrative (*écriture feminine*) in the novel displaces traditional conceptions of author and authority, thus dismantling preconceived perceptions of power located in Western patriarchy. Consequently, the authority of language (logos) situated within the binary nature of patriarchal thought is challenged and put up for questioning.

Disturbing Authority through the Medium of Language

In *El Señor Presidente,* Asturias utilizes the medium of language as one of the principal manners of destabilizing the mythical powers of the dictator. His narrative discourse does not follow traditional canonical patterns of meaning based on (or produced by) binary oppositions and can be more closely approximated to Cixous' *écriture feminine.* In her article "Modernity, Postmodernity, and Novelistic Form," Françoise Perus speaks of the relation that *El Señor Presidente* establishes with language: "1) the possibility of a disassociation between language and its object, and thus the liberation of the object from the mythical power of language; 2) the recognition, tacit if not explicit, of the relativity of all language; 3) the possibility of escaping from opaque and closed prison-house of language, or of discourse, that led Roland Barthes to claim, in his acceptance of speech that 'all language is totalitarian.'"[29] In the opening passage of the novel the reader witnesses the breaking down of language in the innovative, sonorous recreations of Asturias's narrative: "¡Alumbra, lumbre de alumbre, Luzbel de piedralumbre! . . . alumbra, lumber de alumbre . . . alumbra, alumbre!" (*ESP* 1) [Boom, bloom alum-bright, Lucifer of alunite, over the somber tomb! . . . Boom, bloom alum-bright . . . bloom, boom] (7). The deconstruction of the symbolic order of language (logos) is accomplished by the distance between verbal utterance and its relationship to coded meaning. The sonorous qualities of this chant along with the repetitiveness of phonemes recall the prelanguage utterances that Cixous associates with the linguistic stage prior to the symbolic order.

Among others, Jean Marie Saint-Lu has studied this opening passage of the novel carefully and has identified the sounds of the words with the bells of a "toque de muertos" [death bells].[30] Although the sonorous qualities of the paragraph refer to death, the repetitive use of the verb *alumbrar,* which is defined as "to light up/to enlighten/to give birth to," refers to life and life-giving qualities.[31] Saint-Lu states that the negative meaning evoked by the death bells is not declared through words, but through phonemes, or in other words, at the level of the articulation of language.[32] Thus, the level of articulation of language precedes the symbolic order, which equates language with meaning. Saint-Lu suggests that this paragraph is a manifestation of the multiple inversions of signs that appear in the novel. Light/darkness, life/death, and giving life/taking away life are all pairs of binary oppositions that will be presented and deconstructed in the course of this novel.

According to Gerald Martin, el Pelele is a symbol of alienation and suffering and is depicted as "completamente subdesarrollado" in the novel: he is crazed, he is a beggar, he has no mother, and he has no voice.[33] El Pelele, the homeless child in the novel, continually searches for shelter in homes, temples, stores, but he is thrown out and rejected from everywhere: "sin atender a su fatiga de bestia ni a sus ojos que pesar de su inconsciencia, suplicaban perdón con la mirada" (*ESP* 10). He longed for a mother who would sing to him and ease the pain of his physical and mental wounds. Ironically, he manages to find happiness among the heap of stinking garbage in the garbage dump: "Sentíase feliz desde la puntita de la lengua hasta la puntita de los pies" (*ESP* 25) [He felt happy from the tip of his toungue to the tip of his toes] (25).

In the novel, el Pelele transcends the confines of language and reality as he communicates with the apparition of the Virgin of the Carmen without using words: "Por *señas* le contó el Pelele lo mucho que le gustaba masticar cera, y ella, entre seria y sonriente, le dijo que tomara una de las candelas encendidas en su altar" (*ESP* 24; emphasis in the original) [The Zany explained by signs how much he enjoyed chewing wax; and half-smiling, half-serious, she told him to take one of the lighted tapers from the altar] (25). In his temporary dreamlike status of sleep and delirium he is comforted by a three-foot Virgin who understands his unspoken language and gently sings to him a popular Spanish healing children's rhyme as she massages his hurt leg: "¡Sana, sana, culito de rana, siete peditos para vos y tu nana!" (*ESP* 25) [Get well, get well, my little frog's bottom, seven little farts for you and your mamma!] (25). Once again, the chanting, cooing song of the mother, representative of the preverbal stage, is significant because it competes with the oppressive patriarchal order of the dictatorship.

One of the ways in which the narrative loosens the grips of hegemony manifested and maintained through the president's intricate relationship with his subjects is by the disassociation between language and coded meaning. This strategy reflects one of the principal objectives of feminine writing, which can be defined as a revolutionary narrative that challenges the relationship of power located in patriarchal thought. In Asturias's novel, words seem to lose their value, thus dissociating meaning with the power of language. In chapter 25 illogical concepts are presented as the norm when Miguel Cara de Ángel saves the life of General Farfán by informing him that he could be eliminated if he did not gain the confidence of the president. Miguel advises him that some effective ways to get on the good side of the president is to commit a crime ["cometer un delito"] or blackmail defenseless people in public ["ultrajar públicamente a las personas indefensas"] (*ESP* 164). Both agreed that the annihilation of one of the president's own that had turned against him would certainly be the best way of getting in his good favor: "El delito de sangre era ideal; la supresión de un prójimo constituía la adhesión más completa del ciudadano al Señor Presidente" (*ESP* 164). Like Tohil, the god of fire, the president required the blood of his subjects to feed his source of power. The very man that Miguel was saving would be the one to turn him in, who ironically was following his own good advice. Thus the power of language loses its value as a binary system when concepts such as good/bad and moral/immoral collapse, revealing a distorted sense of values.

In *El Señor Presidente,* Asturias plays with traditional concepts of binary oppositions by twisting them, inverting them, and creating new ways of interpreting reality. Throughout the novel, Asturias personifies inanimate objects, but he does so in such a perverse, unique way that it creates a novelistic presence in harmony with its protagonists. In the following sentence he personifies the shadow of a tree that is compared to the freshness of a river, which connects the reader with a bird who sings:

> ¡Soy la Manzana-Rosa del Ave del Paraíso, soy la vida, la mitad de mi cuerpo es mentira y la mitad es verdad; soy rosa y soy manzana, doy a todos un ojo de vidrio y un ojo de verdad: los que ven con mi ojo de vidrio ven porque sueñan, los que ven con mi ojo de verdad ven porque miran! (*ESP* 23)
>
> [I am the Rose-Apple of the Bird of Paradise, I am life, half my body is a lie the other half is truth; I am a rose and I am an apple, I give to everyone one glass eye and one real eye; those who see with my glass eye see because they dream, those who see with my real eye see because they are looking!] (24)

Contrasting ideas contradict traditional paradigms and conceptions of the real world by offering new imagery and new ways of perceiving.

The *ojo de vidrio* is linked to a subsequent chapter with that same title and refers to the hallucination that Rodas Genaro experiences after witnessing the murder of el Pelele and learning of the kidnapping of Camila, General Canales's daughter. The all-knowing eye invaded the home of Genaro, brushing up against the body of his young wife and over the cradle of his newly born child. It continued to grow bigger and bigger until it encompassed the whole room and the life of the culpable Genaro, who would later become one of the principal players in the perverse machinations of the dictator: "El ojo creció en la sombra con tanta rápidez, que en un segundo abarcó las paredes, el piso, el techo, las casas, su vida, su hijo." (*ESP* 56) [In the darkness the eye grew rapidly bigger and bigger, until it covered the walls, the floor, the ceiling, the roof, the houses, his whole life, his child] (58). On the one hand, this glass eye is manifested out of the guilt and horror of Genaro seeing a crazy man die, but on the other hand it is representative of the all-seeing and all-knowing eye of the dictator whose power is mythical and based on corruption. It is ironical that the perceived distorted reality of the growing eye, *ojo de vidrio* representative of *mentiras*/lies, is more real than the objective perception of reality based on truth.

Throughout the novel, harrowing, grotesque images of women are conveyed in the narrative, revealing the critical status to which feminine imagery has succumbed, due to the repressive nature of the patriarchal figure of the dictator. Before Genaro is confronted with the hallucinogenic presence of the moving eye, he sees a ghost of a woman's skeleton, whose only feminine attributes remaining were "los senos caídos, flácidos y velludos como ratas colgando sobre la trampa de las costillas" (55) [the sunken breasts, limp and hairy like rats, hanging over the framework of the ribs] (57). The juxtaposition of the all-seeing eye with the flaccid breasts of a skeletal phantom of a woman marks the suppression of the feminine sphere in the novel and accentuates the excess force of dominant patriarchal power.

The Archetypal Image of the Good Mother in Crisis

In Lacanian theory, the loss of the maternal body and the desire for the mother, or imaginary unity with her, must be repressed. Upon entry into the symbolic order, the unconscious opens up, which is the primary repression of the desire for symbolic unity with the mother.[34] Cixous proposes a utopian place, a primeval female space that is free of sex roles, otherness, the law of the father, and in which the self is still linked with the voice of the mother.[35] Throughout Asturias's novel the severe repression of the maternal preoedipal stage is accomplished through the exaggeration of a phallogocentric order, where law and order impose their power and corruption upon the subalterns. In Cixousian theory, this silenced voice of the mother is associated with *écriture feminine* and can be linked to the archetypal good mother, known for her nurturing qualities.

Throughout *El Señor Presidente* it becomes evident that the archetypal symbol of the good mother, which encompasses life, birth, warmth, nourishment, protection, fertility, growth, and abundance, is indeed in crisis. The novel opens with the depiction of "aquella sociedad extraña" [that strange society] where both the drunk man and the idiot Pelele join together in lamenting and crying out loud for their absent mothers ["reclamaba a su madre llorando como un niño"] (*ESP* 8). This vivid imagery of a child crying for his mother accentuates the moral deficiencies of a society under a dictatorship. The opening scene of unsheltered beggars, idiots, and drunks on the steps of the cathedral introduces the cold, impersonal setting of the sociopolitical situation of the country and serves as a microcosm of the instability and absurdity of a totalitarian government during a reign of terror.

The absence of the feminine archetype is also evident in several key characters throughout the novel. For example, Camila, the daughter of General Canales, is motherless and spent her summers at her aunt and uncle's house and considered them to be a second family to her. When Miguel tries to situate Camila in the house of her aunt and uncle after her father flees from the president, they reject her, leaving her a veritable orphan. Likewise, el Señor Presidente himself is not married and is lacking the nurturing qualities associated with his regime, which may have offset his horrific actions or curbed the violent acts that he inflicted on so many people.[36] Similarly, Miguel Cara de Ángel is said to have committed countless heartless crimes without experiencing any sense of remorse. It is only when he falls in love with Camila that he is able to feel a sense of compassion for the first time since the death of his mother.

One of the most disturbing scenes in the novel was the torture of a mother, the innocent victim Niña Fedina, who was believed to have been privy to information about the escape of General Canales. During her interrogation the officials tortured her by not letting her nurse her newborn baby while the hungry cry of her child rung in her ears for hours. The judge advocate repeatedly asked the question to which she did not know the response as he proceeded to threaten her with the life of her child: "Desde hace dos horas está llorando, y es en el balde que busque donde está . . . ¡Llora de hambre y se morirá de hambre si usted no me dice el paradero del general!" (*ESP* 107) [He's been crying for the last two hours, and it's no use your trying to find him. . . . He's crying of hunger and he'll die of hunger if you don't tell me where the general is] (115). In an attempt to find out the location of the general, the judge advocate ordered her to crush quicklime while she endured the desperate cries of her son. It is in this scene where the primal instincts of the archetypal mother are not only denied but also tormented by the mother's inability to attend to her starving baby. Niña Fedina's failure to produce the desired discourse of the legal order demonstrates her powerlessness within this system and results in the separation of the mother/child dyad.

The reader witnesses a literal enactment of the invasion of the symbolic order (law) that removes the child from its mother's bodily form. After four and a half hours of working arduously with the quicklime, Niña Fedina can hear no other voice but the wailing of her starving child. At twenty to five, the guards abandon her on the floor, where she lie in a state of desperation and delirium. While a viscous stream flowed down from her lips, milk whiter than the lime itself was flowing from her breasts (117). Ironically, the life-giving fluids previously associated with nourishment, protection, and growth are futile in the mother's childless state. She later wakes up in her dark, cold prison cell, only to find the dying, frozen body of her son lying in her lap as limp as a ragdoll. The child revives momentarily and seizes his mother's breast, however when he tasted the sharp bitterness of lime on her nipple he refused to take the breast and began crying again. Niña Fedina cries out for help, but her desperate shouts to the prison guards were ignored as her child died slowly in her arms: "¡Ay, mi hijo se me muere! ¡Ay, mi vida, mi pedacito, mi vida! . . . ¡Vengan, por Dios! ¡Abran! ¡Por Dios, abran!" (*ESP* 109) [Oh my son is dying! Oh my life, my little one! . . . Open up, for God's sake, open the door!] (117). The novel reveals an image of the archetypal mother who is desperate to nurture and feed her baby and a corrupt political system that has deliberately prohibited her from fulfilling her primordial duties. The frustration and sheer agony that Niña Fedina suffers by not being able to give her child the flowing milk of her breasts accentuates the jeopardy of the image of the feminine and its life-giving forces, which is consistent throughout the novel. Niña Fedina resists the objective world of this oppressive reality and takes refuge in her delirium by becoming the living tomb for her dead child. Similar images of mothers in crisis ensue throughout the novel, highlighting the authoritarian nature of hegemonic Western patriarchy, characteristic of this military-imposed dictatorship.

An unexpected premonitory scene that foresees the future of Niña Fedina and highlights the abusive nature of the symbolic order in the novel takes place as she waits in the cold prison cell for her appointment with the judge advocate. Here she is confronted by haunting images of a distorted symbolic order that continues to threaten her as she sees the word of God beside a phallus and the number thirteen on top of an enormous testicle (109): "Y se veían la palabra de Dios junto a un falo, un número 13 sobre un testículo monstruoso" (ESP, 101). She is even more tormented as she looks down and witnesses an army of ants carrying off a dead cockroach, which she strangely perceives as female genitals being carried off by their own hair towards the beds of vice [Niña Fedina, bajo la impresión de los dibujos, creyó ver un sexo arrastrado por su propio vello hacia las camas de vicio] (*ESP* 101). A distorted symbolic world denoted by signs and crude language contrasts with the life-giving forces that Niña Fedina encompasses in the novel. This twisted perception of reality foreshadows her future destiny of being depleted of her maternal duties and sold to a whorehouse.

Water Imagery and Its Link to the Presymbolic

Throughout *El Señor Presidente* there are various problematic images of water that denote the crisis of the female voice as well as provide a means of resistance and a place of refuge within the symbolic order of the novel. For Cixous biblical and mythical allusions are associated with water or oceanic imagery: "We ourselves are the sea, sand, coral, seaweed, beaches, tides, swimmers, children, waves."[37] For countless mythologies, water is the feminine element par excellence and reflects the comforting security of the mother's womb.[38]

In chapter 2 of part 1 of the novel, the police station is described as the place where it always seems to rain, "donde parecía llover siempre," and in the long dark halls of the station, women wait to give their scant breakfast to the prisoners, be it their husbands, sons or loved ones: "Entre ellas se contaban sus penas en voz baja, sin dejar de llorar, enjugándose el llanto con la punta del rebozo" (*ESP* 12) [The women were telling each other their troubles in low voices, crying all the while, and mopping their tears with the ends of their shawls] (12). The presence of the incessant rain coupled with the continuous crying of women, bathed in tears, depicts imagery of the nurturing process in crisis. The cold wet hallways of the police station where women wait to hear news of the death of their loved ones contrast dramatically with the warm, loving place of the mother's womb, where one is in comfort while waiting to be born.

In the novel, the general's daughter's union with the preverbal space of the ocean provides the only positive reference of the mother/child dyad, which otherwise has been eradicated under the paternalistic reign of the dictator. The chapter that introduces Camila relates the feminine qualities of the ocean with the preverbal or imaginary stage as indicated by Jaques Lacan, with its allusion to the young girl's reunion with her deceased mother through the embryonic motion of the sea.[39] The chapter opens with Camila looking at herself in front of the mirror as she recalls how she does not like being treated like a child by her cousins. The mirror stage, according to Lacan, marks the entrance of the speaking subject into the symbolic order of the phallus, denoted by the acquisition of language. Masculine and feminine subjects are said to enter into the symbolic order differently. While men pass through the castration complex, women are believed to be more closely tied to the imaginary. Within the stagnant, stifling house of her father, Camila passes her idle time looking at photographs and comparing still images to the people she sees on the street. Looking at the still images induces in her a state of drowsiness as she considers the hidden meanings of the inscriptions associated with the symbolic order: "Untándola somnolencias de crepúsculo y presentimientos de dedicatoria" (*ESP* 72) [They all induced (in Camila) a sense of crepuscular drowsiness, coupled with superstitious feelings about their inscriptions] (78).

In this mesmerized state Camila remembers nostalgically her first visit to the ocean, whereby she is moved from the still world of photographs and her father's house to the lulling motion of the sea: "La inmensidad en movimiento. Ella en movimiento. Todo lo que en ella estaba inmóvil, en movimiento" (*ESP* 73) [Immensity in motion. Herself in motion. Everything in her that was by nature still was in motion] (79). Like the memory of her mother, she recognizes the ocean by seeing it previously in pictures: "Me lo sabía de memoria en fotografía" (*ESP* 73) [I know it already by heart from photographs] (79). The deafening waves drown out the words of the aunts, whose stiff regime symbolizes the law of the father, while Camila is momentarily thrust into a place where language is silenced (preverbal) [El oleaje ensordecedor ahogaba las palabras de sus tías] (*ESP* 73). When she approaches the water to get a better look, the ocean throws her a liquid slap, wetting her feet and taking with it her hat. At this juncture, Camila yells out a threat to the sea as she gasps "Ah . . . mar!" and without realizing it she has proclaimed the word *amar,* to love, for the very first time (*ESP* 74). This chapter highlights Camila's link to the preverbal order through her relationship with the embryonic imagery of the ocean. While a logical sequence of maturation would be denoted by the repression of the imaginary, or the preverbal stage, and the subsequent entrance into the symbolic order of the law (representative in this case of her father, the general), Camila reverts back to the space of the mother through her relationship with the salty smells and lulling motion of the sea.

Up until this juncture Camila had lived in the loveless still world of her father, denoted by the military, still photographs and the lack of physical contact. Her visit to the ocean with its salty water reunites her with the comforting security and movement of the mother's womb. Camila reenacts the first sensations between mother and child, reminiscent of the preoedipus stage, on the beach by smelling and kissing her salty skin: "¿Por qué se besó los brazos en la playa respirando el olor de su piel asoleada y salobre?" (*ESP* 74) [Why did she kiss her own arms there on the beach, breathing in the smell of her sun-drenched, salty skin?] (81). Camila normally avoided physical contact with her frigid aunts, who would coldly kiss her through their veiled faces ["La besaron sus tías sin levantarse el velito del sombrero"] (*ESP* 72). She is mesmerized by the smell of the ocean on her skin, a sensation that had been missing from her relationship with her father and nanny, who she did not sniff when she kissed: "Camila había besado a su papá y a su nana, sin olerlos" (*ESP* 75). Situated in the midst of the sea air, Camila recalls her desire to kiss her salty flesh, "con las ventanas de la nariz abiertas, ansiosas, anhelantes" (*ESP* 75) [with her nostrils flaring, eager, and greedy] (81). The contact established with the ocean in this chapter links Camila to the imaginary world of the mother, positing her as a resistant force of the oppressive symbolic order of the president.

The novelist uses female protagonists to establish connections with the semiotic world, which according to Lacan, is repressed upon entrance into the symbolic order. It is through protagonists, such as Camila, Niña Fedina, and Señora Carvajal that the novel provides a glimmer of hope and form of resistance against the patriarchal presence of the dictator. Cara de Ángel's love for Camila leads him to undergo a complete transformation, and he ultimately breaks away from the symbolic order of the president. Similarly, the subversive nature of the narrative exposes the hegemonic hold that the dictator holds over the subaltern and works to displace traditional concepts of language and meaning according to rationalist thought.

The Parodization of Power

As stated previously, Asturias reveals the power sources of the dictator, which were previously perceived to be monolithic. According to Carlos Wyld Ospina, Estrada Cabrera's rule was characterized by fear and subjugation: "Estrada Cabrera governed through fear. He committed atrocities because of this fear. Because of fear he lived by distrust, by instigations and deceits."[40] The novel exposes and subverts the mechanical, puppetlike actions of the people under the president, thus providing an initiative to break away from the perpetuation of this power.

According to Michel Foucault, negative power exerted by the state, as in the case of a dictatorship, is based upon a whole network of relations, which serves as a kind of metapower. This metapower, which is essentially structured around a certain number of great prohibition functions, can only take hold and secure its footing where it is rooted in a whole series of multiple and indefinite power relations that supply the necessary basis for the great negative forms of power.[41] By implementing innovative metaphors throughout the text, Asturias exposes and subverts the metapower that supports and feeds into the overpowering dominance of the dictatorship.

As previously discussed, one of the ways in which the dictator of the novel maintains his hegemony over his people is through language. Asturias reveals the importance of language in the perpetuation and mystification of the president through the epistolary form of chapter 23. This chapter is made up of sixteen letters sent to the president on April 28 from the different spies that provide him with the knowledge and power that he needs in order to stifle his opposition. The contents of the letters reveal a disconnected world motivated by fear and treason. Neighbor turns against neighbor, brother against brother, and savior against victim. It seems that nobody escapes the tyranny of betrayal that seeps out of this depraved societal network, a society that ironically mirrors the despicable relationship between the beggars Asturias established in chapter 1:

> Se juntaban a dormir en el Portal del Señor sin más lazo común que la miseria, maldiciendo uno de otros, insultándose a regañadientes con tirria de enemigos que se buscan pleito, riñiendo muchas veces a codazos y algunos con tierra y todo, revolcones en los que, tras escupirse, rabiosos, se mordían. Ni almohada ni confianza halló jamás esta familia de parientes del basurero. (*ESP* 7)
>
> [With nothing in common but their destitution, they mustered to sleep together in the Porch of Our Lord, cursing, insulting and jostling each other, picking quarrels with old enemies, or throwing earth and rubbish, even rolling on the ground and spitting and biting with rage. This confraternity of the dunghill had never known pillows or mutual trust.] (7)

Asturias uses this same language within the novel in order to debase the integrity of authoritative officials, such as the police, who maintain the power of the dictator. In chapter 2 of the novel, authoritative figures of the police force are subverted and made to appear infantile by comparing their chubby cheeks to buttocks ["los cachetes como nalgas"] and their mustaches to dribbles of chocolate ["los bigotes como babas de chocolate"] (*ESP* 13). The puppetlike actions of the authors of this metapower (the police officers in this case), including those who wrote letters to the president, are revealed for their mechanical adherence to the dominant order and are captured more completely by Asturias's language and metaphors.

Similarly, the actions of the puppet master of chapter 8, who tries to scare the children by making his puppets cry, does not reveal a simple cause and effect reaction, but shows more vividly the disconnected sense of humanity that exists under this type of rule. Instead of producing the desired response from the children, they seem to be so desensitized to abuse and pain, they laugh at the hideous presentation of the crying, mistreated puppets (*ESP* 51–52). Instead of feeling a sense of commiseration for the abused puppets, the children laughed upon seeing them cry ["Los niños reían de ver llorar"], and even laughed upon seeing them hit ["Los niños reían de ver pegar"] (*ESP* 51–52). The puppet master's wife, perplexed by the children's reaction, searches for a language that can best express the contradictory results of such a morbid spectacle. When Doña Venjamon argued with her husband, she always added syllables to her words, like safety valves to prevent an explosion ["iba agregando sílabas a las palabras como válvulas de escape para no estallar"] (*ESP* 52). Her inventions of such words as "¡Ilógico!" "¡relógico!" "¡Ilololológico!" and "¡Recontralógico!" [Relogical! Relogical! Recontralogical! Recontrarelogical!] capture the absurdity of the present reality of the novel in creative and unexpected linguistic ways (*ESP* 52). The dissolution of binary oppositions and the employment of innovative metaphors in the novel defy traditional rational modes of thinking and force the reader to move beyond an objective, realistic reading of the novel.

In "Modernity, Postmodernity, and Novelistic Form in Latin America" (1994), Françoise Perus states that as soon as the artistic project goes beyond stylization of the discourses involved and begins to question dominant discourses and practices "the symbolic figure is generally situated in the context of the public square or the popular fair, with the resulting parody and carnivalization of all the crystallizations or solidifications of dominant discourse."[42] The crystallization of the mythical perception of el Señor Presidente becomes evident in chapter 14 when he is asked by his people to address them from the balcony. It is the one-year anniversary of his near assassination and women weep with gratitude upon still having their worthy leader with them. He is introduced as the "muy ilustre protector de las clases necesitadas, que vela por nosotros con amor de padre" [illustrious protector of the poorer classes, who watches over us with a father's love] (98). The orator cries out "¡Viva el presidente Constitucional de la República, Jefe del Partido liberal, Benemérito de la Patria, Protector de la mujer desválida, del niño y de la institución!" (*ESP* 90) [Long live the Constitutional President of the Republic, Benefactor of his Country, Head of the great Liberal Party, and Liberal-hearted Protector of Studious Youth!] (97). The image portrayed is so empowering, the moment so real, that even the *ilustre presidente* sheds a tear at the benevolence of his mythical figure. Upon hearing him sniffle, Cara de Ángel begs the president to come in as to not be too affected by the crowd ["El populacho le afecta el corazón"] (*ESP* 90). However, when word gets out that General Canales has escaped and loud shots are heard, some guests wet their pants out of fright. This type of flowing water accentuates the reality of fear produced by the regime of el Señor Presidente, one that contradicts with the life-giving forces of flowing water related to the presymbolic order.

Displaced Heroes

Perus states that the protagonists of novels like *El Señor Presidente* experience a violent and tumultuous catharsis within the process of *bildungsroman,* which will become representative of a collective unconscious.[43] This becomes evident in the transformation of Cara de Ángel, who rejects the symbolic order of the president and turns to the profound love that he feels for Camila. Within the construction of the novel and the comparisons of the role of the dictator to the omniscient presence of God, Miguel Cara de Ángel's fall from grace simulates Lucifer's fall from the grace of God. Yet the narrative discourse of the novel reveals that this mythical image of the dictator is inverted and that he is truly the diabolical force that oppresses the inhabitants of the country. Miguel's fall from grace or transformation becomes evident in the second part of the novel by the elimination of the epithets "era bello y malo como Satán," by which he is addressed in the beginning of novel. According to Juan Antonio Rosado, Cara de Ángel represents the tragic hero who experiences a type of renaissance upon separating from the symbolic order; however, this rebirth is seen as inverted: "Miguel is reborn in a different way; he abandons his previous life, and from this Genesis he travels towards the Apocalypse, as he fails in his adventure."[44] Because Miguel originated within the binary nature of a patriarchal discourse of language he is destined to die because there is no place for opposition within the language of a dictatorship.

Although his journey is thwarted by the symbolic order of the political establishment, in many ways Miguel Cara de Ángel is able to transcend the limitations of this order. In "Babylonian Mythology in 'El Señor Presidente'" (1967), Richard J. Callan claims that Miguel expresses an unconscious awareness of his metaphysical triumph when he is arrested and beaten by Major Farfán at the end of the novel (418). He shouts: "Pegue, no se detenga, no tenga miedo; que para eso soy hombre, y el fuete es arma de castrados!" (*ESP* 252) [Go on hit me, don't stop, don't be afraid; I'm a man, and only eunuchs use whips!] (270). Ironically, Miguel, who considers himself to be the real man ["para eso soy hombre"], is associated with his rejection of the symbolic order of the law, which is characterized as an exaggerated patriarchal order that enforces its rule through the imposition of language and force. At this juncture, Miguel's speech reverses traditionally accepted relations of masculine/active and feminine/passive as he disempowers his captor from a position of passivity and victimization. In this passage Miguel depicts his captor as being the emasculated one, pertaining to [los] "castrados" [eunuchs], for adhering to the illogical symbolic discourse of the president. Conversely, the male hero of the novel is associated with his appropriation of the space of love and giving denoted by his relationship with Camila and her association with the presymbolic order.[45]

Paradoxically, the evolved masculine subject of the novel does not emerge out of the repression of the imaginary and proceed to the entrance into the symbolic order, but is found by his approximation to the space of love, and the presymbolic order, which according to Lacanian theory is genderless. Cixous alludes to this nonexclusive space in the following passage in the "Laugh of the Medusa": "When I write, it's everything that we don't know we can be that is written out of me, without exclusions, without stipulation, and everything we will be calls us to the unflagging, intoxicating, unappeasable search for love. In one another we will never be lacking" (348). Miguel's trajectory and position in the novel reflect Cixous' proposal of a bisexual subject, that displaces feminine and masculine markers of gender and moves towards a more complete, but genderless, subject. Similarly,

Miguel's cathartic break from the established order of the law serves as an exemplary model of the desired status of the collective unconscious, as suggested by Perus. Through feminine writing, concepts of difference and exclusion are dissolved, thus eliminating the barriers imposed on the speaking subject by gender.[46]

Prelanguage

According to Toril Moi, Cixous affirms that feminine writing is linked to the mother as source and origin of the voice to be heard. The writer searches to find its source in the preoedipal stage before the child's acquisition of language, thus before the child can name and identify its surroundings. The voice is nameless. Cixous relates this theory to feminine writing and states that the speaking voice is in a space outside the logical order of time (eternity), a space that allows no naming and no syntax.[47] In *El Señor Presidente,* Asturias introduces characters and a narrative that resist the authoritative discourse of the law, thus reflecting a feminine writing by its approximation to the preoedipal stage and its connections to the mother's body.

In chapter 31, a governmental official responds to the desperate pleas of Señora Carvajal by telling her to go see the president and beg for her husband's life. Otherwise, according to the law ["conforme a la ley"], he may be sentenced to death and shot within twenty-four hours (*ESP* 200). Carvajal's wife was either unable or refused to ingest the symbolic discourse of the president as she timorously responded: "¡le, le, le!" (*ESP* 200) [La-La-La!] (215). The official proceeded to explain to her the literal superiority of the symbolic order of the law over her need to protect her husband: "La ley es superior a los hombres, señora, y salvo que el Señor Presidente lo indulte" (*ESP* 200) [The law comes before individuals, Señora, and unless the President reprieves him] (215). Again, she was unable to accept the decision of the law and found herself speechless [No pudo hablar. . . . No pudo hablar] (*ESP* 200). In her speechless state of shock, she continued to fight for the safety of her husband as she found herself in a stagnant, useless existence as she rushed to speak to the president: "Necesitaba salvar a su marido. Pero no llegaban . . . pero no llegaban. . . . Llegar, pedir y salvarlo, pero no llegaban." (*ESP* 201) [She must save her husband. But still they hadn't got there. . . .

She must get there, beg for her husband's life and save him . . . but still they hadn't arrived] (216).

In the following passage, Mrs. Carvajal's insistent commands to the driver were of no avail as the carriage did not move: "Más rienda. . . . Necesitaba salvar a su marido. . . . más rienda." (*ESP* 200) [Faster. . . . She must save her husband. . . . Faster] (215). The carriage, which is described as being stretched out like the bellows of a camera, defies logical concepts of time and space as it refuses to respond to the señora's desires: "Pero el vehículo no rodaba, ella sentía que no rodaba, rodaban sólo las ruedas de adelante, ella sentía que los de atrás se iba quedando atrás, que el carruaje se iba alargando como el acordeón" (*ESP* 200–201) [But the carriage wouldn't move, she could feel that it wasn't moving, only the front wheels were turning, she could feel the back wheels lagging behind so that the carriage was lengthening out like the bellows of a camera] (216). This static depiction of the carriage reflects Carvajal's feelings of powerlessness within the oppressive order of the dictator. Cixous has argued that although it is nearly impossible to define a feminine practice of writing, "it will always surpass the discourse that regulates the phallocentric system; it does and will take place in areas other than those subordinated to philosophico-theoretical domination."[48] In the previous scene, the use of a narrative defying logical concepts of time and space and Carvajal's refusal to accept defeat provide a means of resistance to this phallogocentric order.

Asturias also creates new words with onomatopoeic sounds that reflect the prelanguage stage associated with feminine writing. When Niña Fedina awaits her audience with the judge magistrate and is confronted by the distorted symbolic world of the cold prison cell, she takes refuge in the preverbal chanting dedicated to the Virgin Mary as she thinks about her child: "*Ora pro nobis . . . / Ora pro nobis . . . / Ora pro nobis . . . / Ora pro nobis . . . / Ora pro nobis . . . / Ora pro nobis . . . / Ora pro nobis . . . / Ora pro nobis . . .* " (*ESP* 102; cursives in original). In a state of desperation, Niña Fedina directs her prayers to the Virgin Mary while the repetition of this religious litany momentarily places her in a safe place. The constant repetition of the chant, as well as the use of cursive letters in the text, recalls a preverbal order connected to the mother's body. As she suffers in the dark, cold prison cell, outside the city people are depicted for their mechanical like actions as they honor the celebration of the president of the republic: "Fuera, seguía la fiesta, la manta de las vistas en lugar del patíbulo y la vuelta al parque de los escalvos atados a la noria" (*ESP* 103) [Outside the celebrations went on, with the cinema screen standing like a scaffold and people walking round the garden like slaves round a water-wheel] (111). Ironically, neither those found inside the prison walls nor those outside could claim a true sense of freedom within the phallogocentric order of the dictator. Thus, traditional barriers such as inside/outside and freedom/incarceration are subverted in the novel. Niña Fedina, however, finds refuge by creating a mental space in which to escape: "Reanimada, hizo esfuerzos para pensarse libre y lo consiguió. Vióse en su casa, entre sus cosas y sus conocidos, diciendo a la Juanita: '¡adiós, me alegro de verla!'" (*ESP* 103) [Rallying her forces, she made an effort to imagine she was free, and succeeded. She pictured herself at home among her belongings and friends, saying to Juanita: "Goodbye, it was lovely to see you!"] (111).

The different ways in which syntax is disturbed and disjointed ideas are connected in the novel are other ways in which the medium of language is subverted and replaced by another that reflects the presymbolic stage. In "The Laugh of the Medusa," Cixous claims that the "sweeping away [of] syntax" achieved in feminine writing disturbs the symbolic order that is maintained by the phallus (342). In the following passage, Asturias cuts sentences, breaks up words, and adds repetitions of sounds that disrupt traditional syntactical constructions and create new sounds and images: "la car-car-car-jada, del aire del aire. . . la car-car-car-jada" (*ESP* 9) [la-la-laughter from the air. . . from the air. . . la-la-laughter] (9). Similarly, many of the scenes that Asturias describes are like cinematic vignettes in movies. When Camila contemplates the ocean for the first time, she is drawn into images of movement and compares her experience to the movie pictures: "Todo en movimiento. Nada estable. Retratos y retratos confundiéndose, revolviéndose, saltando en pedazos para formar una visión fugaz a cada instante, en un estado que no era sólido, ni líquido, ni gaseoso, sino el estado en que la vida está en el mar" (*ESP* 74) [Everything in motion. Nothing stable. Pictures mingling with other pictures, shifting, breaking into pieces to form a new image every second, in a state that was not solid, nor liquid, nor gaseous, but which was the state of the life in the sea] (80). This way of viewing reality in movement, seeing the whole by a reduction of its many parts, is an effective technique that the novelist employs in order to reveal the many facets that maintain the power of the dictator in place. The rupture from rationalism and logic in the text dislocates the discourse of authority located in patriarchal thought.

Cixous tries to escape the prison house of patriarchal language based on binary oppositions in her feminine writing and searches for a linguistic space that defies difference or exclusion. Similarly, Asturias's narrative in the novel does not fit into traditional conceptions of signifiers based on presence and absence and does not follow traditional patterns of difference relegated to the symbolic order. El Señor Presidente is never identified in the novel; neither is his country. One of the only indications that the reader has in knowing that it takes place in Guatemala is the name of the newspaper where Camila and Miguel Cara de Ángel's wedding announcement came out. Also the choice of colloquial language laden with Mayan origins encompasses a heterogeneous voice that competes with monolithic traits of intellectualism previously encoded in nation-building novels promoting rationalism and civilization.

Hope for Resistance

In "La visión trágica de Miguel Ángel Asturias en *El Señor Presidente*" (2000), Juan Antonio Rosado argues that the novel expresses a sense of hopelessness with regard to the sociopolitical state of affairs. This sense of hopelessness is repeated throughout the text and is reflected in the judge advocate's discourse towards his servant who tried to help Señora Carvajal locate the dead body of her husband. The judge advocate clearly explains to his servant that in his house the first thing everyone has to learn, including the cat, is that there are never any grounds of hope of any kind for anyone ["no se dan esperanzas de ninguna especie a nadie"] (*ESP* 217). I believe that the very nature of deconstruction and subversion of traditional paradigms that operates within the narrative provide hope of displacing the authority of an all-consuming totalitarian power. In addition, the crisis of the good mother discussed earlier shows the reader the need to incorporate nurturing qualities, which are presently deficient within the power sources in the novel.

Despite the nurturing deficiencies in the novel, it is the female protagonists who serve as a means of resistance, which at some level provides an element of hope. Camila's near-death experience serves as a catalyst for the transformation of Cara de Ángel. He must promise to take the road of good and resist the tyrannical order of the president in order to save Camila's life. Although his transformation leads to his death at the end of the novel, his death marks the liberty of the student and the sacristan, who have pledged to initiate a revolution during their incarceration. His love for Camila also resulted in the birth of a baby, which is representative of a new generation and hope for the future.

Similarly, Niña Fedina resists and perseveres through her concentration on her baby's cries during her torture. She does not give in even when he dies because she finds a safe place in her madness by keeping her dead baby warm. Even when he dies, she does not cease to nourish him in the only way that she can, by providing for him a living tomb. Also, when she is in the *prostíbulo* (brothel) upon the realization of the death of her baby, she evokes compassion and human feelings in the other prostitutes, who clean up the brothel in order to give him a decent funeral. The narrator explains that it was as if all of them had lost a child that night. A half-drunk woman, with one of her breasts bare, chewing on a cigar, repeated the following song amid floods of tears (153):

¡Dormite, niñito
cabeza de ayote
que si no te dormís
te come el coyote!
¡Dormite, mi vida
que tengo que hacer,
lavar los pañales
sentarme a coser!

(*ESP* 143; cursives in original)

[Sleep, my little boy,
My pumpkin-head,
for if not, the wolf
will kill you dead!
Sleep, my life,
for I must go
to wash your linen
and sit down to sew!]

(153)

The consolidation of the prostitutes during this tragic moment depicts a space in time (although brief) where difference is put aside while all women share in the mourning process. Meanwhile, the metaphorical implications of the lullaby are directly related to the threatening presence of a corrupt power (*el coyote*). The child has escaped this oppressive order through death whereas Niña Fedina resists defeat and takes refuge in her madness. This type of madness, manifested by her refusal to stop nurturing her baby and her inability to succumb to the symbolic order, also provides a means of resistance.

One of the few voices in the novel that challenges the authoritative discourse of the state is that of an anonymous woman who condemns the mistreatment of Niña Fedina. As she is dragged through the streets being beaten by the officials, no one speaks out in her defense except for one woman coming from the market. Even when she is told to be quiet, the woman continues her invective against the unacceptable behavior of the soldiers towards Niña Fedina (*ESP* 93). Her speech exposes the soldiers for who they are because of their brutal behavior towards the innocent: "¡Calzonudos! . . . ¡Para lo que les sirven las armas!" (*ESP* 86) [So that's what your weapons are for, is it, you cowardly blackguards?] (93). Even though the soldiers threatened her with physical harm if she did not shut up ["Cállese . . . o la rompemos!"/Shut up . . . or we'll bash your face in!], the woman continued to speak. Unlike the rest of the president's subjects, who absorbed the narrative of the dictator out of fear, this woman refused and continued to speak out against the brutal officials: "¡La rompemos, qué mismas! ¡Eso era lo único que nos faltaba . . . ¡Partida de piojosos . . . , ajar a la gente por gusto!" (*ESP* 86) [Bash my face in indeed! That's enough of that, you lousy lot . . . , insulting people just for the fun of it!] (93).

The wife of Carvajal is another figure in the novel that does not cede to the dominant voice of the officials. She feverishly tries to get to the president's house to beg for the life of her husband. When she is refused, she proceeds to the prison where he is executed and presses her body up against the wall so that she can somehow be closer to her husband in his moment of grief: "Miedo, frío, asco; se sobrepuso a todo por estrecharse a la muralla que repetiría el eco de la descarga" (*ESP* 204) [Fear, cold, disgust, she overcame them all in order to press herself against the wall which would echo the sound of the shots] (219). Like Niña Fedina, she continues to love and to fight for her husband despite his imminent death. I see her tenacity and perseverance as a form of resistance against the totalitarianism of the government as she silently challenges the executioners to murder in cold blood one of their own. Her discourse reveals the dehumanization of the political regime that prohibits its subjects of expressing any form of compassion and encourages them to turn on each other if only to save their own hide.

As can be expected, Señora Carvajal was treated as an outcast as she walked through the neighborhood trying to get a petition to locate and retrieve the dead body of her husband. Doors were slammed, messages unanswered, and appointments cancelled. As she wandered from house to house, she was received coldly by the townspeople, who were afraid to show the grief they felt for her husband's death for fear of being taken for enemies of the government (*ESP* 211). The disillusioned widow was treated "peor que la pobreza, peor que el vómito negro, peor que la fiebre amarilla" [worse than the poor, worse than black vomit, worse than yellow fever]; yet when she returned to her home, anonymous letters poured in ["le llovían 'anónimos'"], demonstrating a resolute form of resistance of a people willing to share their misfortunes with the widow (*ESP* 211). Despite the overwhelming oppression administered by the hegemonic order of the dictatorship, a small but unyielding sense of resistance seeps out and refuses to be silenced and/or absorbed into the dominant discourse of the president. Through his employment of a subversive narrative and his use of relentless protagonists who refuse to stop loving and nurturing, Asturias provides a glimmer of hope in an otherwise sinister existence.

As my analysis has shown, in *El Señor Presidente,* Asturias paints a nightmarish, disoriented reality characterized by the fragmentation of traditional images and the innovativeness of language. Within this discombobulated depiction, the archetypal symbol of mother, which is associated with fertility, reproduction, and abundance, suffers helplessly under the tyrannical corruption of a totalitarian government. Nonetheless, the narrative of the novel challenges traditional historiography, which is based on an objective perception of reality, by resisting traditional ways of narrating and storytelling. The breakdown of language, the mixture of fantasy and reality, the fragmentation of syntax and ideas reveal a feminine writing that works to subvert logocentric ideology and results in an explosion of signs, and an open-ended text. As a result, the dichotomous paradigm of civilization and barbarity is shattered and replaced by an innovative narrative, which strives to eliminate concepts of difference. Although Asturias did not publish his novel until after the dictatorships of both Cabrera and Ubico, his novel provides a testimony to the resistance of an oppressive patriarchal authoritarianism that has continued to be a recurring phenomenon in Spanish America after independence. His use of feminine imagery and a subversive narrative becomes instrumental in disrupting a distorted symbolic order, representative of the paternal law of the dictatorship.

Conclusion: Bigendered Nations

SIGNIFICANT STUDIES IN PSYCHOLOGY AND PSYCHOANALYSIS THAT have recognized the dualistic nature of gender have often been overlooked by many femininsts given the fervent nature of gender studies in current literary theory.[1] It is somewhat ironic that modern concepts of gender are still perceived within the terms of binary oppositions despite the drive to deconstruct these detrimental codes that continue to haunt misogynist discourse and attribute power to the masculine side of the spectrum. French feminists have looked towards Jacques Lacan and Jacques Derrida in order to examine the binary nature of gender that they believe to be located in language and originates in the emergence of the speaking subject into the symbolic order. Following Derrida's theory of *différance,* Hélène Cixous expounds on the nature of patriarchal binary thought that corresponds to the underlying opposition between man/masculine and woman/feminine, which she argues is heavily embedded in the patriarchal value system. According to Toril Moi, in her theory of feminine writing Cixous tries to escape the boundaries of binary oppositions located in Western patriarchal thought (104).[2] Recent queer theory has also dedicated its efforts to dissolving the binary nature of gender codes in order to subvert the hegemonic status of heterosexuality in current society. Judith Butler has made exemplary strides in her theories concerning the influence of the discourse of power on the social constructions of gender and thus refers to it as a form of "drag" or a "free floating artifice." Although many writers and critics have emphasized this movement away from binding, antithetical codes of gendered perception and power in modern representations of subjects in the media and literature, it is important to establish that the crux of the breakdown of these gender codes can be attributed to earlier writers who employed gender troping in their contestation to masculinist hegemonic institutions that threatened their very subjectivity.

Throughout history, many intellectuals have utilized gendered binary oppositions in order to appropriate, reappropriate, or maintain the status of power in the political arena, and in doing so they have consciously or unconsciously broken away from these codes, thus opening up their texts to new spaces for interpretation. From Esteban Echeverría's *El matadero* (1839) to Miguel Ángel Asturias's *El Señor Presidente* (1946), published a century later, visually portrayed gendered subjects are employed in order to warn the reader of the excessive masculinist force administered by hegemonic institutions of dominance and authority. In *El matadero,* Echeverría's meticulous construction of the Other as barbaric highlights traditional conceptions of masculinity and its position of dominance. By casting the Unitarian in the subordinate role, he reinforces traditional power structures of gender, where the feminine subject is found literally on the bottom of the sexual equation (*boca abajo*) in a position of inferiority. The Unitarian heroically dies, perhaps in an attempt to refuse to be penetrated, thus revealing some remnant of virility according to traditional codes of *machismo.* His death, however, marks the defeat of the opposition on the political stage of the power struggle, signaling a sense of urgency and the need to change national [gendered] relations of power.

The use of gendered representations of power is highly visible in this early nineteenth-century short story, a characteristic that is repeated in all of the narrative works discussed in this study, despite the evolution or transformation that the gendered national subject assumes. In my reading of José Martí's *Amistad funesta,* the visual reenactment of the culminating stage of hysteria, or *attitudes passionnelles,* is enacted by Lucía and results in the death of Sol del Valle, or the projected spirit of South America, while Juan sits idly by and witnesses this horrific crime. Similarly the masculine characteristics attributed to the female character in Rómulo Gallegos's *Doña Bárbara* refers to the pathological *caudillista* nature of the Gómez dictatorship. The male national subject in the novel must reappropriate these codes of masculinity while he disempowers his opponent, Doña Bárbara/Gómez. In Asturias's *El Señor Presidente* the agonizing cries of Niña Fedina, who cannot feed her newborn baby, provide a literal and visual portrayal of the dominance of the patriarchal order over the traditional role of the mother. Asturias provides clear, vivid examples of the excessive dominance of the patriarchal order over the feminine subordinate and demonstrates the critical status of the feminine sphere within this type of dictatorial government.

In all of these texts a significant characteristic traditionally ascribed to the feminine, *ternura,*/nurturing, is described for its deficiency in the opposing dominant order. Ironically, the national subject and/or national order in all of these works move away from overtly masculine concepts of power and are thus ambiguously structured with regard to both traditional and contemporaneous perceptions of gender. Many writers sought to alter hegemonic forms of masculinity and proposed national subjects that maintained characteristics of *ternura* or nurturing, thus promoting a more evolved sense of nation.

A historical result of the wars of independence was the proliferation of the masculinist *caudillista* leaders who would continue to assume the role of dictator in many Latin American countries throughout the nineteenth and twentieth centuries. In addition, as Latin American nations emerged into an era of modernity, many countries had to define themselves and respond to more powerful nations, such as the United States and many parts of Europe. The intelligentsia of these countries often used gendered representations of the Other in order to persuade their readers of the detrimental effects of the hegemonic *machista* nature of dictatorships or the imposing presence of imperialist nations, incorporating a representation that they would feminize in order to reverse the representative locus of power.

According to William David Foster, gender is neither an exclusively social construction nor is it a matter of biological essentialism, rather "one can debate the proportional interaction of the biological and the constructive, but the point is that the body and its subjectivity interact with social circumstances that, therefore, impinge on the body-subjectivity compound so that meaning moves back and forth between them."[3] Foster argues that one of the issues that arises when gender serves as the basis of a sociopolitical allegory is "the excesses of meaning that can be shown to be problematic for the efficient working of the allegorical proposition at issue."[4]

In this crisscrossing of gender codes that was manipulated in order to realize the status of power, traditional codes based on the binary status of gender are simultaneously displaced or deconstructed, thus opening spaces for reinterpretations of gender. It is my consensus that within this turbulent and transitory period in Latin America, conceptualizations of gender move away from biological essentialism and become more symbolic of a power struggle, where these representatives of power display ambiguous or even androgynous characteristics.

Paradoxically, all of the writers included in this study have advocated for a bigendered or androgynous sense of nation that blurs the binary aspects of feminine and masculine in the manner proposed by feminist and psychoanalytical critical theorists. In *El matadero,* Echeverría shows how the abject portrayal of the hypermasculine characteristics of Matasiete and the overtly passive helplessness of the Unitarian are two extremes that are unacceptable in a progressive society. Unlike traditional readings of the text, Joan Lee Skinner's analysis suggests that Echeverría advocated a dialogue between Unitarians and Federalists: "'El matadero' uses the rape of the young man to dramatize the consequences of antithetical political discourses at work.[5] The rape is a grotesque parody of Echeverría's own earlier calls for national reconciliation; rather than a marriage of the two parties, 'El matadero' presents the violent, sexual abuse of the liberals by the Federalists."[6] The seemingly homoerotic relation between the two men not only reenacts the gendered struggle for power, but also highlights the inability of both parties to communicate and therefore come to a compromise. In his 1846 revision of the *Dogma socialista,* which originally served as the political platform for the Generation of '37, Echeverría laments the polarized status of Argentine society.[7] Although he praises the Unitarians for their progressive beliefs and their advocacy for education, he claims that they are out of touch with Argentine reality.[8] Skinner states: "Echeverría insistently writes and rewrites both political and sexual dualities into his text, but he does so in order to critique the polarization that has led to a situation in which political disagreements can only be expressed through violence" (222). Based on Skinner's analysis, a political compromise between these opposing gendered subjects would lie somewhere between a hypermasculine and a powerlessly feminine subject, thus positing the proposed male national subject for its ambiguously gendered or even androgynous portrayal.

José Martí also contests the masculinst hegemonic presence of the United States that threatens the subjectivity of the Latin American national subject. In his 1886 letter to Manuel Mercado, Martí expressed feelings of alienation and loss of autonomy as he described himself as "una cierva despedazada por las mordidas de los perros que se rufugia para morir en el último tronco" [a young deer being torn apart by (the bites of) dogs, who finally takes refuge in a remote (tree) trunk to die].[9] Throughout this letter, Martí describes himself at the verge of defeat, being swallowed up by the city in which he resides, a city that ironically provides the opposing force from which he constructs a sense of nationalism. The Cuban exile retaliates by manipulating traditional conceptualizations of gender in order to reverse commonly perceived relations of power. In his writings Martí challenges nineteenth-century Western ideology based on the scientific investigations of Darwin and inspired by the progressive tenets of positivism that linked degeneracy with gender and race. According to many scientific treatises, as well as popular travel journals of the nineteenth century, Latin America was perceived as being primitive and uncivilized, thus casting it into the realm of feminized Other. While this feminized Other was marginalized from authoritative discourse and discounted during a crucial era of nation building, Martí succeeded in appropriating hegemonic discourse, only to turn it on its heels. In this way he opened a space for the formation of the Latin American subject by incorporating him into a new improved space of modernity, one which would be free from the clutches of colonialism and, more importantly, imperialism.

Martí does not simply reverse traditional concepts of gender in his utopist vision of the Latin American national subject; in his many writings he promotes a union of the progressive forces of reason with the often discounted qualities of the soul. In an essay entitled "Graduation Day," published in June 1884, he advocates the education of women so that they can be adequate counterparts to male citizens: "Thus, when a man has need of one who understands his sorrow, admires his virtue, and stimulates his mind, he will not have to go searching outside of his home, as now."[10] He then employs the metaphor of nature to man when he compares a tree putting roots in the ground to the husband being able to sink his "roots into [the] warm and loving soul" of a woman. The reader then witnesses the metonymy of images of gender onto nation when Martí argues that the feminine should be a necessary component in the national image: "Moreover, like water, nations seek a level surface. Every nation, if it is to save itself, requires a certain component of feminine intellect and qualities. Just as no child is born without a father and mother, so there is no nation without happy communion between the virile and feminine elements of the spirit. Though unaware of their own excess, the nations are dying of a hypertrophied strength that bewilders and intoxicates them, makes them haughty and causes pain and upheaval, just as a hypertrophying of feeling and art would weaken them and make them effeminate."[11] In his many essays and in his novel, *Amistad funesta,* Martí urges his readers not to indulge in the excesses of materialism that he had previously identified in the North American soul. In the previous passage, he identifies both the "hypertrophied strength" and the "hypertrophying of feeling and art" to be inadequate characteristics of the ideal national subject. Thus, in his utopian project of nation, Martí advocates an even balance of feminine and masculine characteristics.

Rómulo Gallegos's *Doña Bárbara* reveals similar goals in that it also visually portrays an exaggerated appropriation of power that is easier to envision when these pathological masculinist characteristics pertain to a woman. Images of inappropriate quantities of masculine traits are envisioned on this overly seductive, overtly masculine woman, which was a conceptualization of the female that was not widely accepted in the beginning of the twentieth century. His recodification of gender codes in the novel signal the need for a redistribution of power on the national scale as he promotes his new national male image. Although Gallegos replaces one patriarchal system for another, his promotion of an ambiguously or more bigendered national subject, which encompasses both masculine characteristics of *machismo* and traditional feminine characteristics of nurturing, provide a revolutionary national model in this early twentieth-century text.

A bisexual reading of Asturias's dictator novel reveals an open-ended text that revels in the explosion of signs and language, whose principal motive can be that of the dissolution of binary oppositions.[12] His subversion of the patriarchal regime of the president is complemented by his recognition of a feminine order in crisis, suffering under a patented male-dominated regime. Asturias's female characters, as well as the subalterns that refuse to ingest the symbolic order of law and language in the novel, form a means of resistance that shows some sense of hope for the future. Miguel Cara de Ángel's untraditional position as the (national) hero of the novel provides an impetus for the break from the symbolic order of the president. Although he is destined to die within this order, the dissolution of binary oppositions throughout the novel releases the determinacy of fixed meanings characteristic of language based on patriarchal thought. His movement towards the presymbolic space of the mother's body by his association and love for Camila, posits him in a genderless space of love that can be compared with Cixous' bisexual subject. Asturias's novel differs from others discussed in this work in that he does not attempt to implement a new order that would replace the old. His innovative approach of dismantling language as the principal power source of the dictator disrupts the binary nature of language and its dominance over the speaking subject. Similarly his parodization of the patriarchal figure of the president in the novel serves as a critique of the masculinist hegemonic nature of dictators, whose accumulation of power is based on the subordination of the feminine.[13]

In an age when gender and sex are perceived to move away from the biological essence of the body, one can more easily see how concepts of gender pass through the bodies politic, revealing more clearly that gender is often manifested by the discourse of power. In the texts included in this study, the oppositional writers have contested masculinist hegemonic institutions and have advocated for a bigendered space of the nation. Many have employed visual representations to show the extreme to which a masculinist regime has gone.

Returning to Diana Taylor's reaction to the violent erotic reenactment of power in Pavlovsky's *Paso de dos,* I must ask myself: "Is the opposition equally guilty of emasculating, feminizing and marginalizing the 'Other'" in the national struggle for identity, as Diana Taylor suggested? If so what are the underlying reasons behind this gendered reversal of power? In the case of *Paso de dos,* Pavlovsky employs a grotesque visual representation of the gendered oppressive force of power over the subaltern who was emasculated, feminized, and powerless during the military junta in Argentina. However, I must conclude that this was not done to reinforce concepts of power, but to include the audience in what Taylor terms "percepticide," which is the population's reaction to spectacles of power.[14] Pavlovsky, as a trained psychiatrist, must realize that the victim/subaltern has to first acknowledge the problem in order to begin the healing process, and in his play he provokes a collective healing on a national stage. The disturbing complicit actions of the victim highlight the importance of the role of complacency and acceptance within this abusive relation of power. In their works, Echeverría, Martí, Gallegos, and Asturias portray not only the pathological abuse of power within the imposing hegemonic institutions, but also the traditional passive role of the presumabe subalterns in an endeaver to release them from the discourse of power to which they fall victim.

In the conclusion of *Disappearing Acts,* Taylor continues to question the ineffective reaction of those who participate in what she terms percepticide. She argues that the modern viewing audience has learned to disidentify or separate themselves completely with cases of abuse and genocide that are broadcast in today's multimedia. She advocates a better spect-actor, one who does not keep quiet, but speaks out against heinous crimes, such as those committed during the military occupation in Argentina. I argue that, like Pavlovsky, the writers included in this work used visual portrayals of gendered subjects in their endeavor to visually exploit the hegemonic masculinist corruption of power that imposed itself upon the nation. Through their writings they strove to not only educate their readers but also to alter contemporaneous hegemonic forces that threatened their very subjectivity.

Unlike modern versions of percepticide, where the viewer is desensitized to the multiple, endless visual representations of violence, abuse, and genocide that is shown in today's multimedia, late nineteenth- and early twentieth-century writers depended on visual gendered portrayals of the abuse of power as a means of instigating change on the national level. I conclude that gender troping was a strategic endeavor utilized to reverse contemporaneous mechanisms of power within the controlled space of the novel, as well as an effective means of contesting hegemony on a national and/or international scale. As a result, new subjects and spaces were introduced into the literary milieu. As I have discovered, these new subjects and narratives defy traditional perceptions of masculinity and femininity, and thus complement present-day theorizations of gender that both challenge and transcend the confines of biological determinism.

In her book *Reading the Body Politic,* Latin American feminist Amy Kaminsky calls for a broader perception of feminism and more diverse goals. She argues that feminist theory is at an impasse and that the subject is no longer stable because the identity that enables identity politics is in question. When examining the different variables of oppressed women, including race, class, sexuality, ethnicity, age, religion, and geopolitical position, she states: "If we imagine them as the grid of an intricate plaid we can see women separated out from each other, but also woven together into an elaborate pattern."[15] However, given the innumerable circumstances of hegemonic masculinst institutions and forms of government throughout history and across the national spectrum, including expansionism, imperialism, dictatorships, and world leaders such as Adolph Hitler, who advocated genocide based on xenophobia and difference, can we not include "feminized" men into this intricate pattern of representation of the oppressed? In speaking of the geopolitical notion of gender and gender politics, should we not alter our stance from separate and individual disciplines to a unified front, including diverse types and disciplines, against these excessive masculinist forms of leadership that shape our ways of perceiving the world within a biased oppositional perception of Us versus Them? Should we not promote evolving forms of masculinity that accompany progressive forms of femininity in an attempt to level the playing field?

When speaking of Latin American feminism, Kaminsky states: "Connected as it is to a progressive, usually leftist, political program, Latin American feminism does not see itself as eternally oppositional. It struggles toward change, confident that change can occur" (26). Under the umbrella of (Latin American) feminism in this passage, could we not argue that Echeverría, Martí, Gallegos, and Asturias advocated for similar goals? In the diverse categorization of oppositional discourses that seem to be cropping up like weeds in all fields of study, perhaps a more thorough approach when embarking on an academic work would be to look for the commonalities between disciplines that can complement our works and help us achieve our objectives.

Notes

Preface

1. Excluding Cuba, which did not gain its independence from Spain until 1898.

2. My use of *hegemony* is based on Antonio Gramsci's modern concept of the term, which expresses not only the interests of a ruling class, but also the acceptance of the status quo by those subordinated to it. See Raymond Williams, *Marxism and Literature* (Oxford: Oxford University Press, 1977).

3. In "Lucía: ¿funesta?" Juan Carlos González Espitia explores the political implications of Martí's intention of changing the novel's title from *Amistad funesta* to *Lucía Jerez* and signing the novel with his own name. This work will be discussed further in chapter 2, part 1.

4. An exception is Roberto González Echevarría's analysis of *Doña Bárbara,* which departs from traditional readings and offers a profound rethinking of the novel. See Roberto González Echevarría, *Voice of the Masters: Writing and Authority in Modern Latin American Narrative* (Austin: University of Texas Press, 1985).

Introduction

1. Diana Taylor, *Disappearing Acts: Spectacles of Gender and Nationalism in Argentina's "Dirty War"* (Durham, NC: Duke University Press, 1997) and Eduardo A. Pavlovsky, *Paso de dos* (Buenos Aires: Ediciones Búsqueda de Ayllu, 1990).

2. Esteban Echeverría, "El matadero," in *El matadero, ensayos estéticos y prosa varia,* ed., Fernando Burgos (Hanover, NH: Ediciones del Norte, 1992), 55–105.

3. Translations from "The Slaughterhouse" are from Seymour Menton, *The Spanish American Short Story: A Critical Anthology* (Los Angeles: UCLA Latin American Center Publications, 1980), 3–22.

4. A *chiripá* is a course blanket worn by the *gauchos* over their trousers and tied between their legs (Menton 9).

5. Elaine Showalter, *Speaking of Gender* (New York: Routledge, 1989), 3.

6. Anne Cranny-Francis, *Engendered Fiction: Analysing Gender in the Pro-*

duction and Reception of Texts (Kensington, NSW, Australia: NSWU Press, 1992), 1.

7. Toril Moi, ed., *Sexual/Textual Politics: Feminist Literary Theory* (London: Routledge, 1985).

8. "Una polaridad de opuestos basada en la analogía sexual organiza nuestra lengua y a través de ella, dirige nuestra manera de percibir el mundo." Sara Castro-Klarén, "La crítica literaria feminista y la escritora en América Latina," in *La sartén por el mango. Encuentro de escritoras latinoamericanas,* ed., Patricia González and Elena Ortega (Río Piedras, Argentina: Ediciones Huracán, 1985), 29.

9. "La lógica binaria que separa al hombre de la mujer también se establece dentro del discurso del poder." Francine Masiello, "Discurso de mujeres, lenguaje del poder: reflexiones sobre la crítica feminista a mediados de la década del 80," *Hispamérica* 45 (1986): 54.

10. Sara Castro-Klarén, Sylvia Molloy, and Beatriz Sarlo, eds., *Women's Writing in Latin America: An Anthology* (Boulder, CO: Westview Press, 1991), 16.

11. Sara Castro-Klarén, "The Novelness of a Possible Poetics for Women," in *Cultural and Historical Grounding for Hispanic and Luso-Brazilian Feminist Literary Criticism,* ed., Hernan Vidal (Minneapolis, MN: Institute for the Study of Ideologies and Literature, 1989), 95–106.

12. Judith Butler, *Gender Trouble: Feminism and the Subversion of Identity* (New York: Routledge, 1990).

13. The use of gendered language in the formation of (national) identity is by no means a new concept, only one that is being examined more closely in this work in relation to the formation of ambiguously gendered national subjects. For an analysis of the incorporation of gender bias in the formation of US politics, see Mark E. Kann, *The Gendering of American Politics: Founding Mothers, Founding Fathers, and Political Patriarchy* (Westport, CT: Praeger Publishers, 1999).

14. In *The Conquest of America: The Question of the Other,* Tzvetan Todorov points to Columbus's perception of the Indians as "culturally virgin" or "a blank page awaiting the Spanish and Christian inscription" (New York: Harper Perennial, 1992), 36.

15. Todorov, *The Conquest of America,* 35.

16. According to Toril Moi, Aristotle described the female "by virtue of a certain lack of qualities," and he added that we should regard the female nature as "afflicted with a natural defectiveness" (xv).

17. Christopher Columbus, *Diaro. The voyage of Christopher Columbus: Columbus's Own Journal of Discovery,* trans., John Cummins (New York: St. Martin's Press, 1992), 111 and 152.

18. In his letter to Isabella and Ferdinand October 16, 1492, Columbus writes that the Amerindians are disposed "to be made to build cities, to be taught to wear clothes and to adopt our customs" (Todorov, *The Conquest of America,* 43).

19. Octavio Paz, *El laberinto de soledad* (México City: Fondo de Cultura Económica, 1959). Translation of this work is found in Octavio Paz, *The Labyrinth of Solitude: Life and Thought in Mexico,* trans., Lysander Kemp (New York: Grove Press, 1962).

20. According to John Charles Chasteen, nativism was the winning strategy for independence-minded Creoles because it glorified the idea of an American identity based on birthplace before nations existed in Latin America. See John Charles Chasteen, *Born in Blood and Fire: A Concise History of Latin America* (New York: Norton, 2001), 105.

21. Tulio Halperín Donghi, "Argentine Counterpoint: Rise of the Nation, Rise of the State," in *Beyond Imagined Communities: Reading and Writing the Nation in Nineteenth-Century Latin America,* ed. Sara Castro Klarén and John Charles Chasteen (Washington, D.C.: Woodrow Wilson Center Press, 2003), 38.

22. David Bushnell, *The Emergence of Latin America in the Nineteenth Century* (New York: Oxford University Press, 1994), 121.

23. Ibid., 124.

24. Ibid., 120.

25. Ibid., 123.

26. Ibid., 124.

27. Juan Carlos Mercado, *Building a Nation: The Case of Echeverría* (Lanham, MD: University Press of America, 1995), 76.

28. Bushnell, *The Emergence of Latin America in the Nineteenth Century,* 126.

29. Ibid., 30.

30. Halperín Donghi, "Argentine Counterpoint," 46.

31. Ibid.

32. Quoted in José B. Álverez, "The Dialectics of Homoeroticism in Cuban Narrative," in *Chicano/Latino Homoerotic Identities* (New York: Garland, 1999), 247.

33. Michael Aronna, *Pueblos enfermos: The Discourse of Illness in the Turn of the Century Spanish and Latin American National Essay* (North Carolina Studies in the Romance Languages and Literatures, no. 262. Chapel Hill: UNC Department of Romance Languages, 1999), 16.

34. Ibid., 16.

35. Hegel, Georg Wilhelm Friedrich, *Lectures on the Philosophy of World History: Introduction, Reason in History,* trans. H. B. Nisbet (Cambridge: Cambridge University Press, 1980), 164–65.

36. Aronna, *Pueblos enfermos,* 16.

37. Ibid.

38. These two nineteenth-century philosophers were known for their extreme pessimism and their misogynist views. While Schopenhauer saw woman as a complete subordinate, Nietzsche linked her in her sexuality to a jungle beast that could only be tamed through violence. See Sander L. Gilman, *Difference and Pathology: Stereotypes of Sexuality, Race, and Madness* (Ithaca, NY: Cornell University Press, 1985), 71.

39. Aronna, *Pueblos enfermos,* 19–20.

40. Mercado, *Building a Nation,* 55.

41. Ibid.

42. Nicolas Shumway, *The Invention of Argentina* (Berkeley: University of California Press, 1991), 34.

43. Ibid., 112.

44. Quoted in Shumway, *The Invention of Argentina,* 37.

45. Ibid. Shumway observes that although Alberdi modified these racial comments in later chapters, he duly notes that "as indicators of a generational view, his words are self-explanatory" (37).

46. Quoted in Shumway, 126–27.

47. Domingo Faustino Sarmiento, *Facundo: civilización y barbarie* (Madrid: Cátedra, 1990).

48. Doris Sommer, *Foundational Fictions: The National Romances of Latin America* (Berkeley: University of California Press, 1991), 67.

49. Translations from this text are from Domingo Faustino Sarmiento, *Life in the Argentine Republic in the Days of the Tyrants; or, Civilization and Barbarism* (New York: Hafner, 1960).

50. Mercado, *Building a Nation,* 82.

51. José Piedra, "Nationalizing Sissies," in *Entiendes¿: Queer Readings, Hispanic Writings,* ed., Emilie L. Bergmann and Paul Julian Smith (Durham, NC: Duke University Press, 1995), 372.

52. Kathleen Lois Johnson, "Reflections in the Text: Self Portraits in Selected Modernist Novels" (PhD diss., University of North Carolina, Chapel Hill, 2001), 14.

53. Sommer, *Foundational Fictions,* 87.

54. Michel Foucault, *The History of Sexuality,* trans., Robert Hurley (New York: Vintage Books, 1990), 11 and 54.

55. Mikhail Mikhailovich Bakhtin, *The Dialogic Imagination,* ed., Michael Holquist, trans., Caryl Emerson and Michael Holquist (Austin: University of Texas Press, 1990), 293.

56. Charles Darwin, *The Descent of Man and Selection in Relation to Sex* (Princeton, NJ: Princeton University Press, 1981), 328–29. In this popular scientific treatise, Darwin attributes the superiority of man over woman to natural selection (the general struggle for life) or sexual selection (the contest of rival males). He states: "They [men] generally have to undergo, during manhood, a severe struggle in order to maintain themselves and their families; and this will tend to keep up or even increase their mental powers, and, as a consequence, the present inequality between the sexes" (329).

57. Elaine Showalter, *The Female Malady: Women, Madness, and Culture in England, 1830–1980* (New York: Pantheon Books, 1985), 122.

58. Ibid.

59. Ibid.

60. Sharon Magnarelli, *The Lost Rib: Female Characters in the Spanish-American Novel* (Lewisburg, MD: Bucknell University Press, 1985), 15.

61. The majority of the theorizations of gender discussed in the following sections became popular after the publications of *El matadero* and *Facundo* and will be utilized for the analysis of the three novels discussed in detail in the subsequent chapters: José Martí's *Amistad funesta* (1885), Rómulo Gallegos's *Doña Bárbara* (1929), and Miguel Ángel Asturias's *El Señor Presidente* (1946).

62. Georges Didi-Huberman, *Invention of Hysteria: Charcot and the Photographic Iconography of the Salpêtrière,* trans., Alisa Hartz (Cambridge, MA: MIT University Press, 2003), xi.

63. Showalter, *The Female Malady,* 148.

64. Didi-Huberman, *Invention of Hysteria,* xi. Although men also suffered from hysteria, they were not admitted to the Salpêtrière Hospital until 1881 and were not photographed until 1888. Even so, hysteria continued to be associated with the feminine and the asylum as the "medicalized inversion of the brothel" (Didi-Huberman 80).

65. Showalter, *The Female Malady,* 151.

66. Cesare Lombroso, *The Female Offender* (New York: Appleton, 1895), xvi.

67. Gilman, *Difference and Pathology,* 25.

68. The perception of the black female during the nineteenth century was based on her having a "primitive" sexual appetite, explicated by her "primitive" genitalia. Eighteenth-century travelers to Southern Africa, including François Levaillant and John Barrow, had described the "Hottentot apron," a hypertrophy of the labia and nymphae caused by the manipulation of the genitalia, a characteristic considered beautiful among the Hottentots and Bushman (Gilman 85).

69. Gilman, *Difference and Pathology,* 85.

70. Ibid., 105.

71. Quoted in Gilman, *Difference and Pathology,* 105.

72. Gilman, *Difference and Pathology,* 105.

73. Ibid., 102. A. J. B Parent-Duchatelet, the most widely read anthropological expert of the early nineteenth century in Paris, argued that the "peculiar plumpness" of prostitutes was due to "the great number of hot baths that the major part of these women take" or perhaps to their lassitude, rising at ten or eleven in the morning, "leading an animal life" (quoted in Gilman 94).

74. Ibid., 102.

75. Ibid., 105.

76. In Pablo Picasso's 1901 version of Olympia, she is presented as a sexualized black woman with broad hips and revealed genitalia. Gilman argues that Picasso based his reading of Olympia on the image of the primitive female as sexual object as found in the lower-class prostitutes painted by Van Gogh and the Tahitian maidens painted by Gauguin (102).

77. While Parent-Duchatelet denies that prostitution alters the genitalia, he does observe that prostitutes are subject to certain pathologies, including tumors, abscesses, and the gradual development through disease of an altered appearance (95).

78. Quoted in Bram Dijkstra, *Idols of Perversity: Fantasies of Feminine Evil in Fin-de-siècle Culture* (New York: Oxford University Press, 1986), 14.

79. Johnson, "Reflections in the Text," iii.

80. Cathy Login Jrade, *Modernismo, Modernity and the Development of Spanish American Literature* (Austin: University of Texas Press, 1998), 69.

81. Allen, Esther, ed., *José Martí: Selected Writings* (New York: Penguin Books, 2002), 70.

82. Maureen Ahern, ed., *A Rosario Castellanos Reader: An Anthology of Her Poetry, Short Fiction, Essays, and Drama* (Austin: University of Texas Press, 1988).

83. Jean Franco, "Beyond Ethnocentrism: Gender, Power, and the Third-World Intelligentsia," in *Marxism and the Interpretation of Culture,* ed., Cary Nelson and Lawrence Grossberg (Urbana: University of Illinois Press, 1988), 503–15.

84. Debra A. Castillo, *Talking Back: Toward a Latin American Feminist Literary Criticism* (Ithaca, NY: Cornell University Press, 1992), 16.

85. Francine Masiello, *Between Civilization and Barbarism: Women, Nation and Literary Culture in Modern Argentina* (Lincoln: University of Nebraska Press, 1982), 92.

86. Doris Sommer also notes that roughly between 1850 and 1880, romances were projecting civil societies through patriotic heroes who were remarkably feminized and heroines who were remarkably active and resourceful, even though by the end of the novel the women dutifully submitted to their men (15–16).

87. Quoted by Sommer, *Foundational Fictions*, 95.

88. Sommer, *Foundational Fictions*, 83–113. As stated previously, Shumway also notes the unifying motives of the Generation of 37, yet he points out some of their shortcomings, which are made apparent in such paradigmatic texts as *Facundo* and *El matadero*. References to the latter will be made in the conclusion of this work.

89. Ibid., 217–18.

90. Alan Sinfield, *The Wilde Century: Effeminacy, Oscar Wilde, and the Queer Movement* (New York: Columbia University Press, 1994).

91. Ibid., 41.

92. Ibid., 52.

93. Sylvia Molloy, "Too Wilde for Comfort: Desire and Ideology in Fin-de-Siecle Latin America," *Social Text* 31–32 (1992): 187–201.

94. Ibid., 198.

95. Quoted and translated in Sylvia Molloy; "Politics of Posing," in *Hispanisms and Homosexualities*, ed., Sylvia Molloy and Robert McKee Irwin (Durham, NC: Duke University Press, 1998), 149.

96. See Molloy, "Politics of Posing," 141–60.

97. Gilman, *Difference and Pathology*, 94

98. Quoted in Gilman, 95.

99. Quoted in Shoshana Felman, "Women and Madness: The Critical Phallacy," in *Feminisms: An Anthology of Literary Theory and Criticism*, ed., Robyn R. Warhol and Diane Price Herndl, (New Brunswick, NJ: Rutgers University Press, 1991), 6.

100. One must also consider the many Rosas followers, some of whom to this day defend the many accomplishments of his regime. Shumway argues that despite its backwardness and cruelty, Rosas's government was very successful in many ways. The economy grew significantly under his rule, new lands were liberated, and he got along quite well with the British (120). In addition, he enjoyed immense popularity among the masses and even his archrival, Sarmiento, confesses "out of respect for historical truth [that] there was never a government more popular, more desired nor more supported by public opinion" (Sarmiento, *Vida de Juan Facundo Quiroga* 130) (quoted in Shumway 118).

101. John Lynch, *Argentine Dictator: Juan Manuel de Rosas, 1829–1852* (Oxford: Clarendon Press, 1981), 165.

102. Ibid., 201–46.

103. R. W. Connell locates the constitution of hegemonic masculinity in the boy's struggle to establish distance from the mother and negate his own femininity, and the man's need to enforce the subordination of women as the con-

dition of sustaining his own masculinity (27–28). Connell concludes that although masculinity is a rich and plentiful character structure, the "specific richness of hegemonic masculinity is oppressive, being founded on, and enforcing, the subordination of women." See R. W. Connell, *Which Way is Up?: Essays on Sex, Class, and Culture* (Sydney, Australia: Allen and Unwin, 1983).

104. David William Foster refers to the paternalistic authority created by Juan Domingo Perón's masculinist image as general, president, and "Father of the Nation" as a model of hegemonic Western patriarchy. This critic describes Perón as being "hypermasculine" in his implementation of a male authoritarianism and his use of militarism, oppression, and coercion in order to maintain his status of power (*Sexual Textualities* 118–19).

Chapter 1. Feminizing the Other

1. In *Divergent Modernities* (2001), Julio Ramos argues that in the prologue to Juan Antonio Pérez Bonalde's "Niágara," Martí identifies the privatization of art with an exile from the polis and thus "supersedes through the invention of new interventions and reterritorializations" (xxxvii). Through the forging of these new spaces, we begin to see the nature and creation of a sense of *Latinoamericanismo,* or Latin Americanism, that becomes a recurring theme in his later writings. See Julio Ramos, *Divergent Modernities: Culture and Politics in Nineteenth-Century Latin America* (Durham, NC: Duke University Press, 2001).

2. Enrique Anderson Imbert, "La prosa poética de José Martí: a propósito de Amistad funesta," in *Memoria del Congreso de Escritores Martianos; febrero 20 a 27 de 1953* (Havana: Comisión Nacional Organizadora de los Actos y Ediciones del Centenario y del Monumento de Martí, 1953), 579.

3. A detailed account of the use of gender troping in Martí's chronicles and essays will be provided in chapter 1 in order to establish the Cuban patriot's anti-imperialist rhetoric in the early years of his residence in the United States. This will then serve as the foundation for an analysis of parallel political ideas expressed in his novel.

4. Martí used the image of the uncontrollable juggernaut in his essay "El Congreso de Washington," which will be discussed in more detail later in this chapter.

5. Aronna, *Pueblos enfermos,* 13.

6. Ibid., 16. This type of thinking continues the eighteenth-century polemic of the proposed inferiority of Latin America instigated by Georg Louis Leclerc de Buffon. Buffon argued in his *Histoire des quadrupeds* (Paris 1742) that the absence of large animals in America was due to the fact that this continent was the last to emerge from the ocean. As a result of this observation, a heated debate arose about the maturity of the peoples of the Americas in relation to those born in Europe. See María Salgado, "Maniero's *De vitis aliquot mexicanorum* or Biography as Political Agenda," *Dieciocho* 21.2 (1998): 211–12.

7. Beatriz Pita, "Engendering Critique: Race, Class, and Gender in Ruiz de Burton and Martí," in *José Martí's "Our America": From National to Hemi-*

spheric Cultural Studies, ed. Jeffrey Belnap and Raúl Fernández (Durham, NC: Duke University Press, 1998), 129–44.

8. Chasteen, *Born in Blood and Fire,* 114.

9. Mary Louise Pratt, *Imperial Eyes: Travel Writing and Transculturalization* (London: Routledge, 1992), 113.

10. Ibid., 125.

11. Ibid., 126.

12. Otis A. Singletary, *The Mexican War* (Chicago: The University of Chicago Press, 1960), 14.

13. Ibid., 150.

14. Robert W. Johannsen, *To the Halls of the Montezumas: The Mexican War in the American Imagination* (New York: Oxford University Press, 1985), 165. Years later in an article published in a Mexico City newspaper entitled "The Cutting Case" (1886), Martí addresses a conflict that occurred on the US-Mexican border and refers to the "ignorance to which the great majority of this country remains to the respect of the originality, resilience, intelligence, hardships, strengths and hard work that make Mexico a country to be respected." He then adopts a unison voice of all Latin Americans with regard to erroneous perceptions held by US officials of Latin Americans as he states: "They think we are sugar-coated, vice-ridden peoples, devoid of the titanic force that, in enormous struggles, we have long manifested." See José Martí, *Selected Writings* (New York: Penguin Books, 2002), 182.

15. Singletary, *The Mexican War,* 161.

16. Martha Menchaca, "Chicano Indianism: A Historical Account of Racial Repression in the United States," *American Ethnologist* 20.3 (1993): 586.

17. Allen Nevins, *Hamilton Fish: The Inner History of the Grant Administration* (New York: Dodd, Mead, 1936), 180.

18. Jules R. Benjamin, *The United States and the Origins of the Cuban Revolution: An Empire of Liberty in an Age of National Liberation* (Princeton, NJ: Princeton University Press, 1990), 8.

19. In *The American Chronicles of José Martí,* Susana Rotker states: "Martí is the exile who looks and comments upon the structure of power that has rejected and threatened to silence him. In the act of observing/writing, he recreates . . . not only the system of representation but also the means of appropriating elements of the dominant culture from a different location and impregnating them with alternate, independent meanings" (95).

20. José Martí, "The Truth about the United States," in *José Martí Reader: Writings on the Americas,* ed., Deborah Shnookal and Mirta Muñiz (Melbourne, Australia: Ocean Press, 1999), 173.

21. Pita, "Engendering Critique," 142.

22. Quoted in Pita, "Engendering Critique," 142.

23. John M. Kirk, "José Martí and the United States: A Further Interpretation," *Journal of Latin American Studies* 9.2 (November 1977): 275–90.

24. Quoted in Kirk, "José Martí and the United States," 285.

25. Unless otherwise indicated, all translations of José Martí's works including his novel, *Amistad funesta,* are my own.

26. Kirk claims that the two contributing factors that led to Martí's radicalization towards the United States were the first Inter-American Conference in

1889 and the International Monetary Conference in 1891. In the Inter-American Conference, Latin American delegates were persuaded of the value of having closer ties with the "most powerful country in the Americas" (285). Kirk states: "The American press continually listed the advantages to be gained by the various Latin American Republics through closer ties with the United States, while at the same time advocating hard-line treatment for those countries that turned down such an opportunity" (285–86). During the second conference, Latin American countries were encouraged to sever their economic ties with Europe and to increase their trade with North America (286).

27. See Philip S. Foner, ed., *Inside the Monster: Writings on the United States and American Imperialism,* trans., Elinor Randall, Luis A. Baralt, Juan de Onís, and Roslyn Held (New York: Monthly Review Press, 1975), 41; and Susana Rotker, *The American Chronicles of José Martí: Journalism and Modernity in Spanish America* (Hanover, NH: University Press of New England, 2000), 85.

28. Susana Rotker, "The Political Gaze," in *José Martí's "Our America": From National to Hemispheric Cultural Studies,* ed., Jeffrey Belnap and Raúl Fernández, 69.

29. Quoted in Foner, *Inside the Monster,* 243.

30. Foner, *Inside the Monster,* 249–51.

31. Quoted in Foner, *Inside the Monster,* 249–51.

32. José Martí, *Obras completas.* vol. 2 (Havana: Editorial Lex, 1946), 1502. Future references to this work will be referred to as *Oc.*

33. David Healy, *James G. Blaine and Latin America* (Columbia: University of Missouri Press, 2001), 5.

34. Quoted in Healy, *James G. Blaine and Latin America,* 5.

35. Healy, *James G. Blaine and Latin America,* 7.

36. Ibid., 1–20.

37. David M Pletcher, *The Awkward Years: American Foreign Relations under Garfield and Arthur* (Columbia: University of Missouri Press, 1962).

38. Ibid., 63–68.

39. Healy, *James G. Blaine and Latin America,* 21–36.

40. Ibid., 54–73.

41. Ibid., 126.

42. Ibid., 127.

43. Ibid.

44. Ibid., 128.

45. Ibid.

46. Quoted in Foner, *Inside the Monster,* 42.

47. Rotker, *The American Chronicles of José Martí,* 84.

48. José Martí, "Prologue to Poema del Niágara," in Julio Ramos's *Divergent Modernities: Culture and Politics in Nineteenth-Century Latin America* (Durham, NC: Duke University Press, 2001), appendix 2, 304–5.

49. Ibid.

50. Rotker, *The American Chronicles of José Martí,* 5.

51. Blanche Zacharie Baralt, *El Martí que yo conocí* (Havana: Centro de Estudios Martianos: Editorial Pueblo y Educación, 1990), 198.

52. Alejandro Mejías-López notes the significant contrast between both char-

acters, specifically with Lucía's relationship to the color black, darkness, depravity, and the telluric. He argues that her name has its origins in Saint Lucy, traditionally known as the patron saint of the blind, or those who cannot see light and are condemned to darkness. See Alejandro Mejías-López, "La novela modernista hispanoamericana: Definición y estudio de sus inicios" (PhD diss., University of Michigan, 1995), 152.

53. José Martí, "Our America," in Julio Ramos's *Divergent Modernities: Culture and Politics in Nineteenth-Century Latin America,* appendix 1, 296.

Chapter 2. Unveiling the Mask

1. Gilman, *Difference and Pathology,* 106.
2. See Aronna, *Pueblos enfermos.*
3. Pedro Pablo Rodríguez, "'Definir, avisar, poner en guardia . . .' Visión Martiana de Estados Unidos en La América," *in José Martí y Los Estados Unidos* (Havana: Centro de Estudios Martianos, 1988), 79–93.
4. In *The American Chronicles of José Martí,* Susan Rotker states that the "transforming gaze" of José Martí was not always accepted by fellow Spanish American men of letters "who were more anxious to live the identification with the United States as a model for their countries' development than to distance themselves from that nation with criticism" (101). Venezuelan Fausto Teodoro Aldrey of *La Opinión Nacional* requested that Martí alter his judgments about the United States, and Argentine Bartolomé Mitre of *La Nación* suppressed entire paragraphs of Martí's works (Rotker 101).
5. *The Pequeño Larousse* defines *intimidad* as: "Amistad íntima" [intimate friendship] giving the example of "vivir en la mayor intimidad con un amigo" [living in great confidence with a friend] (Sinon. *Amistad, confianza, familiaridad* [friendship, confidence, familiarity]) (589).
6. Quoted in Rodríguez, "Definir, avisar, poner en guardia . . . ," 81.
7. Beatriz Pita argues that in "El Congreso de Washington" (1889), Martí "renders the imperialist designs on Latin American via a 'masculinization' of the Anglo-Saxon and the United States, and counters by asserting the equally 'virile' qualities of Latin America" (137). In this later essay written by Martí, the employment of the metaphor of intimacy as well as gendered tropes are utilized in order to persuade his reader of the imminent dangers of a union with the United States: "Es la hora próxima en que le acerque demandando *relaciones íntimas* un pueblo *emprendedor y pujante* que *la* desconoce y *la* desdena. Y como los *pueblos viriles,* que se han hecho de sí propios con la escopeta y la ley, aman y sólo aman a los pueblos viriles" (quoted in Pita, "Engendering Critique," 138; her emphasis).
8. Mauricio Nuñez Rodríguez claims that although this periodical was considered a family magazine directed primarily towards a female audience, its circulation to twenty-two countries in Latin America and the Caribbean reflected a much broader audience, due to its coverage of Latin American topics (10).
9. It is believed that between 1891 and 1892 Martí wrote the prologue to the novel, originally named *Amistad funesta.* He would later rename it *Lucía Jerez,*

signing it with his own name rather than with the pen name Adelaida Baralt. In his studies concerning the novel, González Espitia explores the political implications of the change of title and of signing the novel with his name. This critic addresses this second edition of the novel as being different from the first. Following this line of thought, my study will focus on the first edition, published in *El Latino-Americano* in 1885.

10. In his analysis of the novel, Anderson Imbert addresses the impressionistic and symbolic relevance of the novel (575 and 604–7).

11. All excerpts are taken from José Martí, *Lucía Jerez,* ed. Manuel Pedro González (Madrid: Gredos, 1969). Future references to this text will be abbreviated *LJ.*

12. In the biographical sketch entitled "Charles Darwin" (1882), Martí strategically builds up the reputation of this world-renowned scientist, only so that he can subvert the fervor to which scientific ideology was adopted in the nineteenth century. By carefully linking Darwinist ideas of evolution to his impressions of South America, Martí succeeds in building up the image of Spanish American national identity, as he simultaneously tears down a theory that contributed to negative perceptions of Latin Americans as the subaltern Other.

13. Foner, *Inside the Monster,* 340–42.

14. Ibid.

15. Ibid.

16. I believe that Martí addresses the negative implications of the influence of both the United States and France in the novel; however, due to the intense nature in which he was involved in US elections, government, and foreign relations while residing in the United States, I argue that the imminent threat to which Martí alludes is North America. In *Escenas norteamericanas,* Martí proclaims that the neurosis of Paris is nothing compared to the excessive characteristics of the United States: "'La neurosis de Paris' dicen los diarios de Francia: ¡por qué no han venido a ver esta otra neurosis! . . . Nadie se duerme, nadie se despierta, nadie está sentado; todo es galope, escape, asalto, estrepitosa caída, eminente triunfo" (363).

17. Translation from Schnookal and Muñiz, *José Martí Reader,* 58.

18. Translation from Luis A. Baralt, *Martí on the U.S.A* (Carbondale: Southern Illinois University Press, 1966), 197.

19. José Martí, "Coney Island," in Julio Ramos's *Divergent Modernities: Culture and Politics in Nineteenth-Century Latin America,* appendix 3, 320.

20. Allen, *José Martí: Selected Writings,* 155.

21. Enrique Anderson Imbert claims that Martí's references for [Juan's] speaking and writing poetry, and his struggles for justice, to his necessity for the love of a woman are precise due to the proximity of his model, [which was] in the mirror: "Las referencias a su modo de hablar y de escribir poesía, a sus luchas por la justicia, a su necesidad de amor de mujer son concretas porque el modelo estaba cerca, en el espejo" ("La prosa poética de José Martí," 587).

22. In Martí's biographical sketches of North American poets Ralph Waldo Emerson (1803–82), Walt Whitman (1819–92), and Henry Wadsworth Longfellow (1807–82), he praises these qualities in fellow literary men and holds them above the base desires of the common man in North America.

23. "Esta identidad daña a la novela y disminuye a Juan Jerez, que ni con

mucho alcanza la talla de su creador, pero el lector enterado no puede divorciarlo de él" (*LJ* 42).

24. "Es una de las criaturas apasionadas por querer vivir más y más y, sin embargo, envueltas en un hálito de muerte, en conflicto con sí mismas, vitales anti-racionales, agónicas, paradójicas, con un sentimiento trágico de la vida que la emparienta con las criaturas de Unamuno" (Anderson Imbert, "La prosa poética de José Martí," 106).

25. Quoted in Showalter, *The Female Malady*, 132.

26. In 1879 Maudsley concluded that girls are more likely to suffer during adolescence because their reproductive organs are already fully developed; their physical activity is limited; social limitations require that they refrain from sexual activity before marriage; and their menstrual cycle was believed to be the cause of periodical disturbances (*The Female Malady* 130).

27. In the prologue of *Lucía Jerez*, Martí writes: "En la novela había de haber mucho amor; alguna muerte; muchas muchachas, ninguna pasión pecaminosa; y nada que no fuese del mayor agrado de los padres de familia y de los señores sacerdotes" (González 37).

28. Showalter, *The Female Malady*, 133.

29. Jaqueline Cruz, "Esclava vencedora: la mujer en la obra literaria de José Martí," *Hispania* 75.1 (March 1992): 30.

30. José Martí, *Obras completas en los Estados Unidos* (Havana: Editorial Nacional de Cuba, 1963), 299.

31. Ibid.

32. Many Latin American leaders following independence had appropriated French philosopher Auguste Comte's (1798–1847) theory of positivism. In his prologue to "Niágara" Martí utilizes the metaphor of the "surgeon's scalpel" in order to criticize the sterile tendencies of this movement, which he argued would lead to the deformation and death of poetic verses (Ramos 313). According to Ramos, the critique of positivism was a frequent theme in the literary field since the 1880s because it prohibited the emergence of new ideas and ignored the more spiritual side of the formation of the subject (xxxix).

33. Cruz, "Esclava vencedora," 31.

34. Allen, *José Martí: Selected Writings*, 156

35. Louis A. Pérez, Jr., *Cuba and the United States: Ties of Singular Intimacy* (Athens: University of Georgia Press, 2003), xvi.

36. After the Ten Year War (1868–78) Cuba had lost former sugar markets and suffered an economic depression that would continue into the 1880s (Pérez, *Ties of Singular Intimacy* 55–56).

37. In *Ties of Singular Intimacy* (2003), Louis Pérez, Jr., examines the interrelated interests of both Cuba and the United Sates. He states: "North Americans considered Cuba essential to the politico-military security of the United States; Cubans looked upon the United States as vital to the socioeconomic well-being of the island. Through the nineteenth century, Cubans became increasingly dependent upon the United States as a market, as a provider of consumer goods and foodstuffs, as a source of credit and capital, and as a defender of the status quo" (xvi).

38. In her analysis of the novel, Joan Torres-Pou notes the highly erotic nature of this scene. See Joan Torres-Pou, "El e[x]terno femenino: aspectos de

la representación de la mujer en la literatura latinoamericana del siglo XIX" (PhD diss., Emory University, 1998).

39. "Los regalos que le hace a Sol son su forma de reducir sus remordimientos por los grandes celos que siente y son una forma de manipular a Sol." See Rosalinda Gayoso Wright, "Un estudio psicológico de la caracterización en Amistad funesta" (PhD diss., Florida State University, 1996), 67.

40. Showalter, *The Female Malady,* 148.

41. Ibid., 150.

42. Ibid., 130.

43. In *Idols of Perversity,* Bram Dijkstra claims that a common depiction of hysteria in nineteenth-century art was women admiring their reflection in mirrors or in water images. He states: "These were the hysterics, the womb-driven women, forever narcissistically in search of their own reflection. . . . Their disposition is profoundly egotistical, and their absorbing preoccupation with themselves makes them love scandal and a public sensation" (219).

44. Showalter, *The Female Malady,* 130.

45. Ibid.

46. Ibid., 134.

47. José Martí, *Obras escogidas, tomo dos* (Havana: Editora Política, 1979), 83.

48. Ibid., 87.

49. During the nineteenth century, many Cubans and US officials believed that Cuba would be annexed to the United States (Pérez 2003, 36–43).

50. Olga Uribe, "La mujer como invención de lo posible," *Revista de Crítica Literaria Latinoamericana* 5.30 (1989): 27.

51. See González Espitia, "Lucía: ¿funesta?" 10.

52. Keja Lys Valens, "Between Women: Desire in Caribbean Literatures" (PhD diss., Harvard University, 2004).

Part II. Loosening the Grips of Hegemony through Narrative

1. Nicholas Abercrombie, Stephen Hill, and Bryan S. Turner, eds., *The Penguin Dictionary of Sociology* (London: Penguin 2000), 162.

2. David William Foster and Diana Taylor have scrutinized the use of gender in the governmental regimes of Juan Domingo Perón (1895–1974) and the military junta of the "Dirty War" in Argentina (1976–83), arguing that authoritarian masculinity was a significant feature in exerting and maintaining control over the people. Furthermore, in his book *Which Way Is Up?* masculinist theorist R. W. Connell states: "To sustain masculinity and male power on the largest scale requires an arbitrary differentiation among men that constructs some of them as hyper-masculine and others as effeminate" (76).

3. See Taylor, *Disappearing Acts,* 9.

4. Wilfred L Guerin, *A Handbook of Critical Approaches to Literature* (New York: Oxford University Press, 1999), 334.

5. "Pero en el siglo XX se intenta más bien elaborar sujetos masculinos nacionales en espacios rurales que rescaten un espíritu nacional que va desa-

pareciendo, luchen contra la intervención económica y política foránea, neutralicen la hegemonía cultural del gigante del Norte, y retraten el carácter latino de las culturas no-anglosajonas de este continente" (my translation). See César Valverde, "Masculinidad en la narrativa hispanoamericana: Hegemonía, transgresión y desconstrucción" (PhD diss., University of California, 1997), 128.

6. Julie Skurski attests that critics widely viewed *Doña Bárbara* as a nationalist reworking of prevailing positivist notions of progress and regarded it as a descendent of Domingo Sarmiento's 1845 denunciation of rural *caudillismo, Facundo:* "Sarmiento, an Argentine reformer and statesman, had also promoted popular education and was once president of his country. However, he sought to imitate and import European and US models of progress and disparaged the rural population." See Julie Skurski, "The Ambiguities of Authenticity in Latin America: *Doña Bárbara* and the Construction of National Identity," *Poetics Today* 15.4 (Winter 1994): 619.

7. Foster, *Sexual Textualities,* 118–19.

8. See part 1.

9. In "Rómulo Gallegos's *Doña Bárbara:* Toward a Radical Reading" (1993), Claudette Rosegreen-Williams presents a more radical reading of the novel and examines the racist, sexist, and class-related undertones found in the narrative. She argues that Gallegos has essentially succeeded in replacing one feudal system for another. She states: "He [Gallegos] has cleverly dissimulated the ulterior motive behind his stated nationalistic intentions, and his whole project becomes tainted with more than a little hypocrisy. . . . He will merely replace feudal anarchy with feudal order" (284).

10. For Butler, gender differs from sex in that sex is biologically determined, while gender is socially constructed.

11. Williams, *Marxism and Literature,* 109–11.

Chapter 3. "Transgendering"

1. See Part I.

2. "Novelas como *Don Segundo Sombra* y *Doña Bárbara,* ante la amenaza de la fragmentación nacional y la penetración de fronteras establecidas, busquen crear una fuerte identidad argentina y venezolana a través de personajes masculinos fuertes y emprendedores" (Valverde 129; my translation). Unless otherwise noted, all translations referring to the novel are mine, excluding translations of the text itself.

3. Quoted in Carlos J. Alonso, "'Otra sería mi historia:' Allegorical Exhaustion in *Doña Bárbara,*" *Modern Language Notes* 104.2 (March 1989): 1.

4. Juan Liscano cites the three planes of Doña Bárbara as personal, symbolic, and mythical: "a su existencia de mujerona frustrada," "representación de vida salvaje y feudal, como personificación de la llanura," and "la Fémina primordial . . . emparentada con Kali y Lamia, con Lilith y Coatlicue" (quoted in Shaw). See Donald Leslie Shaw, *Gallegos: Donã Bárbara* (London: Grant and Cutler, 1972), 44.

5. Sommer, *Foundational Fictions,* 278.

6. Shaw, *Gallegos: Donã Bárbara,* 11
7. Quoted in Alonso, "Otra sería mi historia," 420.
8. Butler, *Gender Trouble,* 10; emphasis in the original.
9. Rómulo Gallegos, *Doña Bárbara* (Madrid: Cátedra, 1997). All references to this work will be addressed as *DB.* All translations will be taken from *Donã Bárbara,* trans. Robert Malloy (New York: Cape and Smith, 1931).
10. The alligator named "el tuerto del Bramador" is symbolic of Doña Bárbara or "la devoradora de hombres." Later on in the text, after Doña Bárbara gradually adopts feminine characteristics, Santos's ranch hands succeed in killing the dreaded animal, which symbolizes her future demise. At this point in the text, Santos had not yet acquired the necessary *hombría* needed to kill the animal himself, despite his good shot.
11. In chapter 10, part 1 the *cacique* of the aborigines placed a curse on the family and its descendants for having stolen their land. The subsequent family quarrels leading to murder and separation can be considered in the novel as a testimony to that curse (93).
12. Marit Melhuus, "Power, Value and the Ambiguous Meanings of Gender," in *Machos, Mistresses, Madonnas: Contesting the Power of Latin American Gender Imagery,* ed., Marit Melhuus and Kristi Anne Stolen (New York: Verso, 1996), 242.
13. Ibid.
14. Doug Yarrington, "Cattle, Corruption, and Venezuelan State Formation during the Regime of Juan Vicente Gómez, 1908–35," *Latin American Research Review* 38.2 (June 2003): 13.
15. Connell claims that the key point of Freud's theory of the fear of castration is the crisis of emotions that leads up to the identification with the father and the eventual substitution of other women for the little boy's attachment to the mother: "[The fear of castration] is not the fear of a particular mutilation, but the threat of the loss of sexual identity" (Connell, *Which Way is Up?* 26).
16. González Echevarría notes that because La Chusmita lies outside of the legal boundary lines, it is considered androgynous: "The palm grove is not a simple origin, a principle giving beginning out of which authority can be spun, but a divided origin: life/death, male/female, inside/outside, beginning/end" (*Myth and Archive,* 53).
17. Moi, *Sexual/Textual Politics,* 108.
18. González Echevarría asserts that Santos, as a lawyer, specializes in the encoding and interpretation of language in its relation to reality (*Voice of the Masters* 48). He argues that while Santos is moved by a need to fix meaning in writing [according to the law], Doña Bárbara "is motivated by the contradictory wish to eradicate all marks and thus induce a chaos of marks and boundaries" (49).
19. In her chapter "Feminism and Hysteria," in *The Female Malady,* Showalter shows how Darwinian psychiatrists classified women who did not follow traditional standards of femininity as "abnormal" or suffering from hysteria.
20. Connell, *Which Way is Up?* 27–28.
21. Jonathan Alexander, "Transgender Rhetorics: (Re) Composing Narratives of the Gendered Body," *College Composition and Communication* 57.1 (2005): 3–4.

22. Eve Kosofsky Sedgwick, *Between Men: English Literature and Male Homosocial Desire* (New York: Columbia University Press, 1985).

23. R. W. Connell, "Masculinities": Reply (in Symposium on R. W. Connell's "Masculinities") *Gender and Society* 12. 4 (August 1998): 476.

24. Ibid., 475.

25. R. W. Connell locates the constitution of hegemonic masculinity in the boy's struggle to establish distance from the mother and negate his own femininity and the man's need to enforce the subordination of women as the condition of sustaining his own masculinity (28). He argues that this form of masculinity, albeit representative of capitalism and most contemporary social institutions, "is by no means evenly spread among men" (*Which Way is Up?* 42).

26. R. W. Connell, "A Whole New World: Remaking Masculinity in the Context of the Environmental Movement," *Gender and Society* 4.4 (December 1990): 454.

27. In chapter 2, part 2 "Los amansadores," Santos is portrayed as a kind and gentle educator of Marisela. In this chapter he is depicted for his spiritual, feminine side as opposed to the rugged *macho* activities displayed in the *llano.* Santos even helps Marisela to design dresses, providing them with excessive details: He states: "Esto me ha resultado un poco sobrecargado. Tiene de todo, alforzas, faralaes" (148).

28. Yarrington claims that Gómez established a tremendous variety of business partnerships with other state officials throughout his political career, but partnerships in the cattle trade always served as the focal point of his economic activity ("Cattle, Corruption, and Venezuelan State Formation . . . " 16).

29. According to Yarrington, the Gómez regime existed fundamentally as a business enterprise to monopolize wealth generated within the agrarian economy and to distribute it among the men who made up the official faction in power. Because these business enterprises relied on political power for their profitability, many of which functioned as partnerships among officials at various levels of the regime's hierarchy, they played a powerful integrative role in consolidating the regime (ibid).

30. Ibid., 71.

31. Ibid.

32. Sommer suggests that Gallegos's writings reflect the positivist ideologues who admired Gómez's paternal position in "a barbarous childlike country like Venezuela" (281). She states: "One wonders if Gallegos admired him [Gómez] too; he certainly admits fascination for the dictator's incarnation into 'the appealing body of a woman' (literally her 'appetizing flesh')" (Sommer 1991, 281).

33. Ernest A. Johnson, Jr., "The Meaning of Civilización and Barbarie in *Doña Bárbara,*" *Hispania* 39. 4 (December 1956): 458.

34. Magnarelli, *The Lost Rib,* 45.

35. Skurski argues that the Creoles did not share a common past with the indigenous people of the nation and they did not embrace Spain because they "saw its legacy as a colonial power as one of social degeneration rather than of community" (611).

36. Quoted in Julie Skurski, "The Ambiguities of Authenticity in Latin America: *Doña Bárbara* and the Construction of National Identity," *Poetics Today* 15.4 (Winter 1994): 615.

37. This idea is representative of Gallegos's legacy to Venezuela in his repeatedly stated motto: "To govern is to educate." See John A. Crow, "The Essays of Rómulo Gallegos," *Hispania* 381 (March 1955): 39.

38. Ernest A. Johnson, Jr., claims: "Santos does not seem as interested in having her [Marisela] taste of the tree of knowledge of good and evil, as he is in having her go beyond that to the feeling from which all else springs: *ternura*. He wants her to have '. . . esa ternura que le falta'" (Johnson 460).

39. All translations pertaining to Gallegos's speech are my own. See Rómulo Gallegos, *Discurso de Rómulo Gallegos,* (Caracas: Imprenta Nacional, 1948), 4.

40. After Gallegos returned to Venezuela in 1935, he was named minister of education, a position in which he served until he was elected president by 72 percent of the vote in 1948. Gallegos ruled for only eight months, after which he was overthrown by a reactionary military coup. See Crow, "The Essays of Rómulo Gallegos," 38.

41. Quoted in Crow, "The Essays of Rómulo Gallegos," 37.

42. Ibid.

43. Skurski attests that gender played a crucial role during the independence years. The male military hero was portrayed as the virile defender of abused national honor, and territory became the sacred icon of independent nationhood (614).

44. It is also Marisela's expertise as a plainswoman that posits her as an authority of Santos's shot. She, like Santos, has evolved, but she maintains significant features of her upbringing in the *llano* that will assist her in her new role of the female counterpart to the ideal national male subject. Thus, gender codes are not restored to their original status, but remain hybrid, reflecting the amalgam nature of the *mestizo* in the promoted national image.

45. In chapter 2, part 2, Gallegos affirms that Marisela's presence serves as a means of maintaining his spiritual side, as well as preventing him from falling into the rustic adaptation of the plains life: "Marisela le servía de defensa contra la adaptación a la rustiquez del medio, fuerza incontrastable con que la vida simple y bravía del desierto le imprime su sello a quien se abandona a ella" (150).

46. Magnarelli, *The Lost Rib,* 45.

47. In his essay "Un ejemplo para todos los días," Gallegos states: "Quien recorra algunos kilómetros de este país . . . no llega nunca al término de su viaje sin que le quiten o le atormenten el sueño las visiones de los pueblos tristes y de las vidas mustias ante cuyas miserias pasó" (quoted in Crow, "The Essays of Rómulo Gallegos," 37).

Chapter 4. *Écriture feminine*

1. See Masiello, *Between Civilization and Barbarism,* 89.

2. Unless otherwise noted, all translations referring to *El Señor Presidente* are mine, excluding those of the text itself.

3. Jack Himelblau, "*El Señor Presidente:* Antecedents, Sources, and Reality," *Hispanic Review* 41.1 (Winter 1973): 43–78.

4. Jack Himelblau notes that even though Asturias had completed *El Señor Presidente* in 1939, originally titled *Tohil,* he was unable to publish it until 1946, because the incidents related to Estrada Cabrera could have easily been interpreted as reflecting the dictatorship of Ubico (49).

5. Himelblau, "El Señor Presidente: Antecedents, Sources, and Reality," 45.

6. Miguel Ángel Asturias, *El Señor Presidente* (Buenos Aires: Editorial Losada, 1966), 9. All future references to this text will be referred to as *ESP.*

7. All translations from this work are taken from Miguel Ángel Asturias, *The President,* trans. Frances Partridge (Prospect Heights, IL: Waveland Press, 1963), 11.

8. Teresa McKenna, "Hegemony in *El Señor Presidente:* A Psychoanalytic Perspective," *Mester* 6 (1977): 100.

9. Ibid.

10. "No hay en toda la novelística hispanoamericana ni en toda la novela contemporánea una obra que represente de modo tan extraordinario y turbador la maléfica y ominosa presencia del poder humano absoluto y su aniquiladora influencia," *Historia de la novela hispanoamericana* (Valparaíso, Chile: Ediciones Universitarias de Valparaíso, 1972), 190.

11. González Echevarría, *Myth and Archive,* 65.

12. Hélène Cixous, "The Laugh of the Medusa," in *Feminisms: An Anthology of Literary Theory and Criticism,* ed., Robyn R. Warhol and Diane Price Herndl (New Brunswick, NJ: Rutgers University Press, 1991), 334–49.

13. According to Jacques Derrida, meaning is never truly present, but only constructed through the potentially endless process of referring to other, absent signifiers. The term *différance,* can be translated as both difference and deferral in English and refers to the open-ended play between the presence of one signifier and the absence of another. Derrida's analysis of language subverts Western philosophical tradition that is based on binary oppositions and undermines what Cixous perceives as the prisonhouse of patriarchal language (Moi, *Sexual/Textual Politics,* 107).

14. Ibid., 108.

15. Clara Juncker, "Writing (With) Cixous," *College English* 50.4 (April 1988): 425. This critic states that French feminists are careful to distinguish between biological females and a feminine linguistic position, which can be denoted by the quotation marks around "woman" (426).

16. Cixous, "The Laugh of the Medusa," 339

17. Susan Sellers, ed., *The Hélène Cixous Reader* (New York: Routledge, 1994), 37–39.

18. According to Toril Moi, Cixous is skeptical about the use of the term *feminine writing,* which she argues reinforces the opposing terms, *masculine* and *feminine.* In an effort to move beyond binary oppositions she promotes a bisexuality, which is multiple, variable, and ever-changing, consisting as it does of the "non-exclusion either of the difference or of one sex" (quoted in Moi, 109).

19. Quoted in Moi, *Sexual/Textual Politics,* 101.

20. Ibid., 108.

21. Many critics have noted the contradictions found in Cixous' theory and her inability to escape the binary thought located in language. Diane Price Herndl states: "Feminine writing, nonetheless, is seen here to vary along gen-

der lines, to correspond to culturally determined gender codes: *His* language is rational, logical, hierarchal, and linear; *her* language is a-rational (if not irrational), contra-logical (if not illogical), resistant to hierarchies, and circular" (*Feminisms* 332; emphasis in the original). The focus of this work, however, is to cite the similarities between Cixous' objective in feminine writing and that of Asturias's in his novel.

22. Taylor, *Disappearing Acts,* 34

23. Ibid.

24. Quoted in *Voices from the Silence: Guatemalan Literature of Resistance,* ed., Marc Zimmerman and Raúl Rojas (Athens: Ohio University Center for International Studies, 1998), 133.

25. "El Señor Presidente es una obra que retrata una dictadura que metafóricamente, se puede comparar con la tela de araña en cuyo centro se halla el dictador esperando por los subalteranos quienes caen en su trampa como moscas." See Luisa Elena Flores, "El diálogo del poder y el poder del diálogo en *El Señor Presidente, Yo el Supremo* y *El gran elector*" (PhD diss., University of Louisville, 2001), 16.

26. "Le hace entender que sólo sirve para recibir órdenes tal como recibió el vómito. Mas aun se da cuenta de que para El Señor Presidente él representa una simple mosca atrapada en el telar de su poder." See Orlando Muni, "Dictadura de la muerte en El Señor Presidente" (master's thesis, University of Cincinnati, 1971), 26.

27. Mónica Zapata, "Las duplicidades del sujeto: *El Señor Presidente,*" *La palabra y el hombre* 96 (1995): 237.

28. Richard J. Callan, "Babylonian Mythology in *El Señor Presidente,*" *Hispania* 50.3 (September 1967): 417.

29. Françoise Perus, "Modernity, Postmodernity, and Novelistic Form in Latin America," in *Latin American Identity and Construction of Difference,* ed., Amaryll Chanady (Minneapolis: University of Minnesota Press, 1994), 45.

30. Quoted by Adriana Sandoval, "El primer capítulo de *El Señor Presidente,*" *Cuadernos Americanos* 83 (2000): 211.

31. *Larousse Spanish English Dictionary,* 1999, s. v. "Alumbrar."

32. "El sema negativo evocado por el toque de muertos no está declarado al nivel de palabras, sino al de los fonemas, o sea, al nivel de la articulación del lenguaje" (quoted in Sandoval 211).

33. Ibid., 213.

34. Moi, *Sexual/Textual Politics,* 99.

35. Guerin, *A Handbook of Critical Approaches to Literature,* 204.

36. In chapter 32 the president reveals that if it were not for his mother, Colonel Parrales Sonriente would have eliminated all of the members of the opposition: "Quise y querré siempre a Parrales Sonriente, y lo iba a hacer general, porque potreó a mis paisanos, porque los puso en cintura, se repasó en ellos y de no ser mi madre acaba con todos para vengarme de lo mucho que tengo que sentirles y que sólo yo sé" (208).

37. Quoted in Moi, *Sexual/Textual Politics,* 117.

38. Moi, *Sexual/Textual Politics,* 117.

39. According to Lacanian theory, the imaginary corresponds to the preoedipal period, when the child believes that it is still a part of the mother and per-

ceives no separation between itself and the world. When the speaking subject enters into the symbolic order denoted by the phallus and the law, it must repress the desire for the mother and the imaginary unity with her (Moi 99).

40. Zimmerman and Rojas, *Voices from the Silence,* 139.

41. Foucault, *The History of Sexuality,* 122.

42. Perus, "Modernity, Postmodernity, and Novelistic Form in Latin America," 63.

43. Ibid., 59.

44. "Miguel vuelve a nacer de modo diferente; hay abandono de la forma de vida anterior, y de ese Génesis viaja hacia Apocalipsis, ya que fracasa en su aventura." See Rosado, "La visión trágica," 220.

45. Their marital union was inspired by the Song of Songs, which is an erotic book in the Bible that transcends the logic of language: "A la muerte únicamente se le puede oponer el amor, porque ambos son igualmente fuertes, como dice El Cantar de los Cantares" (198). It is in this space of love, song, and mental refuge that the novel provides resistance to an oppressive order that threatens the subjectivity of the subaltern.

46. In her analysis of Cixous and her theorization of feminine writing, Susan E. Dunn comments on Cixous' critique of concepts such as logocentrism, or phallogocentrism, characteristic of the patriarchal order. Dunn states: "This post-structuralist framework sets up a definition of bisexuality which is not about the combination of sexualities (androgyny) but the displacement of the terms 'masculinity' and 'femininity.' Bisexuality goes beyond dualism to imagine a multiple subject." See Susan E. Dunn, "The Place That Writes: Locating Hélène Cixous in Feminist Theory" (Stanford Presidential Lectures and Symposia in the Humanities and Arts, 1998), 3.

47. Moi, *Sexual/Textual Politics,* 114.

48. Cixous, "The Laugh of the Medusa," 340.

Conclusion

1. Freud's theory of the bisexual nature of human beings (14); Alfred Adler's belief that the feminine side of the polarity is devalued by culture (17–19); Jung's critical observation that in recent history the feminine has been dominated by the masculine, not that women have been dominated by men. He argued that a certain type of modern man could no longer afford to repress weakness and suggested techniques for talking to one's anima and getting in touch with his feminine side (Connell, *Theorizing Masculinities* 21–22).

2. Cixous utilizes the word *death* because one of the terms would have to destroy the other in order to acquire meaning, which can be considered a contradiction of the most powerful over the weaker that only reinforces the nature of binary thought and hegemony located in interpretations of gender. Moi sums up Cixous' theoretical project as one that disturbs logocentric ideology and, instead of equating femininity with passivity and death, she proclaims woman as the source of life, power, and energy (Moi, *Sexual/Textual Politics* 105).

3. William David Foster, *Sexual Textualities: Essays on Queering Latin American Writing* (Austin: University of Texas Press, 1997), 9.

4. Ibid., 11.

5. Joan Lee Skinner, "Carnality in 'El matadero,'" *Revista de Estudios Hispánicos* 33 (1999): 205–26.

6. Ibid., 223.

7. *El matadero* is estimated to have been written sometime in 1839. According to Skinner, in the initial writings of the *Dogma socialista,* Echevería calls for a democratic reform and recognizes the failures of previous generations. He calls upon the youth to emulate the heroes of the wars of independence in order to peacefully resolve political conflicts between the Unitarians and the Federalists: "La confraternidad de principios producirá la unión y fraternidad de todos los miembros de la familia argentina y concentrará sus anhelos en el sólo objeto de la libertad y engrandecimiento de la Patria" (quoted in Skinner 221).

8. Skinner, "Carnality in 'El matadero,'" 219–20.

9. Martí, *Obras escogidas,* 84.

10. Allen, *José Martí: Selected Writings,* 156.

11. Ibid.

12. See Cixous' theorization of bisexuality in Moi (109) and Dunn (3).

13. See Connell and hegemonic masculinity.

14. Taylor, *Disappearing Acts,* 110.

15. Amy K. Kaminsky, *Reading the Body Politic: Feminist Criticism and Latin American Women Writers* (Minneapolis: University of Minnesota Press, 1993), 24.

Works Cited

Abercrombie, Nicholas, Stephen Hill, and Bryan S. Turner. *The Penguin Dictionary of Sociology.* London: Penguin, 2000.

Alexander, Jonathan. "Transgender Rhetorics: (Re) Composing Narratives of the Gendered Body." *College Composition and Communication* 57.1 (2005): 45–82.

Allen, Esther, ed. *José Martí: Selected Writings.* New York: Penguin Books, 2002.

Alonso, Carlos J. "The Criollista Novel." In *The Cambridge History of Latin American Literature.* Edited by Roberto González Echevarría and Enrique Pupo-Walker, 195–212. Cambridge: Cambridge University Press, 1996.

———. "'Otra sería mi historia': Allegorical Exhaustion in *Doña Bárbara.*" *Modern Language Notes* 104.2 (March 1989): 418–38.

Anderson, Benedict R O'G. *Imagined Communities: Reflections on the Origin and Spread of Nationalism.* London: Verso, 1991.

Anderson Imbert, Enrique. "La prosa poética de José Martí: a propósito de *Amistad funesta.*" In *Memoria del Congreso de Escritores Martianos; febrero 20 a 27 de 1953,* 570–616. Havana: Comisión Nacional Organizadora de los Actos y Ediciones del Centenario y del Monumento de Martí, 1953.

Aronna, Michael. *"Pueblos Enfermos": The Discourse of Illness in the Turn-of-the-Century Spanish and Latin American Essay.* North Carolina Studies in the Romance Languages and Literatures, no. 262. Chapel Hill: UNC Department of Romance Languages, 1999.

Asturias, Miguel Ángel. *El Señor Presidente.* Buenos Aires: Editorial Losada, 1966.

———. *The President.* Translated by Frances Partridge. Prospect Heights, IL: Waveland Press, 1963.

Bakhtin, Mikhail Mikhailovich. *The Dialogic Imagination.* Edited by Michael Holquist. Austin: University of Texas Press, 1990.

Baralt, Blanche Zacharie. *El Martí que yo conocí.* Havana: Centro de Estudios Martianos: Editorial Pueblo y Educación, 1990.

Barquet, Jesús J. "Revelación y enmascaramiento de la personalidad de José Martí en *Amistad funesta.*" Fourth Louisiana Conference on Hispanic Languages & Literatures, LA CHISPA '-83: Selected Proceedings. New Orleans, LA: Tulane University Press, 1983.

Beaupied, Aida. "La transcendencia y dos visiones de la mujer en *Lucía Jérez* de José Martí: La ideal amada inerte y la fuerte mujer fatal." *MIFLC-Review* 2 (1992): 50–64.

Beauvoir, Simone de. *Deuxième sexe* [The Second Sex]. Translated by H. M. Parshley. New York: Knopf, 1953.

Belardinelli Hall, Stella Maris. "Fedina en el mundo surrealista de *El Señor Presidente* de Miguel Ángel Asturias." *MACLAS Latin American Essays* 13 (March 1999): 97–104.

Belnap, Jeffrey Grant, and Raúl Fernández, eds. *José Martí's "Our America": From National to Hemispheric Cultural Studies.* Durham, NC: Duke University Press, 1998.

Benjamin, Jules R. *The United States and the Origins of the Cuban Revolution: An Empire of Liberty in an Age of National Liberation.* Princeton, NJ: Princeton University Press, 1990.

Blest Gana, Alberto. *Martín Rivas: novela de costumbres político-sociales.* Caracas: Biblioteca Ayacucho, 1977.

Bombal, María Luisa. *La última niebla.* Santiago, Chile: Editorial Universitaria, 1992.

Brod, Harry, and Michael Kaufman, eds. *Theorizing Masculinities.* Thousand Oaks, CA: Sage Publications, 1994.

Bushnell, David. *The Emergence of Latin America in the Nineteenth Century.* New York: Oxford University Press, 1994.

Butler, Judith. *Gender Trouble: Feminism and the Subversion of Identity.* New York: Routledge, 1990.

Callan, Richard J. "Babylonian Mythology in *El Señor Presidente.*" *Hispania* 50.3 (September 1967): 417–24.

Calvino, Julio. *Historia, ideología y mito en la narrativa hispanoamericana contemporánea.* Madrid: Editorial Ayuso, 1987.

Castellanos, Rosario, and Maureen Ahern. *A Rosario Castellanos Reader: An Anthology of Her Poetry, Short Fiction, Essays, and Drama.* Texas Pan American Series. Austin: University of Texas Press, 1988.

Castillo, Debra A. *Talking Back: Toward a Latin American Feminist Literary Criticism.* Ithaca, NY: Cornell University Press, 1992.

Castro-Klarén, Sara. "La crítica literaria feminista y la escritora en América Latina." In *La sartén por el mango. Encuentro de escritoras latinoamericanas.* Edited by Patricia González and Elena Ortega, 27–46. Río Piedras, Argentina: Ediciones Huracán, 1985.

———. "The Novelness of a Possible Poetics for Women." In *Cultural and Historical Grounding for Hispanic and Luso-Brazilian Feminist Literary Criticism.* Edited by Hernan Vidal, 95–106. Minneapolis, MN: Institute for the Study of Ideologies and Literature, 1989.

———, Sylvia Molloy, and Beatriz Sarlo, eds. Introduction to In *Women's Writing in Latin America: An Anthology,* 3–34. Boulder, CO: Westview Press, 1991.

Castro Urioste, José. "Poder y resistencia en la escritura de *Doña Bárbara.*" *Explicación de Textos Literarios* 25.1 (1996–97): 41–49.

Chanady, Amaryll, ed. *Latin American Identity and Constructions of Difference.* Minneapolis: University of Minnesota Press, 1994.

Chasteen, John Charles. *Born in Blood and Fire: A Concise History of Latin America.* New York: Norton, 2001.

Chesler, Phyllis. *Women and Madness.* New York: Avon Books, 1973.

Cixous, Hélène. "The Laugh of the Medusa." In *Feminisms: An Anthology, of Literary Theory and Criticism.* Edited by Robyn R. Warhol and Diane Price Herndl, 334–49. New Brunswick, NJ: Rutgers University Press, 1991.

Columbus, Christopher. *Diario. The voyage of Christopher Columbus: Columbus's Own Journal of Discovery.* Translated by John Cummins. New York: St. Martin's Press, 1992.

Connell, R.W. "The Big Picture: Masculinities in Recent World History." *Theory and Society* 22.5 (October 1993): 597–623.

———. "Masculinities": *Reply* (in Symposium on R. W. Connell's "Masculinities"). *Gender and Society* 12.4 (August 1998): 474–77.

———. *Which Way is Up?: Essays on Sex, Class, and Culture.* Sydney, Australia: Allen and Unwin, 1983.

———. "A Whole New World: Remaking Masculinity in the Context of the Environmental Movement." *Gender and Society* 4.4 (December 1990): 452–78.

Cranny-Francis, Anne. *Engendered Fiction: Analysing Gender in the Production and Reception of Texts.* Communication and Culture Series. Kensington, NSW, Australia: NSWU Press, 1992.

Crapol, Edward P. *James G. Blaine: Architect of Empire.* Wilmington, DE: Scholarly Resources, 2000.

Crow, John A. "The Essays of Rómulo Gallegos." *Hispania* 381 (March 1955): 35–40.

Cruz, Jaqueline. "Esclava vencedora: la mujer en la obra literaria de José Martí." *Hispania* 75.1 (March 1992): 30–37.

Darío, Rubén. *Prosas profanas y otros poemas. Antología poética.* Buenos Aires: Editorial Sudamericana, 1996. Darwin, Charles. *The Descent of Man and Selection in Relation to Sex.* 1871. Reprint, Princeton, NJ: Princeton University Press, 1981.

Derrida, Jacques. *The Derrida Reader: Writing Performances.* Edited by Julian Wolfreys. Lincoln: University of Nebraska, 1998.

D'Halmar, Augusto. *Juana Lucero.* Santiago, Chile: Editorial Nascimento, 1973.

Didi-Huberman, Georges. *Invention of Hysteria: Charcot and the Photographic Iconography of the Salpêtrière.* Translated by Alisa Hartz. Cambridge, MA: MIT University Press, 2003.

Dijkstra, Bram. *Idols of Perversity: Fantasies of Feminine Evil in Fin-de-siècle Culture.* New York: Oxford University Press, 1986.

Dunn, Susan E. "The Place That Writes: Locating Hélène Cixous in Feminist Theory." Stanford Presidential Lectures and Symposia in the Humanities and Arts, 1998. 1–Online. Available: *http://prelectur.stanford.edu/lecturers/cixous/dunn.html.*

Eagleton, Mary. *Feminist Literary Theory.* London: Longman, 1991.

Earle, Peter G. "The Female Persona in the Spanish American Essay: An Overview." In *Woman as Myth and Metaphor in Latin American Literature.* Edited by Carmelo Virgilio and Naomi Lindstrom, 79–93. Columbia: University of Missouri Press, 1985.

Echeverría, Esteban. "El matadero." 1938–1940. In *El matadero, ensayos estéticos y prosa varia.* Edited by Fernando Burgos, 55–105. Hanover, NH: Ediciones del Norte, 1992.

———. "The Slaughterhouse." In *The Spanish American Short Story: A Critical Anthology.* Translated by Seymour Menton, 3–22. Los Angeles: UCLA Latin American Center Publications, 1980.

Epstein, Julia, and Kristina Straub, eds. *Body Guards: The Cultural Politics of Gender Ambiguity.* New York: Routledge, 1991.

Falce, Juliet Alison. *Underlying Gender Structures in the Latin American Regionalist Novel.* PhD diss., University of California, Irvine, 1997.

Felman, Shoshana. "Women and Madness: The Critical Phallacy." In *Feminisms: An Anthology of Literary Theory and Criticism.* Edited by Robyn R. Warhol and Diane Price Herndl, 6–19. New Brunswick, NJ: Rutgers University Press, 1991.

Felt Tyler, Alice. *The Foreign Policy of James G. Blaine.* Minneapolis: University of Minnesota Press, 1927.

Flores, Luisa Elena. *El diálogo del poder y el poder del diálogo en El Señor Presidente, Yo el Supremo y El gran elector.* PhD diss., University of Louisville, 2001.

Foner, Philip S., ed. *Inside the Monster: Writings on the United States and American Imperialism.* Translated by Elinor Randall, Luis A. Baralt, Juan de Onís, and Roslyn Held Foner. New York: Monthly Review Press, 1975.

Foster, David William, and Roberto Reis, eds. *Bodies and Biases: Sexualities in Hispanic Cultures and Literatures.* Minneapolis: University of Minnesota Press, 1996.

———. *Sexual Textualities: Essays on Queering Latin American Writing.* Austin: University of Texas Press, 1997.

Foucault, Michel. *The History of Sexuality.* Translated by Robert Hurley. New York: Vintage Books, 1990.

———. "Truth and Power." In *Power/Knowledge: Selected Interviews and Other Writings, 1972–1977.* Edited by Colin Gordon, 78–108. New York: Pantheon Books, 1980.

Franco, Jean. "Apuntes sobre la crítica feminista y la literatura hispanoamericana." *Hispamérica* 15.45 (1986): 31–43.

———. "Beyond Ethnocentrism: Gender, Power, and the Third-World Intelligentsia." In *Marxism and the Interpretation of Culture.* Edited by Cary Nelson and Lawrence Grossberg, 503–15. Urbana: University of Illinois Press, 1988.

———. *Modern Culture of Latin America: Society and the Artist.* Hammondsworth, UK: Penguin, 1970.

———. *Plotting Women: Gender and Representation in Mexico.* New York: Columbia University Press, 1989.

Franklin, Richard L. "Observations on *El Señor Presidente* by Miguel Ángel Asturias." *Hispania* 44.4. (December 1961): 683–85.

Freud, Sigmund. *Neue Folge der Vorlesungen zur Einführung in die Psychoanalyse* [New Introductory Lectures on Psychoanalysis.] Translated by James Strachey. New York: Norton, 1965.

Fuss, Diana. *Essentially Speaking: Feminism, Nature, and Difference.* New York: Routledge, 1989.

Gallegos, Rómulo. *Discurso de Rómulo Gallegos, Presidente de los Estados Unidos de Venezuela, pronunciado en el acto de inauguración de la estatua de Bolívar, en la población de Bolívar, Missouri, Estados Unidos de América, el 5 de julio de 1948.* Caracas: Imprenta Nacional, 1948.

———. *Doña Bárbara.* 1929. Reprint, Madrid: Cátedra, 1997.

———. *Doña Barbara.* Translated by Robert Malloy. New York: Cape and Smith, 1931.

Gálvez, Manuel. *Nacha Regules.* New York: Dutton, 1922.

Gamboa, Federico. *Santa.* Madrid: Cátedra, 1997.

Geddes, Patrick, and J. Arthur Thompson. *The Evolution of Sex.* New York: Humboldt, 1889.

Gil, Juan, ed. *Cristóbal Colón: Textos y documentos completos.* Madrid: Alianza Universidad, 1982.

Gilbert, Sandra M., and Susan Gubar. *The Madwoman in the Attic.* 2nd ed. New Haven, CT: Yale University Press, 1984.

Gilman, Sander L. *Difference and Pathology: Stereotypes of Sexuality, Race, and Madness.* Ithaca, NY: Cornell University Press, 1985.

Goic, Cedomil. *Historia de la novela hispanoamericana.* Valparaíso, Chile: Ediciones Universitarias de Valparaíso, 1972.

Gómez de Avellaneda y Arteaga, Gertrudis. *Sab.* Madrid: Cátedra, 1997.

González Echevarría, Roberto. *Myth and Archive: A Theory of Latin American Narrative.* Cambridge: Cambridge University Press, 1990.

———. *Voice of the Masters: Writing and Authority in Modern Latin American Narrative.* Austin: University of Texas Press, 1985.

———, and Enrique Pupo-Walker, eds. *The Cambridge History of Latin American Literature.* Cambridge: Cambridge University Press, 1996.

González Espitia, Juan Carlos. "Lucía: ¿funesta?" In CD Conferencia Internacional por el equilibrio del mundo (150 aniversario del natalicio de José Martí). Havana, 2003.

Grosz, Elizabeth A. *Sexual Subversions: Three French Feminists.* Sydney, Australia: Allen and Unwin, 1989.

Guerin, Wilfred L. *A Handbook of Critical Approaches to Literature.* New York: Oxford University Press, 1999.

Gutmann, Matthew. *The Meanings of Macho: Being a Man in Mexico City.* Berkeley: University of California Press, 1996.

Halperín Donghi, Tulio. "Argentine Counterpoint: Rise of the Nation, Rise of the State." In *Beyond Imagined Communities: Reading and Writing the Nation in Nineteenth-Century Latin America.* Edited by Sara Castro Klarén and John Charles Chasteen, 33–53. Washington, D.C.: Woodrow Wilson Center Press, 2003.

———. *Historia contemporánea de América Latina.* Buenos Aires: Alianza, 1997.

———, ed. *Sarmiento: Author of a Nation.* Berkeley: University of California Press, 1994.

Healy, David. *James G. Blaine and Latin America.* Columbia: University of Missouri Press, 2001.

Hegel, Georg Wilhelm Friedrich. *Hegel: The Essential Writings.* Edited by Frederick G. Weiss. New York: Harper and Row, 1974.

———. *Lectures on the Philosophy of World History: Introduction, Reason in History.* Translated by H. B. Nisbet. Cambridge: Cambridge University Press, 1980.

Himelblau, Jack. "El Señor Presidente: Antecedents, Sources, and Reality." *Hispanic Review* 41.1 (Winter 1973): 43–78.

Holmberg, Eduardo. *Nelly.* Buenos Aires: Compañía Sud Americana de Billetes de Banco, 1896.

Irving, Washington. *The Voyages of Columbus.* New York: Ungar, 1960.

Isaacs, Jorge. *María.* Madrid: Espasa-Calpe, 1949.

Jehenson, Myriam. *Latin American Women Writers: Class, Race, and Gender.* Albany: State University of New York Press, 1985.

Jiménez, Onilda A. *La mujer en Martí: en su pensamiento, obra y vida.* Miami: Universal, 1999.

Johannsen, Robert W. *To the Halls of the Montezumas: The Mexican War in the American Imagination.* New York: Oxford University Press, 1985.

Johnson, Ernest A., Jr. "The Meaning of Civilización and Barbarie in *Doña Bárbara.*" *Hispania* 39.4 (December 1956): 456–61.

Johnson, Kathleen L. *Reflections in the Text: Self Portraits in Selected Modernist Novels.* PhD diss., University of North Carolina at Chapel Hill, 2001.

José Martí y los Estados Unidos. Havana: Centro de Estudios Martianos, 1998.

Jrade, Cathy Login. *Modernismo, Modernity and the Development of Spanish American Literature.* Austin: University of Texas Press, 1998.

Juana Inés de la Cruz, Margaret Sayers Peden, and Ilan Stavans. *Poems, Protest, and a Dream: Selected Writings.* New York: Penguin Books, 1997.

Juncker, Clara. "Writing (with) Cixous." *College English* 50.4 (April 1988): 424–36.

Kadir, Djelal. *Questing Fictions: Latin America's Family Romance.* Minneapolis: University of Minnesota Press, 1986.

Kaminsky, Amy K. *Reading the Body Politic: Feminist Criticism and Latin American Women Writers.* Minneapolis: University of Minnesota Press, 1993.

Kann, Mark E. *The Gendering of American Politics: Founding Mothers, Founding Fathers, and Political Patriarchy.* Westport, CT: Praeger Publishers, 1999.

Kant, Immanuel. *Observations on the Feeling of the Beautiful and Sublime.* Translated by John T. Goldthwait. Berkeley: University of California Press, 1965.

Kirk, John M. "José Martí and the United States: A Further Interpretation." *Journal of Latin American Studies* 9.2 (November 1977): 275–90.

Kirkpatrick, Gwen. *The Dissonant Legacy of Modernismo: Lugones, Herrera y Reissig, and the Voices of Modern Spanish American Poetry.* Berkeley: University of California Press, 1989.

Lombroso, Cesare. *The Female Offender.* New York: Appleton, 1895.

López Alvarez, Luis. *Conversaciones con Miguel Ángel Asturias.* Cindad Universitaria Rodrigo Facio, Costa Rica: EDUCA, 1976.

Lynch, John. *Argentine Dictator: Juan Manuel de Rosas, 1829—1852.* Oxford: Clarendon Press, 1981.

Magnarelli, Sharon. *The Lost Rib: Female Characters in the Spanish-American Novel.* Lewisburg, MD: Bucknell University Press, 1985.

Mármol, José. *Amalia: A Romance of the Argentine.* Translated by Mary J. Serrano. New York: Dutton, 1919.

Martí, José. *Adúltera: drama inédito.* Havana: Editorial Trópico, 1936.

———. *Inside the Monster: Writings on the United States and American Imperialism.* Edited by Philip S. Foner. New York: Monthly Review Press, 1975.

———. *Lucía Jerez.* Edited by Manuel Pedro González. Madrid: Gredos, 1969.

———. *Lucía Jerez.* Edited by Carlos Javier Morales. Madrid: Cátedra, 2000.

———. *Lucía Jerez.* Edited by Mauricio Rodríguez Núñez. Ciudad de Guatemala: Letra Negra, 2001.

———. *Lucía Jerez y otras narraciones.* Edited by Mercedes Santos Moray. Havana: Editiorial Arte y Literatura, 1975.

———, and Luis Alejandro Baralt. *Martí on the U.S.A.* Carbondale: Southern Illinois University Press, 1966.

———. *Obras completas.* vol. 2, La Habana: Editorial Lex, 1946.

———. *Obras completas en los Estados Unidos.* Havana: Editorial Nacional de Cuba, 1963.

———. *Obras escogidas (1885–octubre 1891).* Vol. 2. Havana: Editora Política, 1979.

Martínez-San Miguel, Yolanda. "Sujetos femeninos en *Amistad funesta* y *Blanca Sol:* el lugar de la mujer en dos novelas latinoamericanas de fin del siglo XIX." *Revista Iberoamericana* 174 (1996): 27–45.

Masiello, Francine. *Between Civilization and Barbarism: Women, Nation and Literary Culture in Modern Argentina.* Lincoln: University of Nebraska Press, 1982.

———. "Discurso de mujeres, lenguaje del poder: reflexiones sobre la crítica feminista a mediados de la década del 80." *Hispamérica* 45 (1986): 53–60.

Matto de Turner, Clorinda. *Aves sin nido.* México City: Editorial Oasis, 1981.

McKenna, Teresa. "Hegemony in *El Señor Presidente:* A Psychoanalytic Perspective." *Mester* 6 (1977): 99–104.

Mejías-López, Alejandro J. *La novela modernista hispanoamericana: Definición y estudio de sus inicios.* PhD diss., University of Michigan, 1995.

Melhuus, Marit. "Power, Value and the Ambiguous Meanings of Gender." In *Machos, Mistresses, Madonnas: Contesting the Power of Latin American Gender Imagery.* Edited by Marit Melhuus and Kristi Anne Stolen, 230–59. New York: Verso, 1996.

Menchaca, Martha. "Chicano Indianism: A Historical Account of Racial Repression in the United States." *American Ethnologist* 20.3 (1993): 583–603.

Mercado, Juan Carlos. *Building a Nation: The Case of Echeverría.* Lanham, MD: University Press of America, 1995.

Moi, Toril, ed. *Sexual/Textual Politics: Feminist Literary Theory.* London: Routledge, 1985.

Molloy, Sylvia. "Politics of Posing." In *Hispanisms and Homosexualities.* Edited by Sylvia Molloy and Robert McKee Irwin, 141–60. Durham, NC: Duke University Press, 1998.

———. "Too Wilde for Comfort: Desire and Ideology in Fin-de-Siecle Latin America." *Social Text* 31–32 (1992): 187–201.

Montero, Oscar. "Modernismo and Homophobia: Darío and Rodó." In *Sex and Sexuality in Latin America.* Edited by Daniel Balderston and Donna J. Guy, 99–117. New York: New York University Press, 1997.

Mosse, George L. *Nationalism and Sexuality: Respectability and Abnormal Sexuality in Modern Europe.* New York: Fertig, 1985.

Muni, Orlando. *Dictadura de la muerte en El Señor Presidente.* MA thesis., University of Cincinnati, 1971.

Nevins, Allen. *Hamilton Fish: The Inner History of the Grant Administration.* New York: Dodd, Mead, 1936.

Pavlovsky, Eduardo A. *Paso de dos.* Buenos Aires: Ediciones Búsqueda de Ayllu, 1990.

Paz, Octavio. *El laberinto de soledad.* México City: Fondo de Cultura Económica, 1959.

———. *The Labyrinth of Solitude: Life and Thought in Mexico.* Translated by Lysander Kemp. New York: Grove Press, 1962.

Pellicer, Rosa. "La mujer en la novela modernista hispanoamericana." *Actas del IX Simposio de la Sociedad Española de Literatura General y Comparada,* Zaragoza, 18–21 de noviembre de 1992. Vol.1. *La mujer: elogio y vituperio.* Zaragoza, Spain: Universidad de Zaragoza, 1994. 291–300.

Pérez, Louis A., Jr. *Cuba and the United States: Ties of Singular Intimacy.* Athens: University of Georgia Press, 2003.

Perus, Françoise. "Modernity, Postmodernity, and Novelistic Form in Latin America." In *Latin American Identity and Construction of Difference.* Edited by Amaryll Chanady, 43–66. Minneapolis: University of Minnesota Press, 1994.

Piedra, José. "Nationalizing Sissies." In *Entiendes?: Queer Readings, Hispanic Writings.* Edited by Emilie L. Bergmann and Paul Julian Smith, 370–409. Durham, NC: Duke University Press, 1995.

Pita, Beatriz. "Engendering Critique: Race, Class, and Gender in Ruiz de Burton and Martí." In *José Martí's "Our America": From National to Hemispheric Cultural Studies.* Edited by Jeffrey Belnap and Raúl Fernández, 129–144. Durham, NC: Duke University Press, 1998.

Pletcher, David M. *The Awkward Years. American Foreign Relations under Garfield and Arthur.* Columbia: University of Missouri Press, 1962.

Pratt, Mary Louise. *Imperial Eyes: Travel Writing and Transculturalization.* London: Routledge, 1992.

Ramos, Julio. *Divergent Modernities: Culture and Politics in Nineteenth-Century Latin America.* Translated by John D. Blanco. Durham, NC: Duke University Press, 2001.

Rodó, José Enrique. *Ariel: Liberalismo y Jacobinismo.* México City: Editorial Porrúa, 1997.

Rodríguez-Luis, Julio, ed. *Re-Reading José Martí: One Hundred Years Later.* Albany: State University of New York Press, 1999.

Rodríguez, Pedro Pablo. "'Definir, avisar, poner en guardia . . .': Visión Martiana de Estados Unidos en La América." In *José Martí y Los Estados Unidos,* 79–93. Havana: Centro de Estudios Martianos, 1988.

Rodríguez, Teresita. *La problemática de la identidad en "El Señor Presidente" de Miguel Ángel Asturias.* Amsterdam: Rodopi, 1989.

Rosa, William. "*Doña Bárbara:* Sexualidad y dominación política." *Escritura: Revista de Teoría y Crítica-Literarias* 12. 23–24 (1987): 89–97.

Rosado, Juan Antonio. "La visión trágica de Miguel Ángel Asturias en *El Señor Presidente.*" *Cuadernos Americanos* 83 (2000): 216–36.

Rosegreen-Williams, Claudette. "Rómulo Gallegos's *Doña Bárbara:* Toward a Radical Rereading." *Symposium* 46.4 (Winter 1993): 279–97.

Rotker, Susana. *The American Chronicles of José Martí: Journalism and Modernity in Spanish America.* Hanover, NH: University Press of New England, 2000.

———. "The Political Gaze." In *José Martí's "Our America": From National to Hemispheric Cultural Studies.* Edited by Jeffrey Belnap and Raúl Fernández, 58–76. Durham, NC: Duke University Press, 1998.

Saint-Lu, Jean Marie. "Hacia un estudio linguístico de la obra de M. A. Asturias: Notas al capítulo XII de *El Señor Presidente.*" *Escritura. Revista de Teoría y Crítica Literarias* 3.5–6 (January–December 1978): 157–75.

Salgado, María A. "Maniero's *De vitis aliquot mexicanorum* or Biography as Political Agenda." *Dieciocho* 21.2 (Fall 1998): 209–18.

Sandoval, Adriana. "El primer capítulo de *El Señor Presidente.*" *Cuadernos Americanos* 83 (2000): 210–15.

Sarmiento, Domingo Faustino. *Facundo: civilización y barbarie.* 1845. Reprint, Madrid: Cátedra, 1990.

———. *Life in the Argentine Republic in the Days of the Tyrants; or, Civilization and Barbarism.* New York: Hafner Publication, 1960.

Sedgwick, Eve Kosofsky. *Between Men: English Literature and Male Homosocial Desire.* New York: Columbia University Press, 1985.

Sellers, Susan, ed. *The Hélène Cixous Reader.* New York: Routledge, 1994.

Shaw, Donald Leslie. *Gallegos: Donã Bárbara.* London: Grant and Cutler, 1972.

Shnookal, Deborah, and Mirta Muñiz. *José Martí Reader: Writings on the Americas.* Melbourne: Ocean Press, 1999.

Showalter, Elaine. *The Female Malady: Women, Madness, and Culture in England, 1830–1980.* New York: Pantheon Books, 1985.

———, ed. *The New Feminist Criticism: Essays on Women, Literature, and Theory.* New York: Pantheon, 1985.

———. *Speaking of Gender.* New York: Routledge, 1989.

Shumway, Nicolas. *The Invention of Argentina.* Berkeley: University of California Press, 1991.

Silva-Beauregard, Paulette. "La feminización del héroe moderno y la novela en *Lucía Jérez* y *El hombre de hierro.*" *Revista-de-Critica-Literaria-Latinoamericana* 26.52 (2000): 135–51.

Sinfield, Alan. *The Wilde Century: Effeminacy, Oscar Wilde, and the Queer Movement.* New York: Columbia University Press, 1994.

Singletary, Otis A. *The Mexican War.* Chicago: The University of Chicago Press, 1960.

Skinner, Joan Lee. "Carnality in 'El matadero.'" *Revista de Estudios Hispánicos* 33 (1999): 205–26.

Skirius, John. "Este centauro de los géneros." In *El ensayo hispanoamericano del siglo XX,* 9–31. México City: Fondo de Cultura Económica.

Skurski, Julie. "The Ambiguities of Authenticity in Latin America: *Doña Bárbara* and the Construction of National Identity." *Poetics Today* 15.4 (Winter 1994): 605–42.

Smith, Paul Julian. *Representing the Other: "Race," Text, and Gender in Spanish and Spanish American Narrative.* Oxford: Clarendon Press, 1992.

Sommer, Doris. *Foundational Fictions. The National Romances of Latin America.* Berkeley: University of California Press, 1991.

Sorensen Goodrich, Diana. *Facundo and the Construction of Argentine Culture.* Austin: University of Texas Press, 1996.

Spencer, Herbert. *The Principles of Sociology.* New York: Appleton, 1901.

Taylor, Diana. *Disappearing Acts: Spectacles of Gender and Nationalism in Argentina's "Dirty War."* Durham, NC: Duke University Press, 1997.

Todorov, Tzvetan. *The Conquest of America: The Question of the Other.* New York: Harper Perennial, 1992.

Torres-Pou, Joan. *El e[x]terno femenino: aspectos de la representación de la mujer en la literatura latinoamericana del siglo XIX.* PhD diss., Emory University, 1998.

Uribe, Olga. "La mujer como invención de lo posible." *Revista de Crítica Literaria Latinoamericana* 15.30 (1989): 25–38.

Ussher, Jane. "The Female Malady and the Medicalization of Sex: The Victorian Madwomen."*Women's Madness, Mysogyny or Mental Illness?* Amherst: University of Massachussetts Press, 1992.

Valens, Keja Lys. *Between Women: Desire in Caribbean Literatures.* PhD diss., Harvard University, 2004.

Valverde, César. *Masculinidad en la narrativa hispanoamericana: Hegemonía, transgresión y Desconstrucción.* PhD diss., University of California, 1997.

Williams, Raymond. *Hegemony.* Oxford: Oxford University Press, 1977.

———. *Marxism and Literature.* Oxford: Oxford University Press, 1977.

Wright, Rosalinda Gayoso. *Un estudio psicológico de la caracterización en Amistad funesta.* PhD diss., Florida State University, 1996.

Yarrington, Doug. "Cattle, Corruption, and Venezuelan State Formation during the Regime of Juan Vicente Gómez, 1908–35." *Latin American Research Review* 38.2 (June 2003): 2–26.

Zapata, Mónica. "Las duplicidades del sujeto: *El Señor Presidente.*" *La palabra y el hombre* 96 (1995): 233–39.

Zeno Gandía, M. *La charca: crónica de un mundo enfermo.* Río Piedras, Puerto Rico: Editorial Edil, 1975.

Zimmerman, Marc, and Raúl Rojas, eds. *Voices from the Silence: Guatemalan Literature of Resistance.* Athens: Ohio University Center for International Studies, 1998.

Zola, Emile. *Nana.* Translated by Douglas Parmée. Oxford: Oxford University Press, 1998.

Index

Page numbers in boldface indicate illustration pages

Fairleigh Dickinson Univ. Teaneck, NJ
3 3208 50005056 2

PQ 7082 .N7 S98 2009
Swier, Patricia Lapolla.
Hybrid nations

Date
Due →

Books returned after due date
are subject to a fine.

Fairleigh Dickinson University Library
Teaneck, New Jersey

T001-15M
11-8-02